Wendy-Ann Paige, [obscured] Scorpio, in Las Veg[obscured] in Los Angeles on the [obscured] to go on the big dipper at the [Magic] Mountain theme park with him. They are living proof that some of the supposedly 'bad matches' can work out beautifully, if somewhat unconventionally. Both born and bred in the United Kingdom, they now spend much of their time travelling the world collecting research for their work in the field of sexual behaviour.

Wendy-Ann describes astrology as a childhood interest which got out of control to the point where she writes on a regular basis for many national publications including the *Daily Star* and, currently, *The Sun*. She gives personal astro-sexual counselling to people whose relationship problems have a celestial, rather than practical origin. Together with Tony, she writes a sex advice column for *ME* magazine and the couple also provide a telephone advice service.

Wendy-Ann and Tony live in London with Jessie the dog, a Capricorn.

Call Wendy-Ann Paige's Sextrology phone line to reveal the secrets of a perfect celestial sex life.

0891 525 199

calls cost 37p per min cheap rate and 49p per min at all other times*

* prices correct at the time of going to press

This phone line is explicit and designed for callers aged 18 or over.

Sextrology

The Lovers' Guide to the Stars

Wendy-Ann Paige

HEADLINE

First published in Great Britain in 1994
by HEADLINE BOOK PUBLISHING

10 9 8 7 6 5 4 3 2 1

ISBN 0 7472 4388 3

Typeset by
Letterpart Limited, Reigate, Surrey

Printed and bound in Great Britain by
Cox & Wyman Ltd, Reading, Berks.

HEADLINE BOOK PUBLISHING
A division of Hodder Headline PLC
338 Euston Road
London NW1 3BH

To Tony
The Most Perfect Scorpio and Lover

The Star Signs

Aries, the Ram: 21 March–20 April
Taurus, the Bull: 21 April–20 May
Gemini, the Twins: 21 May–20 June
Cancer, the Crab: 21 June–20 July
Leo, the Lion: 21 July–21 August
Virgo, the Virgin: 22 August–22 September
Libra, the Scales: 23 September–22 October
Scorpio, the Scorpion: 23 October–22 November
Sagittarius, the Archer: 23 November–20 December
Capricorn, the Mountain Goat: 21 December–19 January
Aquarius, the Waterbearer: 20 January–18 February
Pisces, two Fishes: 19 February–20 March

Contents

Introduction

'What is Sextrology?' I can hear you thinking, so let me explain. In a nutshell, Sextrology is the study of how astrological influences affect each individual star sign's sexual behaviour. If you don't believe that is possible, then maybe this is not the book for you. Or is it simply the case that you are maybe a little nervous of seeing the most intimate details of your sexuality written out in bold print for all to read? Either way, there is no denying that what happened in the Heavens at the exact moment of your birth has shaped your attitude to sex and therefore laid a foundation on which your relationships will be based.

But can we not use this to our advantage? Yes we can, and that's why I've written this book. Meeting potential lovers, going through the preliminaries, the courtship, the sex, the kids and then maybe the divorce are events that seem simply to happen to us. Many people put more thought and logic into choosing a washing machine than a lover and then wonder why it all went wrong.

In Sextrology I aim to give you as much inside knowledge of the male and female of each zodiac sign as I possibly can; I will take you through the first meeting, seduction techniques, the main event of sex itself, what you can expect after a first night and, finally, how to end the relationship if things just don't work out. It is a vital part of any adult's education and teaches you a skill that you won't have learned in school.

Unlike some astrologers who categorically inform us that sign A will never get along with sign B, I disagree. I believe that any member of the zodiac can enjoy a happy and contented lifetime with any other, providing that they take the time to understand each other's character and motivations and make allowances for mutual foibles and weaknesses. I recommend therefore, that you treat this book as a complete course and don't just dive in to your own or your partner's chapter. To achieve your Sextrology qualifications you must sample all twelve signs and their very different approaches to the mating game.

If your own or your current lover's personality does not seem to tally with Sextrology then let me point out that what you will read is the extreme form of each sign's erotic characteristics; it is how they would, or could behave, in an ideal world, free of anything other than astrological influences. There can be other mitigating factors to consider also – rising signs and birthdays that fall on the cusp can make any individual display more than one astrological personality and the pressure of modern-day living combined with input from our friends, our family and our childhood experiences will all eat away at our true celestial identity. For example, Jason Bonham is the son of legendary Led Zeppelin drummer John, and now has a band of his own. The planets have chosen to make him a home-loving Cancerian, but his lifestyle and background have had far more bearing on him than all the planets in the sky put together.

Sextrology is a humorous book written mainly for your pleasure, but I should mention that if you take it seriously and find twelve real-life subjects to study in the flesh, you should remember the dangers that are unfortunately all too real and practise safe sex.

Wendy-Ann Paige

Sextrology

ARIES

FEMALE
Scene 1 **The Meeting**

The purpose of this book is to provide you with an in-depth and truthful look at how the planets have shaped your sexuality, way past the point that you will probably admit to, even to yourself. I do, however, realise that some of you will be leafing through these pages in the hope of discovering the sordid little details of each zodiac sign to help you pick the perfect lover – using it as a sort of owner's manual, just like when you choose a new car.

Well, if you're going to start working your way through the twelve lovely zodiac women, beginning with an Aries lady is a bit like learning to drive in a Ferrari. She's overpowering, amazingly fast and looks best in red. As with Italian sports cars, every man wants one, but few have what it takes to handle her, let alone afford her. Do not let this put you off though, for Aries

7

woman is very much misunderstood. Yes, she is hot to handle and yes, she will stand out in a crowd, but the reasons for putting your keys into her ignition are better than that. This woman was built for performance, she gives years of pleasure and loyalty and even becomes more sought after with age. Take this one home for the night and nothing else will ever quite match up.

So, you've decided to go for it, your motor's running and you need to find a lusty lady Ram – where to now? Locating Aries woman is quite easy, she likes to put herself on show and with a body that's as finely tuned as hers, why not? Check out your local gym – that's her in the why-bother leotard. You could also try an amateur dramatics company, because she knows how to act and will change personality at the flick of a switch. This is worth remembering if she becomes a permanent fixture in your life – one minute she's a whip-cracking, leather-loving dominatrix who loves the idea of tattoos and pierced nipples – the next she's sobbing her heart out over a *Lassie* film. In general, finding her is not the problem, attracting her attention is something else. Here you have a real dilemma. On the one hand, she loves to be flattered – the more you praise her, the lower her resistance. On the other hand – she likes to do the chasing, present yourself on a plate and she'll be sick with disgust. The best line of attack is originality and a sense of humour. Failing that, an act of heroism would do the trick. It might be worth enticing her pet tabby up a tree so that you can rescue it. You'd be guaranteed of having at least one grateful pussy!

We'll assume that you've now decided on your M.O. (If you haven't, you should move on to Taurean ladies right now because Aries woman needs a fast worker.)

So you've got her interested and you're chatting, and first of all, she will flirt. Don't get too excited – she does this to all men and can't help it, it's her natural way. At this stage you have a no better or worse chance than the milkman, the bank manager or your grandad. Now you start to make your less-than-business-like intentions clear. This is where it (thankfully) gets easier. If she is not impressed, she will not toy with your emotions or hormones. She will cut you and your swelling enthusiasm down to size with one savage, brutal comment. For instance, you say, 'How do you like your eggs at breakfast time?' She says, 'Unfertilised, thank you' and walks off. If you're smart this is certainly when you hunt out a Taurus female, as having another stab at the lady Ram will amount to a criticism of her judgement. For this there is no excuse, she is always right and questioning her decisions will provoke fury that makes great men shake in their shoes. If, however, you have managed to arouse her curiosity, then brace yourself. This lady does 0–60 in three seconds and will be fingering the zip of your trousers with all the skill of a Braille reader. Time to exit stage left and find somewhere comfortable.

Scene 2 The Main Event

You may be wondering, 'what happened to foreplay?' I'm afraid you just had it, sunshine! I did just mention that you at this point would be off to find somewhere comfortable. Well, Aries woman's description of comfy could have you reaching for the dictionary. To her, comfortable means different. It means somewhere risky, brightly lit, preferably outdoors and for maximum enjoyment – in public. If England are playing at home, that rules out Wembley Stadium, so you need to think whilst you're still on your feet.

The last resort is your place, but you must leave lights on and curtains open. Aries woman will not be offended if your flatmates are there, but you will be, when she offers to extend her performance, so ask them to leave. She will expect a drink of strong spirit out of a clean glass and will probably ask if you have any drugs. No is the correct answer. Although she considers life too short for all the preliminaries, it's worth knowing that her erogenous zones are around the face. She's a sucker for an ear-nibbler and you could try some eyelid kisses as they make her feel almost ethereal. By now, she'll be ready for action and you better make sure that you are too. Give her a limp reception and you'll know about it – and so will all her friends. One of Aries woman's delights is that for the price of your courage and ingenuity, she is selling you pure sex. With her you get the deal on the day, none of all that 'Once I've got to know you better I'll show you what I can do' stuff. She will rip off your clothes and begin to organise the gymnastics with the skill of an Olympic coach. Don't be fooled that she became so proficient through lots of practice though, her expertise belies the often small number of previous partners. You are one of the chosen few and would do well to respect this. At this stage, your expectation will be gripped in her hands and you will have to watch those long nails on your recently rolled-on Durex All-nighter. (You did remember that, didn't you? Oh dear, you must think quicker than this!)

This lady generally likes to dominate the proceedings and will do so mostly for her pleasure, but of course, by telling you what she wants and how she wants it, your job is made infinitely easier. If you want to climb into the driver's seat, you must have your moves mapped out. He who hesitates will be left holding his own gear stick. Making love with this girl will blow your brains out, she blows most things like that. Oral sex is one of her specialities and she has a tongue muscle that is Schwarzenegger-Approved. There's no need to worry about her only doing half a job either, she loves to taste your success. During the sex act itself, you can expect a lot of noise and a few letters of complaint from the neighbours. She doesn't do it for effect, she really does like to let rip. Mostly she can be found on top as this is the position in which she finds it easier to reach orgasm – this, in case you hadn't realised, is the main objective, and results are all-important. She likes to have one climax as a sort of warm-up to test her decibel level and your performance. After that, she's open to your suggestions, but providing you aim for a nice selection of clitoral, vaginal, G-spot and multiple varieties, you will have acquitted yourself well.

Scene 3 **Extras**

As to whether your relationship develops beyond this point, that will be her choice. Your consent will be written all over your face. Unlike a car, which always seems to give its best performance on the test drive, Aries woman has a very special bonus under her bonnet; it's her brain. It never stops working and thinking of ways to surprise you and delight you both. Over the coming days and weeks, she will revel in taking new sex toys to your bed. Some she will buy in the private shops, others she will have prepared earlier. Do not be surprised if your birthday present is tall blonde and looks very much like Aries woman's best friend. So long as your lady Ram is in control and everything is her suggestion, you will get pleasures that you could only have dreamed about. This is why it's best to keep your fantasies quiet; given enough time, she will think of them anyway.

As for her fantasies, well, she loves to shock and do anything that could be considered crazy or kinky. Her low boredom threshold means that what she fantasises about today could be boring by tomorrow. Because of her love of power, her sexual alter-ego is something of an S&M enthusiast. Whilst she is too soft-hearted to inflict or accept real pain, she loves to play around with whips, canes and chains. That actress in her will want to dress for the part too – rubber, leather, PVC and thigh boots can be found in her wardrobe in varying degrees of outrageousness. Sometimes she'll wear this for a night out. Other girls will make jealous catty comments whilst your mates wonder what it is you've got to keep this woman happy. Just smile, stay silent and maintain an air of smug satisfaction whilst at the same time managing not to let on about the discomfort of those deep scratches on your back and the ache between your legs.

Despite all the wild animalistic behaviour that Aries woman likes to demonstrate to her prey, underneath she really does have a heart of gold. She's generous and loving and will be your best friend. If you are the career type, she will be of more use than all those business meetings on the golf course put together. She's houseproud and would never let it be said that anyone can do anything better than she could.

Scene 4 **The Finale**

Will you keep her? You cannot ever truly own this fiery, independent sign but you can have her on a very long lease, providing you are never short of new tricks. If you have an affair with someone else, she will have two in return, not really to spite you, but to prove to herself that she hasn't lost her appeal. Her temper is frightening yet it's worth going a couple of rounds with her just for the making up. If you lose her, she will disappear from your life as quickly as she arrived, possibly to be repossessed by an old flame. You may never see her again and will be left wondering if it was all a dream.

In short, if you are beginning your astro-sexual education with an Aries lady, you are lucky indeed. From the moment you set eyes on this model of sexual excellence you are hooked. The path through life together may sometimes be bumpy, will take you far from the usual route and you may stray into very unusual territory, but you'll have had a very special experience. This woman is a collector's item for those with discerning erotic tastes and you should watch out for pale imitations.

MALE
Scene 1 **The Meeting**

When God created man, she called him Adam and made him the Aries male. He is the first sign of the zodiac, the first to put sex on the map and the obvious starting point for any woman embarking on a tour of Astro men. Well, since God launched her prototype, times have moved on, design faults have been rectified and there are eleven other delicious varieties to choose from.

For the connoisseurs, however, Aries man remains the original and the best. He is the James Bond of the zodiac. He has a licence to thrill and nobody does it better. His appeal is universal, if sometimes a little clichéd, but once a girl has been through a night of all-action adventure, there is something about this sexy smoothy that has her coming back for repeats time and time again. The big plus to Arien men is that they are all virtually identical. Learn the ropes with one and it will stand you in good stead for the rest – and yes, there will be others. They may not all look the same, talk the same, or walk the same – but they all use the same act.

Right then, if you fancy the role of his leading lady, your first mission is to find him. Here you're in luck – he never attempts to disguise himself and he'll be right where the action is. If you're smart, you'll have done your research and scanned the 'What's On' section of the local papers the week previously and ringed anything with the words 'new' or 'just opened' in the advertisement. Make yourself look gorgeous – that goes without saying – and head off down there. You'll recognise him by his sheer charm, charisma and pure presence. He's the zodiac's superstar – and knows it. Try choosing a place with plenty of mirrors, he is totally incapable of passing one without looking in it.

Aries man is also likely to be your boss because he has to be on top, except when having sex, which is too conventional. He admires an ambitious hard worker so bring yourself to his attention by going to his office and demanding a raise. He'll adore thrashing things out over the table, but don't accept his offer straight away – the thrill of the chase is the key part of the plot. With Aries man you need to think on your feet and quick because this is not a position he wants to keep you in. Decide from the off what you want from him. If it's one night of passion then aim to be his equal. He has a gift for humour and repartee and if you can match him thrust for thrust he will be obliged to take you to bed, and blow you away, but the next morning he'll throw you out. No, this character is so exciting to know that you should make your intentions long term and aiming to be a part of the big picture should be your goal. With all Ariens the problem is one of finding the right opener. The gooey-eyed giggling girly routine will temporarily whet his wolf-like juices but you'll have destroyed yourself as the challenge he needs.

A good piece of advice is to remember that Aries is a Fire sign and nothing fans the flames of their passion more than flattery. Compliment his clothes, which will be expensive, or better still, ask for his advice or opinions. Any subject will do from the stock market to the best local Indian restaurant – present yourself as a damsel in intellectual distress and you've potentially hooked yourself a hero. From the first moment of exchanging conversation, Mr Ram will be plotting ways of exchanging bodily fluids – he's not cheap, he just adores women. Getting him into bed is not a worry, getting the best out of him is now your main concern. If he's not sufficiently captivated, you will be on the receiving end of the Arien quickie which is a great abridged version of the real thing only with no rehearsal, no pauses for breath and an orgasm score weighted in his favour. Oh yes, and it will most likely take place in his parked car. Whilst you are still fumbling about in your bag looking for something oily to aid the re-entry of his rocket – he, with one last glance in the rear view, will be verbally giving you his thanks and phone number before returning to base camp in the bar.

Scene 2 **The Main Event**

The reason why this chap never wins any Oscars for his performance is because it is always overshadowed by the sheer adventure of the whole scene. Though not big on foreplay, he is a master of making a girl feel desirable and will delight in explaining what he's going to do to you in almost gynaecological detail. What goes on between your pubic bones is only a part of what makes a night with him so amazing. If you have grabbed his enthusiasm and been selected for the full works, it's vital to let him lead. Close the lid on any of your own preferences and open your mind to the definite reality of doing all those things you've only ever been told about. If there's any part of your body that you're not entirely familiar with – you should either go home or accept that you're going to be on very friendly terms with it before the evening's through. Aries man has very different ideas from Mother Nature.

The location for the main event is unimportant and indeed, he'd be upset if you had the time to notice. If you do go to his place, bank on it being cluttered in an organised sort of a way and also very unusual. His style of decor is as individual as he is but there's something about the atmosphere that makes you feel wicked. He'll be ready for action before you've even located the bathroom and to be honest, it's not worth looking for condoms as they are against his religion. If you're not sufficiently prepared and don't fancy giving birth to 003½ in nine months, this is your second chance to leave.

Don't worry too much about warming him up – he prefers his own foreplay to come in the bottled or powdered variety, but if you have anything you'd like to try – just yell. He's always open to new ideas. At your own peril, you could try slowly kissing and stroking his lips, as this has incredible results, as does touching any part of his face, and all of this is due to the Arien weak spot being the head. Whilst we're on the subject of head, this is something he loves to do – how well he does it depends on your pain threshold. Performing oral sex on you is viewed matter-of-factly. As long as you smile at the start and scream at the end, then he considers it a job done well. You, however, may get the distinct impression that your clitoris has become some sort of bad guy because those turbo-charged teeth and tongue of Aries man are not going to relent until your defence-less little hot button surrenders in a highly shocked and over-sensitive state.

As for returning the compliment, well, that's taken for granted. If you are one of those girls who considers giving a complete blow-job to be a big favour, you're in the wrong bedroom. Aries man adores oral sex and the good news is that you don't really have to be good at it. Forget all that terribly tricky business of trying to wrap your teeth up in your top lip – the more those molars brush against his flesh, the more he'll lap it up. (Correction, you're supposed to do that!)

His favourite intercourse position is from behind, but he's also tempted by standing up with you lying on a table or similar surface. Despite the frenzied pace of his lovemaking and a ferocity which goes beyond the animalistic, the journey to your orgasms is the ride of a lifetime. It has no regard for all those little tricks that nineties man is supposed to have learned and it almost shows contempt for romance, but once you arrive at that magical destination, you will have experienced that primeval force and unspeakable lust which caused all that upset in the Garden of Eden.

Scene 3 Extras

You may have got the impression by this stage that our hero likes a bit of pain with his pleasure. Well, yes, he does and Aries man can sometimes take this a bit too far without realising his own strength. What is horseplay to him could make you feel as if you've been kicked between the legs by a mule. You need to be upfront from the start and explain what you find enjoyable. He won't mind re-writing his bedroom script as long as you can come up with more inventive ideas. Of course, you may well appreciate his aggressive approach, it all depends on your own star sign. He adores games that involve tying up and spanking (not on him though, silly) and ideally would love a purpose-built playroom complete with every sort of role-playing outfit available. New sexual activities are what makes him tick and he's always searching for that surge of adrenaline that comes with a 'first' of any kind. If he jokes about the recent wife-swapping scandal in the *Daily Sleaze*, you can count on his laughter to be disguising a genuine interest. Don't ever dare him to try it because he will. Group sex fascinates him and he loves the idea of being able to put on a show – give him any hint that you may be keen and don't think that his possessiveness will prevent you from ever having to put your money where your mouth is.

For a real walk on the wild side, this is your man. Despite the rumours he likes to put around the squash club, he can be happy with just one girl and he's smart enough to know when he has met his match. He can be an expert dad, especially to boys but never, ever expect him to change a nappy in public!

Scene 4 **The Finale**

After that first shattering explosion of the first night, Aries man will have left you feeling shaken and yet stirred. Like so many dangerous and risky things in life, this man is totally addictive. He makes good girls into bad girls and bad girls even worse. If he wants you to be a permanent part of his action, there is little you can do. You may escape and settle down to a chocolate-box lifestyle with a Taurean or enjoy the antics of an Aquarian, but once touched by Mr Ram, your fantasies will eventually get round to a sequel. He can be the home-wrecker of the zodiac because he believes the best guy always gets the girl and he, of course, will always be the best. If you want to keep him, all you must do is keep up with him. He'll reward you with a life full of fun, outrageousness and material comforts. As long as his dinner's on the table he won't resent your career and once you've truly broken down his secret defences, he'll occasionally reveal a little boy who needs mothering. If you are the girl who wants to start rolling the final credits, the cause will inevitably be his unpredictability. To order him from your life won't work, but to condemn him to any sort of routine, bed and cocoa by 10.30p.m. and your parents round to dinner every Sunday – that will soon find him preening in the bathroom whilst secretly preparing for his next major assignment . . .

TAURUS

FEMALE
Scene 1 **The Meeting**

If any of you guys are treating this book as a sexual route map, the fact that you've now arrived at Taurus female suggests that Aries woman has got your juices flowing – but perhaps she was a bit too adventurous for your tastes. Well, with Taurus female you can have your cake and eat it. In fact, Taurus women *are* cream cakes. They come in all shapes and sizes and are all basically made from good wholesome ingredients. Unfortunately, these little girls are made up of so much sugar, spice and all things nice that they are too tempting for their own good. They destroy your willpower and once you've had one, the chances are that you will want another.

Taurean women are often portrayed as earthy, mumsy types – wrong, wrong, wrong! This lady is very deceptive. On the outside to casual observers, yes, she may appear straightforward or even straight-laced. What you see, however, is not necessarily what you get. Only once you've nibbled your way into her heart, do you realise what delicious delights she holds. She wickedly satisfies those inner cravings but always leaves you feeling that she's capable of so much more. The rush of energy she creates plays havoc with your insides and ties knots in your tummy.

The good news is that Taurus woman is easy to track drown. You don't really have to go looking as with most other females – she just sort of appears. One minute you're walking down the street, thinking about a cup of tea and that familiar old biscuit tin you've got at home – when all of a sudden, there she is; through the shop window you notice a gorgeous, mouth-watering vision. You know you have to have her and you know it's going to be bad for you. When Taurus woman is young and fresh, what you will recognise her by are her curves. They are perfectly and generously proportioned and are emphasised by the feminine and individual style of clothing which clings and swirls around her body. Her breasts make other women green with envy and make men want to be permanently four months old. Now that you've decided to break your diet of brainless bimbos, how do you attract her interest? More good news – because this woman is open, honest and trusting, she will assume that you are too until time proves differently. She has a genuine appreciation of men and certainly won't be upset by any form of opening line as long as it's not crude or coarse. She has a refreshingly innocent view of the male species and doesn't automatically assume that you want to get her into bed. (If you do, you better keep it well hidden for a while longer.) The key word from now on is Romance. Get it firmly fixed in your head that she is ruled by Venus – planet of passion, poetry and painfully soppy scenarios. Any sensible, articulate and humorous approach will start the friendship ball rolling, but to cross the line from conversation to copulation will require skill and daring worthy of the Milk Tray man. She knows she's good enough to eat, but won't give her cherry away to any Tom, Dick or Harry.

If you have designs on her body, appeal to her love of art. Suggest escorting her to the galleries, the museums and to see *Swan Lake*. A last resort is to offer to show her your etchings – she's traditional enough to fall for this one, so don't worry about drawing a blank. Patience will be your virtue in everything that happens from this point. You may be on first name terms with the entire Bolshoi Ballet before sex becomes part of your programme. When that 'right' moment comes though, you won't always know about it in advance. With some girls, success is calculated by utilising the natural progress chart that lies in the six inches between their upper thigh and their treasure trove. Two inches for the first date, four for the second and so on. Once your middle finger, which has all the determination of a Jack Russell, has managed to tunnel through the last defence – the knicker elastic – you know you're home and dry, well, sort of! With Taurus girl though, forget it. You may spend a year giving foot massages, then go from ankle bracelet to Heaven in one giant step for mankind.

Scene 2 **The Main Event**

So far, she has set the pace and the word 'snail' may have sprung to mind. Now though, you have obviously done something to trigger the full Mills and Boon mode and this woman wants to be taken. The setting will be her place, it's candlelit and comfortable and you will have just finished a meal that was so good it defies description (Taurean ladies are *the* cooks of the zodiac). She won't announce that you are to be the last course, you are supposed to have taken the hint when the small talk stopped and her asparagus tip began getting a blow-job. You must now take the lead and you better do it by the book. Anything unusual, unconventional or kinky can only be introduced once she has entire trust in you and preferably a wedding ring. Assume the role of 'Me Heathcliffe – you Kathy' and it will stand you in good stead. Start at the top because the Taurean sensitive spots are the throat, neck and chest. Little kisses that extend from the ears to the breast, but stop short of the nipple, will turn her to jelly and if you back this up with tiny love bites to the top of her spine you'll soon be on your way to the honey.

Eventually you've reached the stage where her actions, her body language and her whole being are screaming 'Yes'. Your Jack Russell finger is enjoying the walkies of a lifetime and you're just about to release the Pointer in your pants to keep it company. The only real difficulty which occurs when making love to this girl will probably happen at this point. Basically, she has a flair for dramatics and in her fantasies she doesn't surrender without a fight. 'No!'

she yells, 'Don't do it, you mustn't . . . I mustn't . . .'
Terrific, what now? Do you treat her with all the
respect she deserves and chain up Rover and Fido
promising them a romp in some other field, or do you
fling her on the bed with abandoned lust with half
your mind pondering what the penalty is for rape
these days?

The answer is simple – you ease off the pressure and
return to the safe zone around her neck, never
questioning, never stopping and never hinting that
you are attached to an unexploded missile that's in
danger of premature detonation. You've lit her touch-
paper and from here the only way is up. Despite the
fact you've got the impression that she's going to be a
passive partner, you are about to be pleasantly surprised. No matter how much she enjoys her games of
force and resistance, she adores sex and she's kind to
dogs. Her instincts will take over and with one
lightning and very athletic manoeuvre . . . Bingo, boy
meets girl.

For intercourse itself, she prefers to be underneath
which you may find rather predictable, but you will be
rewarded by the way she gazes up at you in awe and
wonderment. She could not look any more enthralled
if she was gazing up at the ceiling of the Sistine
Chapel.

The confirmation that you really are an Old Master
will swell your confidence, your pride and the tools of
your trade. One shattering simultaneous orgasm is
what she wants, so judge your timing. Afterwards,
dispel any thoughts of the cigarette and pizza routine
– the future of this romance depends on your after-
play techniques.

Scene 3 **Extras**

Think about what it would be like to have to eat nouvelle cuisine permanently – you'd be constantly amazed by the techniques and presentation, but still be left at the end of the night craving something a bit more substantial. Well, this is the benefit of life with Taurus woman. She may not be the most imaginative encounter you ever have, but she will be one of the most satisfying. The icing on this particular cake is that as she gets to know you better and the emotional bond between you strengthens, she is increasingly prepared to cater to your rather more exotic sexual appetites. There's not much that she won't at least consider just so long as it's in the name of love.

She's a real sucker for oral sex too; her love of food and the joy of tasting new delicacies means that she's more than happy to swallow your own protein potion. You shouldn't expect her to volunteer her own suggestions for spicing up bedtime, but neither should you make the mistake of thinking that she has no fantasies. Taurus is an Earth sign and as such, what goes on in her mind can be fantastically filthy. Given a choice of blue movies, she'll be scanning the cases looking for ones with four-legged stars. Her earthy characteristics are again the reason why she likes her men to smell like men and not a perfume counter. Taurus girl is a pheromone junkie who is easily intoxicated by fresh sweat and the smell of sex.

Outside the bedroom though, a Taurean partner is the perfect homemaker, wife and mother. She's fiercely loyal, so long as she's sexually fulfilled, is calm in a crisis and more than prepared to bring home the bacon if you fall on lean times. She is practical, patient and comfortingly predictable – some may say she's the perfect woman. If there is a sticky point, it's that as contentment increases, so does her dress size. Although plump should never be classed as a problem, you may have to get used to the idea in ten years' time of having twice the woman you married.

Scene 4 **The Finale**

Taurus woman may be a cream cake, but she'll never be left on the shelf, her qualities are too sought after and her faults so few. If you find one, then I'd advise you to grab the goodies quick because they don't hang around for long. Life together will be sweet and if you ever decide that your passion has gone past its sell-by date, then be honest. Providing she sees it the same way, your separation will be as polite and proper as that first night. If, however, you are a glutton for punishment, then try having a little nibble on the side.

Once she finds out – and she will because Earth signs always have an ear to the ground – you can consider your goose to be cooked. She will never forgive any indiscretion and if you stay together for the sake of the kids, she will never let you forget it. Every aftershave purchase will be met with suspicion, every trip to the pub with a questionnaire, but you'll only have yourself to blame.

Finally, a Taurus gal should be on every man's menu, she's naughty but she's nice and there's not much more you could want.

MALE
Scene 1 **The Meeting**

Action men, such as the Arien variety, are all well and good, but life with one can be rather exhausting. They make no allowances for headaches, period pains and nights when your idea of bliss is a bath, a brandy and bed – on your own. If you're the sort of girl who is a bit long in the tooth for a Barbie and Ken existence, very soon it will cross your mind that the grass could be greener if you explored the field a little more. Well, next stop on your astro-rampage is Taurus man and he's as close to his zodiac symbol as you're going to get. This Bull of a man is meaty and masculine, yet easily tamed, willing to be domesticated and on the inside he is temptingly tender. Unlike some men who constantly chop and change to keep up with the times, Taurus man has remained true to his astral blueprint. Sensuous, solid, successful and reassuringly stubborn – he has retained those basic earthy characteristics which make women want to have his children. The key to Mr Bull's attraction is his dependability; so long as he is loved and well handled, he will work like an ox to keep you in fine style and won't stray into pastures new to nibble on illicit clover. A criticism often levelled is that he's quite primitive in his approach to sex, but what he lacks in refinement is more than made up for with romance.

If this sounds like the sort of animal for you, then you need to know where to find him. Anywhere not too loud and brash would be a good bet. If you are at a party, he'll be the confidently quiet one, not saying much, but listening to everything as he mentally makes notes of those who could either be useful to his career or would look decorative on his duvet. He also tends to love sport. If he's watching then it will be bloodthirsty big boy stuff such as rugby and ice hockey, if he's playing then golf or snooker is more his forte. The least likely places to see him are those which are at all phony or pretentious. He can stomach the occasional soirée with arty types for the sake of love or money, but surround him with an assortment of 'Luvvies' and 'Dahlings' and he won't be able to conceal a facial expression similar to that of treading in something nasty.

Physically he is, well, bull-like! A broad body, set on square hips with stocky legs all wrapped up in a fair bit of flesh. His neck will be short and strong and resting on it will be a wide head topped off with thick wiry hair. The final giveaway will be his voice which is deep and expressive and can be quite animated when he's talking about something he is interested in such as food, music and his family's plans to retire to the coast.

If it seems that I'm giving you lots of clues as to how to recognise him it's because with this guy it is really necessary for you to make the moves. He is very territorial and as such, he treats other people's property with equal respect and won't risk treading on toes to get to you. If you maintain a coy distance from him, no matter how much he likes what he sees, all you can expect is a friendly smile as he passes you the tray of peanuts. Make your intentions a touch clearer, however, and that's a different matter.

There's a famous 'No Trespassing' sign which some farmers attach to their gates. It reads 'To cross this field takes ten minutes . . . The bull can do it in seven.' Remember this advice when planning your pulling strategy. It may take a while for Taurus man to get the hint, but once you are in his private space and acting provocatively, you are waving the red rag that ensures the chase is on. You will definitely enjoy the preliminaries with Mr Bull because you can be relaxed to the point of laziness. It may make you feel better to drape yourself in designer dating gear, but he can't tell the difference between Ozbek and Oxfam, so save your pennies for a fantastic dinner which really is the food of love. Chat-up lines? . . . don't waste your breath, he genuinely likes female conversation and is just as interested in the terrible price of hold-up stockings as he is in getting them off you.

Scene 2 **The Main Event**

If the entire session of lovemaking was to be compared to the face of a clock, starting at midday, foreplay would take you to 8.00p.m., intercourse until 9.00p.m. and afterglow until midnight. This may be viewed scornfully by the never-mind-the-quality-just-feel-the-width boys who think it's the amount of time spent horizontal jogging that makes a girl tick, but Taurus man belongs to the Barry White school of romance. He *lurves* to get you in the mood with husky mutterings and good old-fashioned charm. Unusual approaches are not his style, but the tried and tested methods he employs have been proved to stand the test of time.

So you are in his bedroom and are as confident as you can be that tonight's the night this bull gets down to business. The only reason you're not entirely convinced is because prior to this point you have been through a fair amount of what can only be termed as trial runs.

This guy doesn't really believe in sex on the first night. You've had plenty of times when you've moaned and groaned and you have knocked the stuffing out of an entire three-piece suite, but as yet neither of you has actually got any clothes off, and subsequently, you are at the stage when an orgasm is long overdue. He, however, is finding it hard to keep his physical restraint in line with his principles and has long since run out of reasons to explain those strange stained patches on the front of his trousers.

Well, whether he's decided that he now knows you well enough, or because he suspects that his mum won't fall for another coffee-in-the-lap excuse, your big moment has arrived. The endless kissing, stroking and nibbling are all running true to form and once again, your breasts have been sucked into perfect cones, but this time there is something different. As Barry on the stereo gets to the big instrumental break, you notice that Mr Bull has discovered that there is life below the waistline. If you are, say, Aries woman and have anything out of the ordinary down there, such as a tattoo, an erotic piercing or a balder than usual pubic hairstyle, he will make a polite comment about going to refill your wine glass as he dashes downstairs to phone Scorpio man for advice. If though, everything looks vaguely correct and is modestly moist, then you can lie back and enjoy at least half an hour of an oral wash-and-brush-up. He will treat your most treasured possession with the care of a professional French polisher and if he misses a bit, you must be prepared to tell him. He won't be over the moon if you offer to show him though, because although some men revel in their partner's self-stimulation, he will feel a little miffed and ask you if you do that sort of thing often. On the plus side, however, when you've gone through the 'down a bit, left a bit' routine once, he won't forget. He does possess an excellent ability to retain information and this asset will only let him down if he ever moves on to a new partner. He will give her a fitting using your memorised details and if she's shorter than you, he will probably wonder why she doesn't scream in ecstasy when he rubs her belly button. For intercourse itself, he'd prefer you to be on top which suits most girls fine, but is equally happy to do all the work and won't mind if you just lie there in pure relaxed bliss. He'd rather go for gentle rock than heavy raunch and is capable of satisfying your needs many times over, each orgasm being meticulously sandwiched between ample amounts of fore- and afterplay. Stamina is not something he lacks and Mr White will have sung himself hoarse before Taurus man begins to feel tired.

Scene 3 **Extras**

The innocently romantic and wholly fulfilling first time is a demonstration of what Mr Bull does best. He is not opposed to trying new things and indeed, would do anything to keep his lady love happy, but deep down he is perplexed by hi-tech sex. Lovemaking for him is just that; an expression of his most intimate emotions and a physical outlet for his highly charged drive. He will gladly occupy your two most accessible orifices but the gentleman in him is a bit apprehensive about the third. For the same reason, he will worry about a spot of slapping and spanking but will be more than happy to be on the receiving end if you ever tire of being submissive. Although he is the typical Bull, he is certainly no brute. A beneficial by-product of his determination to be all man is that he accepts you as all woman. When those time-of-the-month troubles occur, he will readily supply you with hugs and hot water bottles and if your haywire hormones make you extra horny, then he will not deprive you of sex. Taurus man is a paragon during pregnancy and a blessing after the birth. When you two become three, his abilities go into overdrive, nothing fuels his driving ambition more than having his own family. When you all drive off for a long weekend to visit his parents who now live by the coast, you can count on him to have arranged a perfect candlelit evening, *sans* baby, complete with enough champagne to temporarily take your mind off stretch marks.

Scene 4 **The Finale**

Taurus man is one of the least likely signs to end an affair. Once you've put a ring on his finger, you may just have well put it through his nose because a partnership with him is for keeps. He guards his possessions well and will snort with rage if they are threatened. He'll forgive an indiscretion or two and will only come to the end of his tether if you turn out to be a compulsive nymphomaniac, but even then, he'll offer to get you some therapy.

If you do decide to put him out to grass, chances are it is because he's fallen into the classic Taurean trap of taking things for granted. As he matures, he gets sloppy and is prone to putting on lots of weight. Sex may become stale for your tastes – even though it's wonderful to receive roses at your office every week, there may be times when you just want to be chained in the bathroom and abused with a wet loofah! He can grow quite mean too – that once-a-year dream holiday loses some of its sparkle when you remember how many coupons he made you cut out and use at the supermarket.

Either way, the end will be painful and emotional. If he leaves you, he'll still want to be your best friend and this can be tricky if you have moved on to a jealous new partner. If you leave him, there are the constant phone calls begging you to return and in the background, singing loudly, is Barry at his gut-wrenching best. Accept that Taurus man loves you the way you are and that is all he requires of you. If you can do this, you will have a friend and partner who offers a special sort of love and romance in this world. If you can't, then it's on with your best Matador hat, a quick pause for breath and off in search of Gemini man.

GEMINI

FEMALE
Scene 1 **The Meeting**

By now I'm assuming that you chaps out there are fully acquainted with the ins and outs of the first two zodiac ladies. After the extremes you have encountered with adventurous Aries and the traditional Taurus, you could be thinking that you have it taped and you can celebrate your newfound sexual knowledge with Gemini woman. Well, if you like your celebrations to come with fireworks, you are in luck. This cracker of a girl is a box of delights; never the same on any two occasions, hugely unpredictable and totally unprepared to give you any sort of clue as to what you're going to get until her fuse is lit – then all you can do is stand clear and wait. The relationship between such a fascinating female and mere mortal man is an uneasy one and not usually destined to last forever, yet most males would gladly risk getting their fingers burnt for the sake of sharing that one

35

sparkling moment in time with her. She will bring out the kid in you, yet it takes a real grown-up to handle her properly. The quality of her display and performance will depend entirely on how much thought and effort you have put in, and even when the party's over and you are left to pick up the pieces wondering if the experience was worth the cost, the answer will be *Yes* – most certainly Yes.

Gemini girl is not the most materialistic character of the zodiac, but does like luxuries as much as the rest of us and if a man can keep her in a style to which she is happy to become accustomed, he has a better than average chance of securing her attention. So before beginning the search for your gunpowder girl, it's best to have saved a reasonable amount of pocket money. There is no one specific place to locate her, as her boredom threshold is low enough to ensure that she is always on the move and never regularly frequenting one particular venue. You are most likely to come across her by chance and when you do, she will be surrounded by a mixed pack of friends. A talented conversationalist, she will be the one who is leading the chat and her ability for social networking is a finely honed skill that keeps her abreast of everything. Cut off her intravenous line to the grapevine and she will wither and die. If by some miracle, she is not to be found talking, you will recognise her first by twinkling eyes that constantly dart from person to person and also by her clothes. To say they are bright is an understatement – how she manages to look stunning in outfits which make other girls look like Coco the clown is one of life's mysteries. Her exterior packaging does serve a purpose though; just as the deadliest snakes have the most exuberant skins, your potential pyrotechnic is wrapped with its own warning. For your own safety and enjoyment, I'm going to give you a couple more tips. First, do not interrupt her debating to suggest meekly dinner and a movie. She will be so insulted by your lack of originality that not only will you get a thumbs-down, but you will be so publicly scorned that you will feel like a Christian at a Roman family get-together. Second, remember that she is ruled by Mercury, planet of the mind. She is eternally curious, thirsts for uncertainty, hungers for change and never satisfies her appetite for knowledge. If you can come up with an opening gambit which appeals to three or more of these traits, then you are in with a sporting chance. If you can't, I'll give you a little hint . . . move straight on to a Cancer lady.

Once you have succeeded in separating her from the rest of the bunch, you are now primed for a one-way ticket to the heavens; she would not leave her friends if she only wanted to talk to you. If all Gemini girl was interested in was verbal intercourse, then it would be more her style to pull up another chair and await your contributions to the discussion. From now on you must have very big sleeves filled with the most imaginative aces – it is accepted that she will provide most of the words during your encounter, but you must provide the catalysts that spark her sexual responses.

Scene 2 The Main Event

Quite where your spontaneous combustion takes place is not the main issue but the more bizarre the better. Everyone knows how a firework behaves when launched into a vast black sky – that's why I bet in the past you've ignited at least one in the kitchen. Well, Gemini girl is the same; bedroom cotton and shag-pile carpet are familiar fabrics to her back and ordinary props will provide a standard performance.

Stimulate her senses by spreading her legs over the studded seat of a seriously powerful motorbike. Enjoy the exhilaration of racing down the moonlit street as the returning Hell's Angel sees what her heels have done to his customised paint job. Pin her against the wall of the post office and then listen as she screams 'Help . . . Rape . . .!, these are the tests of your tenacity. Remember, she is not kinky, she is just curious of your every reaction. By now you may be thinking that there's more chance of you being locked up than getting laid, but never show your fear. If you do, she will push you on to increasingly dangerous liaisons which could end in tears unless your idea of a future sex life with her is hand relief under the visitor's table in one of Her Majesty's guest houses. There is no prescribed order for lovemaking to follow, foreplay is not required and you will have received yours by way of her expertly filthy descriptions of what she intends to do to your phallus. If you are a gent though and do prefer to knock before you enter, let me tell you that the Geminian sensitive spots are the areas between hands and shoulders. Sucking a girl's fingers is fairly usual foreplay but this activity has a greater than average effect on Gemini woman as does lightly stroking her arm or nuzzling her armpit. Making love to the girl born under the sign of the twins can be a minefield; some of the time she wants romance, some of the time raunch and all because you are catering to two personalities. She's as much fun as a threesome and far easier to find. By now, of course, all clothes will have been removed as she likes an uncluttered view and you will have demonstrated your total commitment to the project by not wincing as your best shirt gets mercilessly relieved of its buttons.

With both of your brains fully attuned to the job, she will waste no time in bringing your bodies into line. Her duality inevitably makes her incredibly versatile and she can easily stimulate herself at her own regular pace whilst simultaneously massaging your manhood at a more rapid rate; it's the sexual equivalent of rubbing your tummy whilst patting your head. A word of warning here – she can often be unaware of her own strength, especially with those astrologically gifted fingers. As she takes you in hand, you'd be forgiven for thinking she was trying to start a fire. For intercourse itself her favourite position is any one she hasn't yet tried and once in place, don't count on staying there until lift off. Her frenetic style means that after a couple of seconds she will struggle free to try something different – such as phoning a friend to give a progress report. In fact, her need to chop and change will ensure you are in and out more times than a group of party-goers doing the hokey-cokey. Don't count on Gemini girl to announce her climaxes, she will test you to see if you can tell. If you are particularly good at this game, she may throw in a few fakes just to confuse you further. For all the conundrums of coitus, when you eventually hit your own explosion, you can count on it to be dynamite because Gemini woman certainly gives as good as she gets. Hopefully, you've made no plans for the rest of the night because she believes in life after orgasm. Her favourite place for afterglow is a nightclub where she is quite prepared to go straight from the bed without visiting the bathroom. She will have dazzled you with sex and now wants to shock some strangers by displaying the evidence – and of course, watching their reactions.

Scene 3 **Extras**

The first night has gone with a bang and as with fireworks, Gemini woman is something you want more than just once a year. A relationship with her will make every night an occasion and every day an adventure. Sex will never lose its sparkle but to keep your partnership happy, there needs to be more. You must always be around when she needs you, yet at the same time be prepared to accept her need for independence and that includes nights out with friends of both sexes – jealous types need not apply. As time goes on, your intimate life together will become more outrageous. That non-stop curiosity will lead to a taste for fetishes, not for the sexual pleasure but for the mental stimulation that goes with such pastimes. If you are ever stuck for a present, buy her the latest marital aid or any gadget, gizmo or vegetable that could have alternative uses. It is impossible to embarrass her but she loves you to try and nor will she be shy of discussing any potential relationship problems. She will keep your mind alert, your body active and your friends enthralled. The only price you may pay is never being able to get a word in edgeways. All in all, she's a tonic and a treat, she puts stars in your eyes and wonderment on your face. Handle her with care and life will be out of this world.

Scene 4 **The Finale**

Realising that Gemini woman has two personalities is something that happens on the first encounter, but as time passes you may also suspect that she is capable of leading two lives. Look through her dictionary and the words 'commitment' and 'lifelong' could well have been scored out. The problem is that she is one of the few women who are entirely capable of separating the physical from the emotional – she uses sex as another form of communication. To you she communicates love, to another man, friendship. She may even take a lover of the same sex which is all well and good if you can play too, but that's quite unlikely to happen more than the first exploratory time. So if you are not a sign that can handle constant suspicion and decide that this partnership is burnt out, how do you end it? The sensible way is to arrange your parting so that she makes the move. If you simply tell her it's not working, her logical side will accept it, but her emotional side will guarantee that the back of every door of every public ladies toilet will be embellished with your greatly magnified shortcomings duly ensuring that finding a new lover will require you also to find a new neighbourhood. The answer is simple – to end this union you simply have to become boring. Stop varying your bedroom repertoire and leave your socks on for sex. Insist on showing the same holiday video to all her friends every time they visit. Stop talking to her unless it is to relay tedious details of your day, such as problems with the photocopier. If all else fails, condemn her to a life of housework – you won't see her for dust!

MALE
Scene 1 **The Meeting**

So girls, you have now reached Gemini man and are one quarter of the way through your journey. As well as thinking 'doesn't time fly when you're having fun', you are probably feeling fairly confident about this astro-sex stuff. Each guy conforms to a type and all that's needed is to recognise, remember and respond accordingly – yes? Well, no, actually. Gemini man is different because what you see isn't necessarily what you get. You are now to encounter the salesman of the zodiac, although it's fair to say that you have most likely met him several times already. He was the terribly convincing chappie responsible for your double glazing, your satellite dish and that timeshare in Tenerife. So before you glibly consider letting him in your life, reflect on what happened when you last let him in your front door. Nevertheless, this guy is definitely executive class – he's intelligent, witty, sexy in a sophisticated way and is as smart as they come. Oh yes, and he's successful, he has to be the best at whatever he attempts so if you are keen to get down to physical business with him, what better reasons do you need? The strategy you should employ, whether for a night or a lifetime, is to play him at his own game. Don't present the whole deal straight away, sell him a little at a time to maintain his curiosity, give him plenty of incentives and surprise him with plenty of hidden extras.

Fortunately, locating this man is the easy part, in fact it's avoiding him that sometimes causes the problems. Just like the female counterpart, it's the Geminian gift of the gab that provides his passport to popularity.

There will always be at least a couple of them at any party because seasoned hosts know that he alone can make the difference between an enchanted evening or a feeble fiasco. His talent for chat is unparalleled in the zodiac. He talks with his mouth, his eyes and his hands and is more than capable of holding several conversations at the same time without letting any of the topics slip. It's the verbal equivalent of spinning lots of plates from lots of poles. He also adores stirring up controversy and unless he is kept in check will soon have fierce debating battles raging. When you arrive at a get-together you will instantly know if Gemini man is there because the 'yes's' will be lining up against one wall with the 'no's' pinned against the other. He, by the way, will have surreptitiously disappeared from the discourse about an hour ago when he got bored and can now be found loitering with intent to find something more interesting to do. This is where you come in and you need not be shy of making the first move. If you need final confirmation of his astrological identity, ask him politely to do something simple such as pass the pepper or tell you the time. He won't just give you these things, he'll bargain with you. You say, 'Could you pass the pepper please.' He says, 'Yes I could, but be a really good girl and I'll pass the salt too.' If these words fell from the lips of most other signs, you'd be understandably irritated, but Gemini man exudes such a pleasing persona and sensual sincerity that you can't help but somehow feel you've got a good deal. Now that you've attracted his interest you need to trigger his testosterone and the way to this man's hormones is through his head because his astral ruler is Mercury, the planet of intellect. Having a handy supply of unique one-liners will work well, but answering any of his questions with one of your own is an adequate alternative. Your real ace in the hole is that Gemini man simply can't resist a challenge, but we're not talking all that playing-hard-to-get business, as this tactic will set off his boredom alarm instantly. It's much better to talk about your sole previous lover and sigh wistfully as you explain that despite being wined, dined and draped in jewels, he never really understood you. Also add that you'd live on bread and water if only one man could make the earth move. Tell him that this person would be rewarded with the full force of your repressed and rampant sexuality. In one fell swoop you have set Gemini man a target, a realistic budget and a commission too good to refuse.

Scene 2 **The Main Event**

If you are wise, you will keep your side of the erotic negotiations to a minimum and before you clinch this deal you won't try to extract any promises of permanence. Gemini man likes to be sold as seen and the long term depends entirely on how you treat him as the weeks go by.

As for where you conduct the business; anywhere that's brightly lit and mirrored will suffice. Unlike Gemini woman who is turned on by outrageous locations, the male species is aroused by watching his own performance. He is his own voyeur and being able to see and speak about what is happening is just as important as being able to feel it. Of all his five senses, sight and speech come way before touch. Ask him if he likes oral sex and he will say yes, he does like talking about it!

Once you are down to the nitty gritty you can look forward to your every whim being pandered to. What makes this chap a good lover is what makes him a good salesman; he doesn't just want you to buy his product, he wants you to enjoy it, to believe in it and hopefully recommend it to your friends. Even though you have probably realised by this point that Gemini man does not come with a lifetime guarantee, you still won't be able to resist his trial offer. He will lavish expert foreplay on you, both physical and verbal and every action, every word is designed to coax you, entice you and weaken your resistance. Forget any love-making limitations you may have previously set yourself, his curiosity will lead him to parts of your anatomy that you thought were only visible by X-ray. If you so much as hint that you still possess areas of virgin territory, he'll be there like a shot to stake his claim. It has to be said that stamina is not his main attribute. He isn't, nor does he need to be, a sexual athlete because he knows that the right buttons to press on a woman are in her head. He scorns those sex manuals that insist the average female needs twenty minutes of warm-up. Girls can count on going from, 'I think I need more time,' to 'give me the goods now' in about thirty seconds. Also, Gemini man is not keen on the idea of prolonging sex and covering the same ground twice. The way he sees it is simple; after the preliminaries, he presents his package, you present yours and the object is to get as much mutual satisfaction as quickly as possible. He is not cutting corners, he's just being efficient and it's a lesson many other zodiac males could learn as they persist in twiddling bits that have as much chance of sending you into orbit as a bicycle. To get back to oral sex, for girls who find fellatio a bit hard to swallow, this is your man. He can't deny the pleasures of receiving it but invariably stops you because it means an end to conversation for ten minutes. For the same reason, don't expect to hold his ears and see the top of his head very often either. For intercourse he will want to run through a vast repertoire of positions and he has one for every taste – the more you sample, the happier he'll be just so long as you don't take too long over it. One small foible you should be aware of is that at the climax of your merger, he may prefer to leave a deposit on you, as seeing those results is all important to him.

Scene 3 Extras

Once your union is well and truly cemented, Gemini man will be happy if you can diversify somewhat. He will want to expand both of your horizons and is fascinated by new ideas, gadgets and just about anything that promises to stimulate him mentally or physically. It's actually not as tiring as it sounds because he is just as willing to discuss the theory as try the practice. He is, however, more likely to stay on his home patch if you can live out the occasional fantasy.

I think at this point, I should mention the famous Geminian twin personality. I've not touched on it so far because people born under this sign of the Twins are often accused of being untrustworthy, when, in reality, they are misunderstood and their motives misinterpreted by other signs who cannot think as fast as they do. It is through their sexuality though that the two personalities emerge most clearly. If your Geminian loves luxury, he will be turned on by having sex in a pig sty. If he hates pain, he'll want you to thrash him and if he's all man, don't be surprised if you catch him in your stockings. Whatever you do for him, don't give it away too freely or he might be tempted by the idea of buying it. For all his quirks, Gemini man is one of the zodiac's characters and regardless of how long your encounter lasts, he will have put something in your life that you never knew you needed, but now find it impossible to do without.

Scene 4 **The Finale**

Unfortunately, keeping hold of your high flyer might be tricky, as whilst he's young, Gemini man has to be out in the field, constantly travelling and always looking for fresh conquests and ways to gain more knowledge. Only when he matures is he likely to settle down and the lucky lady who gets a full-time position will benefit from his considerable experience both in and out of the bedroom. The young Geminian does not relish a life of domestication and if one of your early meetings results in him giving you a free gift, he'll be gone quicker than you can say antenatal classes. If you are the rose-covered cottage type, I'm afraid this chap may not live up to your expectations and despite his attractions, you may decide that it's time to return him to his manufacturer – his mum. Stop paying him attention, reject his advances, supervise his socialising and he's sure to start packing his suitcase in search of a more appreciative customer. Honesty will also pay off, if you tell him you're no longer satisfied he will take it well. If he's incurred you any cost or expense, he's fair enough to give you your money back plus a reasonable bonus to compensate for the inconvenience.

One thing he won't do is actually tell you if he wants to call it a day. A relationship with Gemini man never ends, it just changes and he cannot see the problem in exchanging romance for friendship. Even when the final transaction has long since been concluded, he will never be entirely out of your life. As you sit by the mirror that once witnessed some of the most unusual sex you have ever had, you can count on the phone to ring. It will be Gemini man doing a spot of optimistic cold calling that will, no doubt, tempt you to try his unique product just one more time.

CANCER

FEMALE
Scene 1 **The Meeting**

Whether your interests are actual or purely academic, if you are a chap working your way methodically through the zodiac ladies, let me inform you that you've now sampled three of the four astrological elements, i.e. a Fire sign, an Earth sign and an Air sign. If you have optimistic intentions of going for the fourth, you are going to have to clean up your act because the Cancerian female is a Water sign and for the purposes of studying Sextrology can only be likened to a celestial French maid. She will certainly tickle your fancy instantly, but attempting to put your sticky fingerprints all over her straight away will lead you to be the victim of a good stern dressing-down and, believe me, this is not as much fun as it sounds. The conquest of this sign of the Crab is something that requires a good deal of thought, patience and care because she is a real lady with meticulous morals and pristine principles, despite any first impressions. Treat your encounter with her in the same way you would if you were looking for someone to handle the family treasures – after all, hopefully she's going to be handling yours. Finding yourself and keeping a French maid will be a measure of your success and status – without doubt, very few men have the refinement required to ensure a long-term contract and this is what she ideally craves. Before you even begin to consider peeling away her veneers, you must sweep all those preconceived and prehistoric pulling techniques firmly under the carpet and start again. The key to Cancer lady's heart is firmly wrapped in her emotions which are as deep as an ocean and as difficult to fathom. She will readily admit that she has known quite a few men but this is simply because many previous lovers have only skirted around the edges and failed to touch her soul. To experience her passion at its most perfect and polished calls for someone special. If this turns out to be you, you will be repaid by a peep into her sexual store cupboard which holds many wild and wanton wonders.

If you have already been tempted by what you have read and your current sexual situation is vacant then you should waste no time in locating her – ladies like this offer a highly specialised service and are snapped up fast. The first place to try is within her current employment which is likely to be in the field of looking after people, animals or things. She was born to work, but not solely for monetary reward, indeed, your local charity or voluntary organisation will be staffed by at least a couple of these caring creatures.

She could also be a nurse and it's almost worth slipping a disc just to get a sneak preview of her bedside manner.

Failing that, you could resort to placing an advert in your local paper. Describe yourself as dashing, debonair and above all else, desperately trying to recover from recent domestic distress – Cancer woman will answer your call because she cannot bear the thought of human suffering. The best place to pin down a non-working Cancer girl is in her home which is the focal point of her existence and the word 'immaculate' does not even come close to describing it. Without putting ideas into your head, if say, her window should get broken and a chap who's good with his hands should just happen to be passing by, it's only right that he would offer his services, isn't it? You can count on her gratitude being immeasurable and an offer to stay for a quick bite will be yours before you've even had time to consider getting your tool kit out.

Over a period of time you could pop round frequently to see if there's anything else she needs fixing, fastening or fitting, but never suggest the sort of odd job you really have in mind. Do things step by step, secure her trust and then one day, when everything in her house is nailed, filled or screwed you will eventually get the nod to attend to the one thing that isn't – her! Don't get the impression that you can investigate her personal plumbing right there and then, but do take the hint of what's to come as she presses her privileged phone number in your hand with a look that guarantees your manual dexterity is about to take on another dimension.

Scene 2 **The Main Event**

This traditional girl will relish a traditional date and nothing more than an intimate dinner in elegant or quaint surroundings will be expected. After you've taken her home, she will invite you in for a coffee and so far, so good. What it pays to know is that she will never make the first move and without some prior planning you could go through the entire night sipping and chatting, only to face the morning in a state of caffeine-induced neurosis. What I recommend is that on a prior visit you sneakily nobble the coffee machine and with no further ado, whisk her into the bedroom. In actual fact, she will relish your powerful passion and will readily submit to your superior male sexuality – this is no women's libber. Undress her manfully; skilfully enough to prove you know what you're doing, but not with the expert twiddling and unlatching of a safe-cracker. She doesn't expect to be your first, but neither does she want to feel like she's another on your list of 'Things to Do'. As her clothes start to hit the floor, compliment her on every aspect of her body. She is supersensitive about her appearance and any part that you don't praise will be swiftly covered up again. This wonderful innocence conjures up memories of previous virginities that you may have stolen but if you never succeeded as a thief, the first night reactions of Cancer lady are as close as you can get. The only excuse you have for temporarily ceasing the compliments is to kiss her and this is where you discover just what this activity is all about. She could smooch for England and will explore areas of your mouth that even your dentist has not yet been able to reach whilst at the same time giving a tantalising demonstration of what lies ahead. When she does proceed to your lower department there will be no messing about – all those nooks and crannies will be sucked clean with the power of an industrial vacuum and when she clamps her mouth around your own extension hose you will have a real battle preventing her from manually extracting your excitement. Cancer girl can, at this point, have a flair for biting which is her subtle way of testing the speed and authenticity of all your other bodily responses.

Her most favoured intercourse positions are those which require you to do most of the moving and her to use little more than her smile reflexes. You won't mind this initial lack of participation because it reinforces her image of innocence and if she tells you that you're the best she's ever had, you can believe it because she is not prone to bolstering your machismo for effect. If she fails to bestow any such championship on you, you must try harder and anyway, she knows the average male ego ensures that you won't give up until her ecstatic cries have crossed the county line.

It's recommended that you don't opt for anything too adventurous on the first night and, depending on your own sign, it can actually be a relief to find a girl that is satisfied simply by what God gave you rather than the array of near-impossible stunts that some of the glossy magazines recommend. Being fit and self-disciplined, however, are vital attributes to pleasing her. She does not view either of your journeys to orgasm as a race, but will expect you to motor comfortably in fourth gear for most of the night and secretly feels that the one who crosses the climax line first is the loser. Some call her approach to sex lazy – I call it clever.

Scene 3 **Extras**

You may worry after your first night with Cancer woman that your relationship will settle down and lose some of its initial brilliance. This would be a mistake because, unlike some other girls whose contents never live up to the advertising, this lady does not believe in putting all her most valuable assets on display. The more time and trouble you invest in your little French maid, the more she will reveal and you will learn that her quite prim and proper exterior is secretly harbouring an incredibly mucky mind. Remember – the grandest houses have the grubbiest cellars. When Cancer woman feels secure, she will come out of her shell rapidly and will reveal her fantasies and erotic ambitions. Her underlying sexual preference, however, is for submission as she likes her men to crack the whip, so to speak. She has a very special skill for appearing totally compliant and non-demanding yet at the same time always managing to get exactly what she wants from each love-making session. This female Water sign is also known to flow in both directions and it's not unheard of for them secretly to take a female lover – twice the fun, half the guilt. In this situation she will assume the feminine role, love every minute of it and ease her conscience by convincing herself that she's not really that sort of girl, but sometimes things happen. Masturbation is a pastime done in earnest and she's not shy about it. Quite often you will catch her buffing up a nice little shine on her valuables with a variety of household utensils. Don't think she sits on the washing machine purely because she has no breakfast stools either.

Life with this lady gets better all the time; she is

loving, loyal and the perfect person to add quality to your life, your home and your children. She will fight ferociously to defend anything that is dear to either of you and what's more, your mother will adore her. Share your life with her, give her the respect she deserves and you'll clean up!

Scene 4 **The Finale**

Once life as a cosy couple starts sprouting a few cobwebs, Cancer woman will be the first to recognise it and the last to say anything. To end an affair with her is tricky because you have to get rid of her family too and they will have worked their way into your life like woodworm. Talking it out won't help because she will always have a better reason for staying together – such as she is the only one who knows how to operate all the space age kitchen equipment. There are very few reasons why your passion should bite the dust, but one could be her intermittent moodiness and the noise of plate-throwing that precedes it – or it could be that if her maternal instincts are not satisfied, she will take a toyboy lover. The easiest way to ensure her exit is to treat her like a servant. Scatter your most obnoxious used underwear all over the floor, or instead of buying her flowers, leave twenty pence on the table as you rise from the dinner table. These tactics are cruel, but unfortunately too commonly used by men who should know better. Her capacity for tolerance is one of the strongest in the zodiac and often leads to her being badly treated. This is a real pity and many males have found to their cost that they only realise what they had once she's gone and without her, your house is certainly not a home.

MALE
Scene 1 The Meeting

In what seems to be a very short time, we have now arrived at the fourth zodiac male and if you are a girl who is still looking for a chap to take home confidently to meet your father, well, you could be in luck. Dad will love Cancer man even though it will take him a lifetime to work out what exactly it is about this guy that is so reassuringly comfortable. Between you and me, the answer's simple: Mr Crab could easily be your mother! Now don't get me wrong, I'm not saying that sharing a life with him means sharing your make-up bag too, I'm merely highlighting the fact that the reason for Cancer male's familiarity with females, their families and their friends is that he is ruled by the Moon which is astrologically synonymous with motherhood. In him you will find a protector and a peacemaker, a problem-solver and your best pal all rolled into one. This is a person who readily puts your needs before his own and even if you ever break free in search of independence, he will still always be around to pick up the pieces. What sets Cancer male apart from the pack is that he cares. He cares about everything, from the struggles of the Third World to the stresses of the Third Division and what's more, he will invest a lot of time and trouble in trying to sort them out. The down side to all of this, though, is that for the most part Cancer man exudes a cool, calm and unemotional manner; his nervous centre is tucked away deep within that protective Crab shell. Breaking into it is only done with patience and an unspoken promise that your union will be permanent. If it's just a one-night stand you're after, Leo man is next door awaiting your call.

The best locations to hook yourself this real catch of a man are any that you could describe as aquatic, perhaps your local riverbank. This is because he is a Water sign so, regardless of the time of year, he can be found messing around in his element and fishing can be a favourite hobby. Next, you need to eliminate the other two Water signs, but this is relatively easy; sexy show-off Scorpio will be bragging about the size of his tackle, while animal-loving Mr Pisces will be rooting around the shoreline looking for fish to revive, resuscitate and return to the river. Cancer man will probably be standing alone as he's none too competitive and the relaxed, rhythmic movements he makes as he confidently casts his rod in and out should be enough for you to identify him. He wouldn't normally appreciate his concentration being interrupted, but a good opening bid with this man is to ask for advice – he loves to be helpful and will not be able to resist aiding your amateur attempts. As he puts his arms around you to teach you his angling technique, you may imagine you've already reeled him in, but at this stage he's just being friendly. Whatever you may be thinking as you press against his pole, he will not be impressed by any sudden vulgarity, so keep your hands off his flies. It's much better to dangle your bait in far more subtle ways – really keen girls could 'accidentally' stumble into the stream and provide him with an impromptu glimpse of his own Miss Wet T-shirt. This would work quite well because Mr Crab is a breast man, born and bred. If this sounds far too sexist, you could equally flaunt your I.Q. Name dozens of fresh-water fish that he's never heard of and describe in detail their markings, behaviour and breeding habits. With the topic of chat now innocently round to sex, the progress rate should jump up. He may not like forward women, but he is human and will at least offer you a sandwich. The ploy so far has established that you have a common pastime and that he is able to teach you things (a factor that is important to Cancerians). You will also have succeeded in arousing his interest and can now afford to be more daring. Laughingly suggest that if he can net that big angry trout swimming by, you wouldn't mind sharing it with him for breakfast. He will realise he's opened up a whole can of worms but he won't want to hurt your feelings and as far as a date goes, you're home and dry.

Scene 2 **The Main Event**

You may spend many a freezing weekend wading around in your wellies before savouring the warmth of Mr Cancer's bed. It's not that he's shy as is often stated, it's just that he does not see the point of sex for its own sake. He prefers to make love to your whole being and for this he needs as much prior information as possible. His superb memory will have retained any little snippets that you may have let out and when THE night occurs it will begin with him presenting you with your favourite perfume, flowers or wine. He won't expect a gift from you but should you buy him something in silver, he will be enraptured. The biggest compliment this sentimental sign can pay you is to take you to a place that has special significance to him. As he drives you to a large open field, you could start thinking that he's more kinky than he appears but in fact, it's probably the place where he first took the stabilisers off his bike. The real action will take place in his home as here he knows where to locate everything he may need. Foreplay will be extensive and expertly carried out, although it has to be said that the younger males take a while to perfect this art. Until they become more experienced, there is a tendency for the preliminaries to feel more like an examination. All that probing, prodding and concentrated staring reminds you of the school nurse checking for nits – it's that maternal streak again. Regardless of age, all Cancerian men have extra-sensitive nipples and you sucking them will drive him wild and reinforce the parent/offspring role that is so evident in his sexual make-up. His fondness for teaching means that you have to do little other than be an appreciative pupil. Let him dictate the pace and describe the procedures; he loves to explain in great detail what he intends to do and how it's going to make you feel – a sort of 'Janet and John bonk each other senseless'. The more words of encouragement and sighs of enjoyment you utter, the further he'll go and his patience ensures that he will prolong any erotic activity until he's got the message across. Many girls during sex will use the stock exclamation, 'Wow, how did you do that?' It comes from the same phrase book as 'Wow, why has that never happened to me before?' and 'Wow, did you know you're the best lover I've ever had?' As we all know, these words puff up the male chest quicker than a session down the gym. Well with Cancer man, there's no self-satisfied smile and smug raise of one eyebrow, no, this chap will literally stay up all night if necessary endeavouring to explain and show you the answers to these and similar questions. Smart girls will admit to grasping the basics only after at least twenty demonstrations. First-time intercourse is likely to be anywhere except on the bed and a preferred position is for him to stand and hold you while your legs wrap round his waist. He also adores having his manhood massaged by your breasts, so that you can sport his favourite jewellery – a pearl necklace. Oral sex is not high on his sexual curriculum, but if you'd like to perfect the art of fellatio, he's more than happy to let you practise on him. What a man!

Afterglow is very important to him so don't spoil the moment by trying to dash to the bathroom before anything sticky hits the carpet. For him, love means staying put in your mutual passion puddle. If you manage to fall asleep in it, you've made a lover for life.

Scene 3 **Extras**

As I mentioned earlier, Mr Cancer would not like to think that your first night together was a one-off, but after what you have just experienced, I doubt you would either. His love play is so sensually slow and deliberate that many subsequent encounters are needed just to taste his full range of techniques. You can be guaranteed of the sex getting better all the time because that amazing memory of his will have recorded every ooh and ahh you made and his long-term mission is to reproduce them in louder and larger quantities. He is not really what you would call adventurous and when it comes to exploring the entire field of possible sexual activities, he remains quite close to the gate post. Still, he is not averse to the odd spot of role-playing and can get rather keen on the idea of ticking you off for being a naughty girl and then forcing you to accept your punishment. Obviously there are exceptions to every rule and the occasional Crab can be found dabbling in S&M practices, the most common being that he will keep a 'slave'. For the sake of appearance when attending a gathering of fellow Whippers and Thrashers, he will profess to enjoying the whole Sub-Dom scene, but deep down what he really relishes is having someone to keep his house tidy.

Generally though, this is a sign of the zodiac that you should spend some time getting acquainted with, as whatever you invest in your partnership will be returned with interest. Only after an affair with this man do you realise what being cared for is all about.

Scene 4 **The Finale**

If life with your Moon-ruled man should begin to wane, the cause will most likely be his moods. If ever there was a chap who displayed symptoms of PMT, it's him – his tendency to change from mellow to murderous is as regular as the rise and fall of the tides and this can be very aggravating to live with when your own hormones are giving you hell too. Even when his emotions are relatively relaxed, he has an annoying habit of lecturing you about money, and if he's the breadwinner, he will keep you on limited pocket money. Not that you'll ever go without anything – you just won't get the pleasure of buying it. Clothes, by the way, are deemed as luxuries. He has no flair for fashion and will not appreciate you purchasing the latest labels, especially as he can see garments twenty years old in your wardrobe that look exactly the same.

Breaking free from this maternal man requires more than simply leaving home. It's sad to say that just like a Crab, he will never release you unless you wound him and this is most effectively done with criticism. Play on his insecurities such as laughing when he undresses or painting your nails while you have sex. It sounds brutal because it is; you'll end up hating yourself and in only a few days be more than ready to give him a second try. By then it will be too late, his feelings run too deep for forgiveness, so don't attempt to bump into him by strolling down along the riverside – you will never get your hands on his packed lunch again.

LEO

FEMALE
Scene 1 **The Meeting**

With a third of the zodiac's delightful, yet definitely different, ladies now explained, all you ambitious guys could be thinking that it's a case of four down, eight to go. It is not, of course, quite that simple. Leo woman is the gal to separate the men from the boys and she knows it. She is a celestial designer outfit and every man at some point in life wants to slip into one. Ruled by the Sun, she twinkles and sparkles and would ideally love the existence of a Hollywood star, adored by all who gaze upon her. Like most designer ensembles she is usually woven from good, strong fabric which gives her a flair for practicality to see her through some of life's less glamorous patches. Mostly though, by applying her creativity, her lust for luxury and her drop-dead sensuality, she manages to possess an appeal that screams of natural quality and exclusivity. Those men who scorn her as overrated and overpriced are the ones who can't meet the cost of her passion anyway. Both her birth colour and metal are gold, but do not be fooled by what they say about all that glitters – her big, generous heart is moulded by the same substance and her moral fibre is of the highest texture.

Finding a Leo girl to decorate your arm for an evening is not that difficult, but really only amounts to having her on hire. The wherewithal required to have her permanently grace your bedroom is something of a different matter. She can always be found at swanky cocktail parties and events which have a touch of prestige but then there is the problem of fighting it out with her other admirers. My advice is to intercept her before the going gets glitzy and mosey on down to any hairdressing salon that is a cut above the rest; you know the type – they operate under one-name titles such as Frederick, Roberto or Maurice (pronounced More-reece). She is equally likely to be found in any establishment which beautifies and brightens, but the hairdresser's is your best bet since her tresses are often her crowning glory and reflect the mane of the lion which astrologically symbolises her. Leo girl will be sitting in her regular chair being manicured, pedicured and generally pampered. The final confirmation that she's the lass you're after will be provided by More-reece himself as he minces, crimps and simpers in a way strictly reserved for big spenders. The object of your desire will not be too comfortable in her waterproof coverall and curlers and will be silently cursing Maurice for ever deciding to go unisex. If, however, you notice her trying to hide behind her *Cosmo* mag, you will have a major indication that she finds you attractive. If she is totally unbothered about you seeing her mid-coiffeur, then it is reasonable to assume that her loins, at this point, are unstirred. This is where you resort to being flash – whatever she's having, order two. It may prompt funny looks in the locker room later, but at least you'll have Leo girl's attention. She is not what you'd call a golddigger, she's not that keen on dirtying her nails. No, this girl's curiosity is aroused by seeing your wealth a little closer to the surface than that, so let your credit card play Cupid – it can speak more volumes of love to her than all the Shakespearean soliloquies put together. It is vital to add that you must display some breeding and class – when one of Maurice's minions fetches you a coffee, eat your individually wrapped shortbread separately. Dunk your biscuit and it will be the only thing you ever dunk so far as Leo girl is concerned. Inviting her for a date won't be too demanding providing it appeals to the Leo ego-element. A good option would be VIP tickets to a sell-out concert but choose your megastar carefully. Leaving her backstage with Bon Jovi is as sensible as trusting your cat with your kid brother's gerbil.

Scene 2 **The Main Event**

Everything in Leo girl's personal organiser is either filed under F – for friend, or L – for lover and both sections will be pretty well stuffed. After your inventive and probably expensive first date, you will quickly be informed in which you are to be listed. Upon reaching her front door, an 'F' will be told what a truly great guy he is and that Leo woman hopes to see a lot more of him because, considerate creature that she is, she believes he would make a perfect partner for her best friend. As she is very loyal to friends, true you will see more of her, but not the bits you wanted. If though, you are to become an 'L', you will cross the first threshold of the night and be allowed to enter her lavish vestibule.

Ladies born under the sign of the Lion are sometimes mislabelled as pouncers, who leap on a poor lad and relieve him of his clothes before you can say 'contraception!' This is not actually the reality and much of her pleasure is derived by watching your anticipation and admiration play havoc with the straight lines of your neatly pressed trousers. You may fancy having her wrapped around your body, but this is no ready-to-wear woman. She will expect a good degree of saucy fore-talk to enable her to gauge your preferences and then to tailor her performance to suit your requirements.

As with the male Leo, her sensitive spots are all situated along her spine and she does subconsciously choose clothes that unfasten down the back. Don't waste the opportunity to help with her zip; ease it down slowly and sensuously, leaving a trail of kisses as you do so. Give it a quick yank and you only have yourself to blame when she treats you the same way. She prefers to discard her clothes fully before you remove anything, it gives you the chance to observe and praise her athletic form which is usually more than worthy of your compliments. Next she may tease and will saunter, lasciviously naked, to the kitchen to fetch two glasses of best bubbly fully aware that your cork is likely to pop before the bottle's. Pander to the moment and show your contempt for something as trivial as money by pouring the champagne over her and drinking it off slowly. As you now start to get a closer view of her treasures, you will notice that this completely coordinated woman has matching top and tails and you may wonder if her lower curls are shaped by Maurice too. Continue to lick every drop of liquid from every last reservoir and never be so crass as to ask her if she's enjoying it. The mere fact that your nose is now being tickled by her perfect pubes should tell you that she considers you to be the best – so start believing it.

Fellatio is not a favourite activity of hers, not because she's mean, but because she wants your first surge of ecstasy to come from coitus. Also, when highly aroused, she can bite, so think twice before putting any head in this Lion's mouth. Why not now do what she wants and slip into something more comfortable? She is a sign renowned for pelvic prowess and you can be sure that she will fit your manhood like a glove – a surgical glove. Leo lady will fight for supremacy during sex, alternating submission with dominance. Ultimately she opts for positions where you can still see that beautiful body and only she will decide when any climax occurs. She glides down the path to orgasm like a model on a catwalk – slowly, gracefully and with expert timing. When she finally unveils her ultimate euphoria it will be with a gasp and a sigh while all you can do is applaud the style that puts her in a class of her own. Making love with Leo lady is exhilarating and exhausting and totally satisfying. She will possibly fall asleep without needing an encore which will be fine with you. Your whole being, just like your month's salary, will be spent.

Scene 3 **Extras**

Leaving aside everything I've just said, don't be put off this girl if you feel your funds don't run to it. She may have an elaborate exterior, but she's no dummy. She can live happily and modestly if she sees in you the spirit to be successful and more importantly, that you will always love her and respect her without question. Sexually, she willingly attempts to cater to just about every deviant design you may have on her, but this won't happen in an off-the-cuff way. It will take maybe a year for her to reveal her full collection – perhaps longer, as she continually gathers new ideas and accessories to revamp her repertoire.

There are a few no-nos, it has to be said. If you get the urge to sample swinging, she will absolutely rule out another female joining in, but could be tempted by the thought of multiple male encounters. It's wise to not consider group sex at all, because the more she thinks about playing to a bigger audience, the more she'll like it. Nor is she fond of watersports, fantasising about golden showers is one thing, but she'll be horrified if you ever actually rain on her parade. A natural part of her make-up is bossiness and this opens up a wonderful array of games if your high power job causes you to secretly revel in subservient or masochistic notions.

This decadent damsel is most men's ideal and is certainly not just for decoration. For all her fine trappings, she possesses an enduring substance that will fiercely protect you from life's nastier elements and in marriage she has the ability to weave a security blanket around herself and her family. Aspire to attain a Leo female and you can only benefit. With her you can look good, feel good and face the world with confidence.

Scene 4 **The Finale**

When life with this lady starts to fall apart at the seams, it will probably be your fault rather than hers and a classic error is to not give her the space she needs. Just as you wouldn't cram your best outfit into your sock drawer, Leo girl must be given a prime place in your life and also the understanding that she may just want to hang loose with her friends now and again. Remembering and taking her out for special occasions such as birthdays, anniversaries, etc. is compulsory but never treat her as a mere accessory when you have an important function to attend.

She does have foibles of her own too and as she gets older, you may get increasingly tired of always being the one responsible for varying your sexual pattern. Constantly having to keep an eye on the bank balance is equally frustrating especially with her longings for everything unique or individual. One thing is certain, when it's over, it's over. You must think long and hard before severing ties and do not assume that lost love will eventually turn into friendship. In her personal organiser, an F never comes after an L. She won't show it, but she will be hurt and may quickly fall into an unsuitable rebound romance while she recovers from that feeling of being shop-soiled.

Leo girl won't tell the world about your failings behind your back, but will confide in a pal. If it happens to be More-reece, it probably amounts to the same thing.

MALE
Scene 1 **The Meeting**

For all the girls who are studiously following Sextrology by the book and have so far experienced the fun and foibles of the male Aries, Taurus, Gemini and Cancer, I would like to congratulate you for persevering with your expedition. Certain females may have already jumped ship to settle down with one of the afore-mentioned men, but for those who believe in seeing this course right through to Mr Pisces, well, you are in for a treat and a half. Deceptively lurking as the fifth member of the zodiac, Leo man is not just another sign. He is *the* sign of the zodiac. Just like the lion which represents him, he is also King of the sexual jungle – a sort of latter-day Tarzan. He may be the second Fire sign you've encountered, but do not be fooled into thinking he's a carbon copy of Aries man – no, this guy is unchartered territory compared to everything else you have sampled and even to consider lifting his loincloth requires an enormous spirit of adventure and reasonable amounts of self-sacrifice. Before letting your mind drift off to Virgo man who is nowhere near as challenging, let me give you a few good reasons for hanging in there. Number one: he strives for and achieves the ultimate from life and to be his partner means that you get to share in it as well. Number two: he's gorgeous, witty, talented, charming, super-successful, loyal, considerate, brilliant in bed . . . Convinced? I thought so. The list continues and I'm sure you want, with no further ado, to know where to find him.

He is Lord of the Jungle, but this is no apeman, his tastes are refined, lavish and individual and guys like him do not drop off trees. You need to have your plans well mapped out and be prepared to do battle with the other female natives who constantly stalk him. For this particular sexual safari you need to dress the part and however impractical it may be, you will fare much better in anything that is downright glamorous, better still, expensive and glamorous. Your first port of call should be a place or event where Leo man can allow the main two facets of his personality to be freely revealed, these being, first, his love of displaying wealth and power, and second, his even greater and sincere pleasure of being generous and able to help those less fortunate than himself. A charity fund raiser is a prime starting point as is any glittering get-together in the name of a worthy cause. Lower down the scale, your local Lion can be found donating to the village rummage sale, but you can still count on his knick-knacks to be bigger than anyone else's. To recognise him is easy, he is, quite simply, the star attraction. He knows it, he loves it and what's more he's good at it. No one can hold a spotlight as well as he does and for all the jealous mutterings of men who can't hold a candle to him, he is undeniably attractive. Ruled by the Sun, the centre of our solar system, Leo man is the centre of female attention and the sign from which all other zodiac males take their cue. He will be found surrounded by pouting, preening, potential playmates while the surplus rejected and dejected menfolk sulk in a corner licking their wounds. The key to separating him from the pack and hopefully getting him to make a contribution to your own sex appeal is to follow him, flatter him and fall in two paces behind him. The submissive, subservient, gazing up at him through low-ered eyelids routine works every time. For all his superior feline characteristics, Mr Lion will not play cat and mouse with you – if he's married with cubs, there will be none of that typical male sleight of hand which magically removes the wedding ring faster than the female eye can blink. The photos of his family languishing in Leo luxury will be out in a flash which lets you know where you stand and gives him a chance to compare what he's got with what he could be having. It's also a shocking, self-imposed reminder of how unbearably expensive a divorce would be if his animal instincts got the better of him. If, however, the only item in his wallet is cash, he will be entirely upfront in asking you for a date so long as you promise to wear your hair in his favourite style – spread over his pillow.

Scene 2 **The Main Event**

A first date with any new man will give a girl the jitters, but when you are tangling with this guy, the pre-match adrenaline is potent enough to feel illegal. You will have already lost sleep, half a stone and all your principles about doing it on the first night because Leo man will have previously made it clear that he is not turned on by a tease. He would never invite you to his habitat if he thought you weren't game to cuddle his coconuts. The setting for sex with your lion will probably be his lair, but if he has not yet aspired to the kind of opulent splendour he desires, then it will be an exclusive and exorbitantly priced hotel. Dinner, drinks and everyday chitchat could lull you into a false sense of security that maybe it will be possible to escape this particular evening with a coffee and a kiss and perhaps a few days to lose that last bit of cellulite, but as you step into the bedroom to conclude the preliminaries, you will experience at first hand what it's like to be the human equivalent of a gazelle or wildebeest, as Mr Lion will pounce with a speed that defies description.

He dispenses with foreplay because it's not necessary. While other men use the warm-up to plan their next moves, he, through experience and sheer talent, knows how to go straight for the jugular. He can home in on a woman's weak spots blindfolded and once he has you in those strong arms, pulling you against his even stronger enthusiasm, your only desire is to roll over and submit to his frenzied nuzzling, gnawing and nibbling. Leo man makes love as if his life depends on it. Regardless of how long it has been since he feasted on female flesh, he will treat every encounter as if it were to be his last and although it might sound brutal or even barbaric, it awakens delirious feelings of urgency and utopia. Senses that have lain dormant will be revived and all that matters is to be devoured completely, but don't surrender just yet, once you're down you are past the point of no return, so put up a fight and show some spirit.

The most vulnerable area on this man is his back and if you want to risk rousing those reserves of passion that only surface in rare, raw moments, work your fingers firmly down his spine to his tail bone and back again. Kneel in front of him and do this while you swallow him whole but never think for a moment that he will lose control because his aim is to defeat you and drown you in pure sex. You might feel that your life is flashing before you as he sucks the breath from your mouth but then temporarily revives you by breathing fire between your legs. At this point it would be easier to hold back the tide of an ocean than hold back your orgasm, but endeavour to do so. Clench your thighs, think about the pile of ironing you have at home – do whatever it takes because he prefers you both to reach a peak only after he has entered your domain.

Favourite intercourse position for this sign is him on top, or any that makes you appear vulnerable and there he can stay for a remarkable length of time. He will push and thrust until you are near senseless, but this may just as easily be caused by your skull thudding against the bed's headboard. He will orgasm with a roar and expects more than a tiny miaow from you – the climactic cries that please him most are ones which contain the words 'God', 'Jesus', 'Almighty' or basically anyone else he can relate to personally. Afterwards, you can be sure that he won't fall asleep first – he stays awake stroking you gently until you drift into slumber. Yes, he's a considerate lover – he's also double checking that you're fully satisfied and not attempting a furtive solo fumble.

Scene 3 Extras

Your first ferocious and fantastic night with Leo man could, understandably, make you wonder what comes next – will his tastes become even more violent? The answer is no, his lovemaking needs no manufactured thrills or deviant distortions. If anything, he will become more mellow and treat you tenderly like a prized trophy, providing – and that's with a very big P – that you continue to massage his male confidence and pamper him with praise. Unconditional adoration is what he needs and, some would say, deserves. Leo men who start to feel unappreciated can go off the rails and resort to exhibitionism in the form of flashing to kindle female reaction. Pride of place on his body is his penis, the size of which he secretly worries about more than most. In the same way as a financially insecure Leo will leave his biggest car outside the garage, a sexually anxious lion will resort to leaving his dick outside his trousers. Lazy or unattractive Leos who fail to find satisfaction consider that a credit card will do nicely and will often inflate their ego with a high-class hooker at an even more inflated price.

In any relationship, the law of the jungle suggests that, occasionally, a couple may be tempted to toy with the idea of group sex, but surprisingly, Leo man is no swinger. Two Janes to one Tarzan he can handle, but play second fiddle to a stand-in stunt man? No chance.

The real joy of life with your Leo is that he surrounds you with security; physical, financial and emotional and these are the foundations on which great sex is often built. He can be viewed as a Male Chauvinist Pig, but this is often by women who deny him the right to do what he does best – treat you like a lady.

Scene 4 **The Finale**

Girls who leave Leo lovers don't usually do so for routine reasons such as boredom or differing interests, it is invariably the growing inability to tolerate living in someone else's shadow which causes women to weaken and wither away. All the flamboyance and exuberance which once was so attractive can start to irritate you and it's not really his fault. Having, however, persistent party invitations arriving for Mr Lion and Guest can destroy a girl's feelings of individuality and identity and confidence is further shattered when he constantly looks better and fitter than you. To add insult to injury, Leo men become more attractive with age – their power and self-assurance radiate sensual magnetism which draws women of all ages towards them. True, he does not expect you to be Wonderwoman, but female pride ensures you will exhaust yourself trying to be.

When it's time to separate you need to be savage. The quickest way to kill his passion is to ignore him and only speak to criticise him. Force him to question his bedroom prowess by boldly filling your home with calendars of super-hunks, and this will drive him into the arms of another woman to reaffirm his supremacy. Although he won't leave you, his infidelity provides a perfect excuse for you to up sticks and escape. One thing is for sure, life after Leo man is going to seem dull and dreary for a very long time. Catch yourself a lion, strip away his intimidating exterior and savour the pussy cat inside – he'll make you purr.

VIRGO

FEMALE
Scene 1 **The Meeting**

If you have been good male students and are working through your Sextrology degree sign by sign as instructed, you are now nearly fifty per cent of the way there and could be thinking that it's time for a half-term break to recharge those sex-sapped batteries. Unfortunately, no – to achieve top-class honours you must see this course through to the end without hesitation. I am going to make it easy for you, though, and I'm pleased to introduce Virgo lady who is the Calculator of the zodiac. As every scholar knows, this wonderful invention is an indispensable ally which gets you through many tricky moments and remains an asset forever. This, then, is she, a sign so often wrongly tagged as the perennial virgin. It might be wise to clear this one up here and now. Virgo woman is not a prude, her sexuality is as much a part of her personality as anybody

77

else's, but she tucks it safely away in a sensible and practical cover. The only men who ever qualify to take a peep beneath this durable exterior are those who prove they can fulfil her finest of standards. Virgo lady could be the challenge of a lifetime because she believes in realism rather than romance and logic rather than lust. Once you have switched her on to the fact that she can have all four, she will produce passion in the only way she knows how – pure, precise and perfect with no margin for error. All of this adds up to a girl who most certainly should be on your curriculum.

Finding a Virgo lady can sometimes be taxing as she doesn't stick to a routine. She is often where she needs to be instead of where she wants to be and this changes in accordance with whatever project or ambition she is pursuing at the time. Admirably, her aim is one of continual self-improvement and many of her sign have dragged themselves up by their bootlaces to heights which make other females feel dizzy.

In her incredibly well-ordered and meticulously planned life she seldom allocates enough time for meeting potential lovers and takes a philosophical view that Mr Right will cross her path eventually. Prudently, she doesn't waste precious evenings in the noisy, superficial singles bars where everyone pretends to enjoy themselves but finds it impossible even to catch the drift of conversation, let alone a partner. Of all the zodiac signs, she more than most, can be tempted by computer dating, which although not foolproof, appeals to her analytical brain and returns her money if the guy proves to be in breach of his description. Her actual synopsis will read plainly and unassumingly: 'Virgo lady, intelligent, articulate and reasonably attractive requires neat, tidy, cultured partner to share mutual interests.' If she printed the truth and dropped the modesty it would be more like this: 'Very bright, pretty, vivacious Virgoan female desperately in need of go-ahead guy to disrobe me, devour me and drag me down a deviant path of debauchery. Must say Thank You afterwards'. So your starting point is here – sign on the books of your local matchmaking establishment and take your smartest photograph, a pre-prepared list of your exemplary qualities, an open mind and the sense to read between the lines when browsing through Virgo lady's personal profile.

For that all-important first date you must escort her somewhere that appeals to her intellect; take her for a sumptuous dinner and she will view it as wasteful; take her for a romantic riverside stroll beneath the stars and she will question your sanity by informing you that there's a perfectly good dual carriageway you could use and the lighting is better. The best option would be a venue in theatreland to see a show or satirical comic and whilst you're there, buy a season ticket – getting your finger on this calculator's hot button necessitates the investment of time, tact and patience.

Scene 2 **The Main Event**

Over the ensuing weeks you will have got a sneaky feeling that Virgo woman has been operating on half power. That's not to say that she isn't good company – indeed, her conversation is of the highest calibre and some of the words she uses will have had you delving in the dictionary during many a wee small hour. It's just that somehow you have realised that behind that functional facade is a female with enough reserve charge to light up the National Grid, and all you must work out is how to plug into her mains. As far as she is concerned making love, as opposed to sex, will naturally become part of the equation when she has figured you out fully and also when the law of averages states that a guy will only wait so long before finding himself another socket. Don't expect this to be a spontaneous event – she will decide the date and unbeknownst to you will have circled a day in the diary strategically placed between periods to minimalise the chances of pregnancy, tender breasts or erratic temperament. You will get about one week's notice and never again will seven days pass so slowly. When you arrive at her place, her favourite location for lovemaking, there will be no messing about. With her mind made up she is fully committed to getting the show on the road and instead of the customary drink, she will suggest a shower for two which is an intrinsic part of her foreplay and satisfies her fastidious nature.

Once you have stripped her down to her bare components you can count on her body to be firm, feminine and rounded and the part you should be aiming for is her stomach – the Virgoan sensitive spot. Circle the soap around her belly button whilst nuzzling her shoulders and she in return will kiss and caress with the intensity you had hoped for. She won't stop soaping until every last trace of the day's debris is removed and smart guys should paint a phony particle on their penis. Well, maybe that's not a great idea because the best is yet to come. As you reach the bedroom you will be amazed at the confidence and poise she exhibits and you can only cast aside your previous misconceptions that she was going to be shy and naive. Virgo lady will be remarkably familiar with her body and regularly servicing her own working parts means that she has no trouble conveying to you what she wants. She makes it all unbelievably easy as she takes your hand and guides your eager digit to her most responsive equipment. For you, the pressure of all that mental dexterity is removed; you don't have to keep counting how long you've twiddled this before you can start tickling that. Virgo woman couldn't make it any more straightforward if she drew an A–Z on herself. When eventually you get to demonstrate that one into one will go, it is likely to be in a routine position, but unless your tastes are positively perverted, she will try almost any variation you can imagine and her natural curiosity will lead to a few that you haven't. Some of the most adventurous sex she's had will have begun with the words 'I wonder what would happen if . . .?'

You can count on that first night to be a long one. As soon as she has worked out your pleasure formula, she will then try to improve upon it, making slight readjustments and alterations to increase the enjoyment percentage. Not a selfish lover, she does nevertheless, at the pinnacle of her rapture assume her orgasm to be delivered on the dot. With the entire proceedings having gone like clockwork, there is no reason to doubt your timing. Step up the pace as your output starts to surge, utter a couple of words of encouragement and you can be confident that first time coitus scores the ultimate 10 out of 10.

Scene 3 **Extras**

It won't take very long for any man to put two and two together and realise that his Virgoan lady has extremely complex workings when it comes to sex. Once her code has been cracked you can expect to access a very versatile mind which considers no erotic challenge too big. When the first flush of novelty wears off and you both begin the quest of recapturing the excitement, she won't know all the answers straight away, but give her time and she will come up with something. She will read any publication or watch any film that could possibly enlighten her, even the blue variety just so long as it is all in the name of improving her sexual specification. Your joint fantasies may go off at a tangent from so-called 'normal' notions and role-playing games could involve a punishment element with you taking it in turns to chastise each other. There's sure to be some practices which she deems as too rude, crude or dirty to attempt but it's unlikely that you will ever consider them any-way, unless you live particularly close to a farmyard. Whatever they are, you won't miss them, Virgo girl's desire to be the best she can be inevitably leads to some pretty special nights. With her bent for mathematics, you may achieve a real rarity – the male multiple orgasm and whatever the outcome of your relationship, you will never be able to deny that she always tried her hardest. Should your affair ever produce a little addition, she won't be the most maternal of mothers but will approach the situation with the ultimate degree of common sense and rationality. If Virgo junior turns out to be the baby from hell, she will see it as your fault.

The sum total of life with this woman must not be

under-valued. You will come to rely on her totally as she can always cope with a crisis. She issues few instructions, and will be yours forever providing she is treated with care and compassion. Love her and look after her or run the risk of one of your friends recognising her skills and stealing her for good.

Scene 4 **The Finale**

Virgo woman puts up with a lot but when she decides that you are no longer her ideal other half, the most probable cause will be laziness on your part to remain the man she fell for. Be sloppy, slobbish or vulgar for any length of time and her tolerance will evaporate; leave the toothpaste lid off and the toilet seat up and passion will flow down the pan. If you need to get rid of her in a hurry, just let her see you perform in the weekly boys' night out belching contest.

You will know when your number's up because she will have washed, ironed and neatly packed your clothes into several suitcases and left them outside the front door attached to a note that explains with unequivocal reason exactly why this twosome has gone on the blink. An amicable parting is guaranteed, as Virgo female is above all that 'You can have the crockery and I'll have the cuckoo clock' routine. With her you are assured that there will be an equal division of assets and she may throw in a little extra cash to enable you to seek treatment for those terminal bad habits. Virgo girl makes a fairly rapid recovery from romantic bust-ups because she is governed by Mercury, planet of the mind and therefore always lets her head rule her heart.

Consequently, it will be hard to rekindle the spark when you get round to realising what you have lost. She won't answer the phone and whilst you are putting down drink like there is no tomorrow, she will be putting you down to experience.

MALE
Scene 1 **The Meeting**

Okay then girls, the moment has come for a team talk. Despite the revelations of this book and the five astro-hunks that you should have already liaised with in previous pages, I have not yet managed to pinpoint the perfect man. The best I can do at this stage is present the guy who thinks he is. Placed sixth in the zodiac and approaching half time in this sexual stampede lies Virgo male, the Celestial Referee. Other men won't always like him because he is not famous for his sense of humour plus the fact that his cool, calculating, analytical brain is totally inflexible. Consequently, he often lands himself in positions of authority and as a boss he can make decisions which cause verbal aspersions to be cast on his parentage. The reasons why men give him a wide berth are the very reasons why many women can't wait to get his kit off. He exudes power, control and a silent strength which screams out to be challenged. Ladies want to tangle with him for the sheer thrill of dirtying him up a bit. There is more to it than that though; as a partner he will wrap you in rock solid security and give plenty of astute advice as to how to deal with life's nastier characters. He will tirelessly work his way to the top of his league and will stand his ground in the face of any adversity, thus ensuring a life of unbeatable mutual success. Sexually, he is inquisitive rather than impetuous and does tend to work in the set pattern that has stood him in good stead on previous other encounters. Once, however, you have convinced him that you're on his side and you can be trusted, he will be prepared to see love-making from more adventurous angles.

What you should know now is that this chap, who prefers to operate in isolation, won't put himself out to find a partner. He can enjoy life to the full as a long-term bachelor merely having sex when the need arises. If you are only looking to hit it off with him once, you simply have to ask. He will consider your application carefully and probably agree to give you a one-night try out. Even if he's impressed by your talents, afterwards on reflection, he will be dismayed by your unladylike conduct and relegate you to one of his friends. My thoughts are that you should aim to see his deeper and more desirable qualities by becoming the full-time occupant of his little black book. The warm-up to this, nine times out of ten, is going to be friendship and to turn it into romance requires you to do all the running. The best place to find your Virgoan male is at work – he's the guy who's first to arrive and the one who answers the phone at one minute to five in the afternoon when everybody else has coat and briefcase in hand ready for the sixty-second sprint to the elevator. To get his attention, you need to exhibit manners, wisdom, wit and intellect, and to get a date you must make him feel that he could learn something and enhance his life by having you around. Swot up on subjects that are serious or sophisticated and drop educated phrases into your conversation whenever he's about. He still won't ask you out, but the odds have now increased tenfold that he will say yes to a casual coffee or lunchtime hamburger.

I must add that there is just one asset you could have that might produce a faster response should you spy him in a social setting – and that is drop-dead beauty. Casanova he isn't, but neither is he Ray Charles. If you are sufficiently stunning to capture the attention of all the other guys in the place, he will notice like a shot, and good ref that he is, nothing gets him trotting over quicker than a commotion in the corner. Whatever your tactics are to be, a good idea for a proper first date would be an exhibition of state-of-the-art gym equipment or a seminar on alternative medicine. Virgo man is the health freak of the zodiac and it pays to remember it. From this point on there should be no smoking, excessive drinking or the minutest mutterings about anything stronger. If you were a horse, he'd have you dope-tested before climbing on. I'm not saying that he doesn't ever touch addictive substances, but, boy, does he hate himself afterwards.

Scene 2 **The Main Event**

The kick-off to your intimate entwining will be at a prearranged time and the venue will be either of your residences depending on whose turn it is. If he entertained you at home last week he won't mind travelling away to your place for this important event. Don't get the impression that he's taking all this in his stride. Indeed, he couldn't be more aware of what is at stake, you are about to test his stamina, his coordination and his eye for detail so he will certainly come prepared. On arrival a neatly pressed change of clothing will deftly be removed from his holdall and transferred to your wardrobe and whilst in the bedroom he will survey the playing area for potential hazards and also determine where to stand his mobile phone for maximum signal. A light meal eaten to the sound of sentimental love songs is a good way to relax you both and provides him with the opportunity to discuss the preliminaries. Of course he won't make it sound that clinical, he has a charming, almost boyish, foreplay patter and will praise and flatter you with sincerity. Whether you realise it or not though, by the time the action moves from dining room to bedroom he will have determined that what follows is going to be an end-to-end game in which you will both score and can use a modest amount of creative technique to achieve this. Any monkey business or moves that he's not sure of, however, are strictly ruled out for now. Don't be too taken aback if he gets a case of very cold feet at this point and hastily tries to postpone proceedings for a week or two. These are purely first night jitters and you can change his mind by seductively peeling off your clothes in time with the music and then suggesting that he shows you his strip in return. His mind is his biggest erogenous zone and by virtue of the fact he's in your bed, you know you have stimulated that. Physically you should be concentrating on his upper abdominal area to find the highest proportion of erotically charged nerve endings – try licking, stroking or trailing your nails over the skin. He meanwhile will be skilfully working his way down your body noting and commenting on everything he touches. When his hands get within striking distance of your scoring zone, he will amaze you with the knowledge he has about the female anatomy, not so much by what he does, as by what he says. For a lot of the time he won't really do anything, preferring to watch your reactions to his words. Next comes a period of hectic activity as the pace heats up and you roll and scramble attempting to find the best position. Now is when you realise that this is going to go all the way, but to your utter disbelief, Virgo man may suddenly withdraw into the background leaving you to fumble around in complete confusion, and for a horrible moment you won't know if it's game over or a sudden injury. Don't worry – this is part of his strategy, it confirms his importance and bolsters his ego knowing that right now you need his intervention more than anything else in the world. Sure, you could sort matters out for yourself but it would be a hollow victory. Eventually, intercourse will take place in the missionary position unless you have any special requests and his endurance and all-round fitness will be impressive. He is likely to hop straight into the shower afterwards so there will be a pause before you can lie back and enjoy afterglow or, perhaps, an action replay if time permits.

Making love with Virgo man is full of stops, starts and changes of direction which on the face of it are infuriating. If you're honest with yourself, you will concede, just like the average soccer fan, that this is what makes the game exciting, what adds that aggro element to get the blood pumping. Love him or hate him, you can't do without him and as far as that first night goes, I'm sure you'll agree . . . the boy done good.

Scene 3 **Extras**

When your relationship progresses into extra time, Virgo man will come into his own as he is a sign with whom sex gets more, as opposed to less, exciting. Foolish girls who decide against a rematch following his quite conservative debut often make the mistake of thinking that he must have run through his entire field of erotica on that first night. Sensible ladies should stick with it because the next time you get hot and sweaty together, you'll find that Mr Virgo has moved the goalposts. Everything from pre-sex chat to penetration will become more animated and adventurous and the oral content will increase too. Even some of your filthiest fantasies could be fulfilled providing you discuss them with him first. He does not like sexual surprises as they undermine his authority, so whatever you have in mind, don't present him with a *fait accompli*. He can see an unfair tackle from miles away and you will get a firm ticking off. Respect that he's in charge and try introducing your amorous ideas only when he's in full possession of the facts and you can count on him being a sport. When Virgo man matures, he can sometimes develop assorted little kinks and cravings which fall into the voyeuristic category. He may increasingly revel in watching as well as taking part and it has been known for this chap to suggest bringing a couple of muscular reserves into your love play to satisfy this longing. He won't ever force you into it but he will try and convince you that it makes sense.

Despite all the sexual rules and regulations, life with Virgo male is worth it. He may not be the zodiac's most dazzling star, the one who generates glamour and pizzazz, but he is the one who holds things together and makes sense out of life's stupidity and for this you should rate him highly. At the end of the day the score is Sexiness 5 Stability 10.

Scene 4 **The Finale**

Should you want to blow the whistle on your romantic ties, it will be his constant fault-finding and nitpicking that have done the damage. Also, he may not give you much freedom and even at home he can get under your feet as he monitors everything you do. The boot will seldom be on the other foot because there's not much that upsets him. Amazingly, it's possible that he will even tolerate a couple of your indiscretions, but play away from home too often and his pride will be hurt to the point where he's forced to show you the red card.

Either way, he's an Earth sign and this makes him stubborn, so the ultimate decision to split will always be his and, as we know, his word is final. Sometimes, it's only when you leave this man that you realise just how much he cares. Virgo men will go to the ends of the earth to resolve a dispute and such devotion is very touching. I'd recommend that you spend more than a season in the orderly and efficient world of Mr Virgo – after he has packed his bags and gone you can bank on life to be pure chaos.

LIBRA

FEMALE
Scene 1 **The Meeting**

I sincerely hope that all the men reading this revealing guide have enjoyed the sexual secrets contained within the previous six delicious damsels. So far it's all been good, dirty, adult fun but with the introduction of the Libran female, you can look forward to an experience that will bring out the child in you. This woman shares many of her celestial characteristics with that most favoured of kids' toys – the Kite. Ruled by Venus, planet of grace and all things beautiful, she is also an Air sign and seems to float through life without ever getting too concerned about the more serious and earthy aspects of existence. Libran women come in all shapes and sizes yet are instantly noticeable for at least one or two features of extreme attractiveness which can be anything from long luxurious hair to perfectly proportioned pins. Sexually she is a free spirit and will breeze

91

through the full spectrum of every carnal position known to man, providing the man in question has managed to strike the balance of making her feel secure, yet allowing her the freedom she needs to flourish. Even if your intimate arrangement with this girl is a loose one, she can pull off with poise some sensual stunts and tricks that leave many women tied up in knots. As a long-term partner her faults are few – she adds colour, dimension and exhilaration to your union and after many years, the guy in her life will still always want to rush home from work, shower her with little presents, take her out to show her off and then return home to play with her in private.

I can already feel that Libra woman is tugging at your heart strings, or perhaps a little lower, so next you need to know where to find her. Forget about those cattle-market nightclubs and bawdy bars, she won't go there for pleasure and is irritated by drunken boys-about-town practising their pick-up lines on her. A far better location is her natural environment – the great out-doors. Don't get me wrong, she's no Hooray Henrietta complete with horse and hounds, no, she prefers the solitude and peace created by idyllic scenery. The Lake District is positively littered with Librans filling their lungs and taking advantage of the air which is the fuel of their creativity. This is where you'll stumble across her as she paints, sketches or draws, so why not pretend to be an arty type and view her work constructively, maybe asking if there's anything she'd like you to touch up. Do know what you're talking about though, she knows her onions when it comes to art and can spot a forgery a mile away. If you really can't tell the difference between a Picasso and a pistachio, it's wise to appeal to her love of luxury and flash some cash within her eyeshot. Try striking up a casual conversation and mention how you are only in the countryside in search of inspiration to assist you with all next week's turbo-charged negotiations and boardroom powerplays back in the office. True to her astrological character, this lady kite is more than happy to link up with a fellow high flyer.

Next, ask her out to a venue that is aesthetic or exclusive, and fingers crossed and if the wind is in the right direction, she will accept. In actual fact, getting her to say yes is easier than you'd imagine, it's keeping her to the date that's more difficult. Her initial agreement will arise out of flattery, curiosity and her own realisation that she is a girl who functions best with a strong man to handle her. Second thoughts then strike her that perhaps she is being too eager and should show some restraint. Such sitting on the fence is a classic trait of lady Libra and it can be said that the other main way of recognising this sign is from the splinters in her bum. Right up until the moment she appears you can never be sure your date will materialise. Fanatical about her looks and presentation, the eruption of a spot is nothing short of a disaster. She won't be seen in public with a mini-Mount Etna on her chin and until paper bags become fashionable as head gear, don't expect to catch a glimpse of her for at least another four days.

Scene 2 **The Main Event**

Take the aforementioned advice that even when it gets down to the night of nights, nothing with Libra female will ever happen on time. She invented the word 'late' and was largely responsible for 'delayed', 'unpunctual', and 'Where the effing hell is she?' Do try to have patience and remember that you'll only get to tangle with this woman when she deems the conditions to be absolutely right.

After an elegant and unhurried dinner during which you should keep the compliments flowing as freely as the wine, a suggestion to go back to your place must now be made. At this stage she can still possibly manage to resist the lure of your body, so casually mention the bottles of pink champagne you have chilling in the fridge; like a moth to a flame she won't be able to help herself. A short time and several glasses later, you will begin to suspect that this girl has the makings of being another sort of artist. Whatever you do, don't try to keep up with her – she can't just drink you under the table, she'll drink you right down to the basement and if you match her sip for sip, your bulging enthusiasm will start pointing that way too. Despite all this, she still remains elegant and relatively composed, and although the percentage of silly giggles and accidental hiccups increase, it's all done in an utterly charming way. This is when Libra woman turns the passion timetable on its head; just as you are pondering the pros and cons of hand on the thigh as opposed to little kisses on the cleavage, she, with button-busting force, will rip off her blouse and stare at you expectantly. Obviously, any guy is going to need a few moments to reassess, but lady Libra will see your hesitation as inexperience and will now assume you're a virgin as she excitedly begins to demonstrate who does what to whom with the help of an empty champers bottle. You could, of course, play along with her misconception, lie back and let her seduce you – she has ideas up her sleeve that will blow you away. The downside however, is that you take the risk of her telling all her friends that she was your first and this is a tad embarrassing if you're pushing 30.

My recommendation, now that she's in full flight, is to fight for some control. The buttocks are Libra's erogenous zone so why not relieve her of her lower garments and then stand suggestively behind her – you can bet your bottom dollar that she will bend forward. Now reach round and gently tug on her nipples, these serve to control her movements left and right and enable you to position her perfectly. Finally, after double checking that your manhood has the right degree of uplift, you can launch into paradise en route to heaven. It's essential that you remain flexible and adaptable to her desires, even if she's having a great time as that famous indecision and unpredictability will cause her to demand that love-making takes a turn in a different direction. You may, just like the average kite flyer, feel that once you've got up there it's pleasant to take the advantage and ride the breeze as it were, but really it is well worth seeing her from as many angles as possible. During intercourse she is captivating to watch as she rolls and rocks back and forth never losing any finesse. She has incredible endurance and will soar to great heights many times during your love-making always ensuring that you do too. After orgasm and when you have both come down to earth, she will need only a few minutes and some liquid refreshment before she's ready to go again. There is very little that the Libra woman won't attempt with enthusiasm and energy and if anything, her performance is only limited by lack of skill on the part of her lover. In terms of erotic imagination, some would say that she is head and shoulders above other females and for this you can only look up to her.

Scene 3 **Extras**

Life with this lusty lady is never dull and she gets a positive thrill out of surprising you. After a hectic day in the office you may arrive home to find candles and caviar on the table and Libra woman wearing nothing more than a smile. If by chance you have brought the boss home with you to discuss your promotion this could be a trifle embarrassing but, looking on the bright side, it will no doubt do more good than all those Saturday mornings on the golf course put together. Don't rule out the possibility that the entire episode was not really the 'accident' it appeared, as this girl will do almost anything to further your career.

Sexually, you can expect a whale of a time as her inventiveness knows no bounds. With her flair for creativity, the settings for your erotic encounters become ever more lavish and the bedroom will be continually redecorated in a theme to suit whatever fantasy is currently in her head. Later in life, Librans are prone to exhibitionism and become hooked on the buzz created by wearing rude or revealing clothing. Taken to an extreme you have a potential flasher on your hands and I'd advise you to keep a check on this, especially if her latest turn-on is connected to handcuffs and big truncheons.

Scene 4 **The Finale**

After all I've said, what possible reasons could there be for wanting this relationship to end? Here are a couple that you might have to contend with. Firstly, Libran women can sometimes be a touch fickle and if you take her for granted or condemn her to a life indoors full of cooking and cleaning, she may start venturing out on her own in search of bluer skies. This is a sign that needs space and will resent it if you try to keep her on too short a leash. Some Libra girls, granted a minority though, can be accused of being rather hollow in the middle and should a domestic crisis strike, she may suddenly remember an old friend or sick relative that she simply has to visit. As she hastily throws an assortment of items into her case, she will kiss you quickly and promise you that whatever the problem is she's certain you will sort it out much better without her around. Another of her foibles is laziness, or to put it more fairly, she loves to sleep. Unless she has to go to work, there is no one single reason good enough for getting her out of bed. She is not the sort to take pleasure from cooking you breakfast and if you are an early riser, you'll have to get used to sorting out your own lunch box.

If you begin feeling that this is purely a fair-weather romance, how do you cut ties? Simple. Invite the most obnoxious friends, cantankerous relatives and noisiest children you can find round to your place for a long weekend. Just as they arrive, suddenly remember that you too have a sick relation to visit in the next county and promise to be back by Monday at the latest. As you kiss her goodbye, you can be confident it's for the last time.

MALE
Scene 1 **The Meeting**

Do you know why horseshoes are considered lucky? I shall tell you. There are seven nail holes in a horseshoe and, traditionally, seven has always been a lucky number. Why am I telling you this? Well, Libra man is the seventh sign of the zodiac and the average girl is going to need all the horseshoes she can get if she has her sights set on long-term security with this guy. Libra man is the naughtiest boy that astrology ever produced – to call him an artful dodger is an understatement. He's unpredictable, unreliable and as crafty as a cartload of monkeys. With sexual supremo Mr Scorpio lurking round the corner, I'm sure you need a very good reason for not skipping this part of your Sextrology education, so here are a few: symbolised by the sign of the Scales he appears diplomatic and just; he has an outrageous and unique sense of humour; he's a brilliant business man and will attain success through fair means or perhaps foul if absolutely necessary, oh, and did I mention that he's also an expert lover? He may display an impish, boyish brain but further down he's all man. With him as your partner you can expect to live life in the fast lane. He seeks continual excitement and desires anything that has a hint of danger. Just like an ambitious child he yearns for the latest, flashiest, most sophisticated version of everything and you can bet he had the biggest conkers in the classroom. The male Libran's quest is simple – he strives for perfection – from himself and everything he touches. Second best is not a phrase in his vocabulary. Capturing him, therefore, is equally straightforward; either you have to be perfect or you must convince him of your belief in his own perfection. Yes, I know he sounds like yet another ego-maniac, but Libra man does deserve to have this part of his make-up well and truly massaged.

So, where do you go to find him? Exhibitions are a good starting point such as boat shows, motor shows and ideal homes. Whereas, say, Virgo man will be looking disgusted at such obvious materialism and Leo man will be buying in bulk, Libra man can be heard declaring . . . 'Got it, seen it, done it, yawn . . . I'd have two if they did them in black' etc. It may, of course, all be an elaborate front but either way it has served the purpose of demoralising the other men and keeping the cash in Libra's wallet. This is your cue. Stroll up to him and loudly ask, 'Is that your Mercedes coupe in the car park? I think you've left the lights on.' These expertly timed words alone should have him thinking honeymoon, but the killer clincher should be an innocent 'If your battery's gone flat, I could give you a jump start.' You can afford to be this brazen without the worry that he will whisk you outside expecting a quick service, this would be much too coarse and vulgar and not at all his style. The trick of snaring Libra man is that after you have made a fairly forceful first move, you should cool it big time as he is a sign for whom the chase is as necessary as the kill. Gentleman that he is, if you present yourself as a woman consumed with a smouldering passion in your heart and fire in your loins, just like Red Adair he will rush to your aid, do his job and then hang up his helmet until a more challenging opportunity comes his way. It is much better to come across as a girl who needs his mind rather than his body so ask for help, assistance or advice. Set him a poser that involves a legal matter – he's symbolised by the Scales of Justice after all, and he is usually quite well up on the law and its procedures. Pretend that you are a witness in an important court case and that you are nervous of what's ahead, maybe he could run through a dummy interrogation with you? This mixture of vulnerability and flattery of his talents should have him planning an evening to take down your particulars in no time at all.

Scene 2 **The Main Event**

Beyond a shadow of a doubt, this is a man who knows how to treat a girl. Even if he is living on a lemonade salary, he will be a champagne date. The preparations begin hours in advance and as any fly on his bathroom wall will verify, the time spent puffing, preening and perfuming is remarkable by a female's standards – for a man, it's unbelievable. He thinks of everything, no appendage or orifice escapes the scrubbing brush and whilst in the shower, purely for your benefit, he'll administer himself a spot of hand relief, firstly to ensure his endurance later and secondly, so he can perfect his orgasmic facial expressions in the mirror. You may laugh, but as we girls know, it's much more pleasant to gaze into the eyes of a guy who looks rapturous rather than constipated.

Expect to be picked up some considerable time after the prearranged hour. He won't be so late that you start to become annoyed, but just late enough to get your adrenaline flowing and heart thumping thus ensuring you won't want to eat too much. Dinner will be romantic, the manager is on first name terms and the credit card will be gold, the same colour in fact as the enamel paint in his brother's model-making kit. Despite the artistic licence that goes into the date, you must remember that from now on, his only objective is to provide you with a sexual pleasure the likes of which you have never experienced before. If his amazing powers of intuition tell him that your juices are already flowing, he may not want to wait until he gets you home so do be prepared if he 'accidentally' drops his napkin under the table. Hopefully you have enough will-power to be patient because what he has to offer really requires some privacy. Try not to come across as overly eager or lascivious – this guy has to feel in control and wants the thrill of your corruption. Deep down he fantasises that you are a virgin and it can be argued that until you have made love with him, you are.

After the meal, he feels safer taking you back to your place. At his home there is always the underlying worry that you will find stray pairs of knickers that most certainly are not Y fronts. Then there's the chance of phone calls from the inhabitants of his little black book. With such an overtly sexual man, you might be tempted to kick off proceedings with the suggestion of a raunchy movie to prove how liberated you are and to misguidedly give him some ideas. This is not actually the best plan of attack, remember that you are dealing with Mr Seen it-done it. The course of action that I would recommend is to do absolutely nothing and wallow in Libra man's seduction technique. He may have a slight build and frame but his knowledge of the female body and instinctive appreciation of what turns a girl on is enormous. The biggest benefit to being bedded by this man is that he gets his satisfaction from seeing and experiencing your pleasure so don't be shy with the vocals. Tell him what you're thinking and how it's feeling and remember to use plenty of superlatives – he responds extremely well to words like biggest, strongest and longest.

With Libra man, there is no need to fake it. We all know what it's like to reach that point in time – roughly after about five minutes of pumping and thrusting – when you realise that your orgasm is approximately another five minutes away but the man in charge of the action is expecting results in two. This is when a phony climax is compulsory to prevent him from writing you off as frigid. Well, with Mr Libra you can take as long as you want, twenty minutes, half an hour, no problem. His perfectly proportioned bottom will be bouncing up and down with the same pace and power as Skippy out on a cross-country run. A night of sex with him will be memorable and won't involve much sleep. Just in case you don't fancy a permanent reminder of the occasion, do be prepared – Libra man is one of the most fertile in the zodiac.

Scene 3 **Extras**

Many girls, after sampling the pleasures of Mr Libra will come to the conclusion that he's the best they have ever had. This is a fact that does not go unnoticed by the man himself and is, unfortunately, the reason why maintaining a long-term relationship with him is so difficult. He is notoriously bad at fidelity and should he notice himself showing early signs of being in love, he will take his temperature and retire to bed with another young corruptible until the symptoms pass. On a superficial level and thanks to his ruler, Venus, he does fall in love often. Three times in one day is not unheard of and he purchases more engagement rings than the buyer for Ratners, but generally unless a girl has the ability and inclination to make every night seem like the first, there is not much chance of wedding bells. Libran men born into the Western world have a deep sense of misfortune that geography placed them in an area where communal living or polygamy is frowned on. An alternative that does suit him is to find employment with a male escort agency, the chance to earn money for doing what he does best is too tempting to turn down.

I think it's wise to take the philosophical view with this chap; seeing as no relationship comes with a lifetime guarantee, you might as well plump for the most satisfying short-term encounter in the zodiac. His bedroom prowess will constantly astound you, his stamina never wanes and his inventiveness is infamous. There is one little ploy you could try if you really can't cope with inferior impostors – that is, to drop very unsubtle hints that his love-making is lacking in some way. It may just take him the rest of his days endeavouring to prove how wrong you are.

Scene 4 **The Finale**

Ending your affair with Libra male is the simplest part of the entire process. For starters you can let yourself slip into a state of plump laziness. Wear tacky ill-fitting clothes that barely cover the results of weeks spent gorging on cream cakes. You will know that he no longer finds you attractive when he introduces you to strangers as 'a friend'. Quite rightly you may consider that having to put on several pounds is a bit excessive just to offload a man, so next you can begin invading his privacy. Let him catch you ransacking his pockets or researching his personal organiser and make a point of phoning him at work every hour. Develop a case of permanent PMT and be as moody as possible. Libra is the sign that craves peace and harmony and regular temper tantrums will be your passport to freedom. At the end of the day though, honesty has to be the best policy. Tell him that you have to go to pursue your career, and he will admire and respect your motives. This strategy leaves the door very much open if, on having enjoyed the other eleven astro-males, you ever feel the desire for one night of uncomplicated, unbeatable sex.

SCORPIO

FEMALE
Scene 1 The Meeting

The fact that you are currently reading through these pages suggests to me that either you like to have the odd read now and again, or there's simply nothing on the television. Hopefully, your reason stems from the former and if so and especially if you're a guy, you are really going to enjoy this part of your Sextrology education. It's common knowledge that Scorpio woman is the most smouldering, sexual lady ever created, but that over-simplifies this highly intriguing female. She is the astrological equivalent of an intensely absorbing mystery novel and we all know how much fun it is to get stuck into one of those. Don't be fooled into thinking that she is an open book though, you could not be more wrong. An affair with her will keep you guessing from start to finish. At times the action will be slow and brooding due to her obsessive and intense emotions, at others it will be violent and volatile. The underlying storyline of a relationship with her, however, is sex. This is the driving force of her existence, the activity that links all aspects of her life together, the very reason she was created and sometimes the cause of her sadness or even her demise. Her life is always eventful as she is a sign of extremes that does not comprehend a middle ground. Her relationships, good or bad, will be fuelled by emotions of epic proportions. She is not a woman to be casually picked up and put down as the whim strikes. She demands and gets complete attention and from the moment a guy slips under her covers he will never be able to get her out of his mind. Should she be turned into a film, it would most certainly be X-rated and whatever her nationality, there's no need for subtitles because the language of love that she speaks is universal. Once she has fallen heavily for a guy and made a mental commitment, her loyalty is immeasurable. Just like your favourite paperback, she will accompany you to the ends of the earth and will tolerate neglect and misuse to stay by your side.

Scorpio woman has *femme fatale* written all over her and is not the easiest girl to recognise, so you may need to do a spot of sleuthing to track her down. Let's look at the astrological evidence. First, she is a Water sign so watery locations have to be a good bet. Second, she is ruled by Pluto and Mars, planets of danger and energy. Any clues yet? Well, yes, you might meet her on the log flume ride at your nearest theme park but this makes no allowance for her love of luxury and all things expensive. If I were you, I'd head off down to the travel agents and loiter with intent around those brochures that advertise skiing adventures, white-water rafting or cruises through the Bermuda Triangle. It's also worth knowing that the Scorpion female is fascinated by the occult and so it's probably her hovering over haunted house weekend breaks. For final confirmation that this is indeed the girl you're after, just look into those eyes – large, staring and unblinking. Many men at this point make the mistake of thinking that the way to attract the Scorpion female's attention is to be equally mysterious, but this is not so. If you follow her around wearing dark glasses and a long overcoat, she will have you down for a simple pervert and will call the cops. The guy that is in with the best chance is the one who displays a sense of humour, after all, every gripping thriller has to have its moments of light relief. Do something outrageous or childish – make an exhibition of yourself, perhaps have a go at getting down on one knee and serenading her. If you find the thought of this far too embarrassing then you're not likely to be a suitable hero. You must remember that her bedroom is an inhibition-free zone so start getting some practice in early. When chatting up this lady you should refrain from asking too many personal questions. Scorpios guard their privacy fiercely and should you be lucky enough to enter into a full-scale affair with her, you will always get the feeling that you are not seeing the real person, merely the character that she chooses to play at the time. A line that works surprisingly well is the old 'My wife doesn't understand me' routine. It's not that she wants to understand you any better, but she revels in the role of mistress – all the attention, all the nice presents, no smelly socks to wash.

Scene 2 **The Main Event**

I've never really understood why two people are more disposed to falling into bed together after a meal as opposed to an evening spent bowling or ice skating, but as the candlelit dinner now seems to be an obligatory part of foreplay, then this should be your invitation. It certainly won't be wasted on Scorpio woman as she loves her food and will be eating out of your hand if you take her to a seafood restaurant or oyster bar. Watching the way those slippery molluscs slide down her throat could be enough in itself for you to want to skip the sweet course and rush her off home but attempting to hurry this girl is a definite no no. Like all good yarns this erotic escapade should have a beginning, middle and end and if you just want to flick through the night only lingering over the dirty bits you can count on your union never reaching the sequel.

The location for love-making will be her place as here is where she feels safe to exhibit her sexuality; neighbours are either broadminded or have moved away following their embarrassment at reporting a murder next door only to find out it was this girl reaching orgasm. Once settled in her home, the prologue to your passion will begin with dialogue. Scorpio woman loves to talk about sex and does so in deep and dulcet tones. For a female so expert at disguise and illusion, she gives away clues to her sexual behaviour surprisingly clearly, if she has a glass in her hand, note the way she slides her fingers up and down the stem and then circles the rim. Men are mesmerised by these actions but you'll soon feel the adrenaline rush as she downs the drink in one. Lady Scorpio will need about half an hour of seductive chat before deciding on whether you are a good guy or a bad guy. To ensure you fall into the first category try to avoid talking about past lovers or mind-blowing erotic escapades – she does not want to hear that. You actually would fare much better with her if you admit to some sort of naivety or sexual deficiency, now that's a real challenge for her. Even more effective is to mention the fact that you have suffered a recent bout of impotence due to pressures of work. That interest she has in the occult will make her determined to raise the dead.

She is likely to leave the room and return in lingerie that most definitely did not come from Marks & Spencer. She has a bit of a fetish about underwear, especially those garments that exaggerate or draw attention to the crotch area. Do bear in mind that this sign is ruled by their genitalia and they will go to great lengths to adorn and decorate these parts, so you can never offend Scorpio woman with gifts of naughty knickers or glamorous G-strings. Try not to look too stunned if she turns out to be sporting erotic piercings and/or tattoos. If your relationship progresses, she would be thrilled if you pledged your commitment by having her name permanently needled onto your manhood. (It's pure bad luck if your Scorpio insists on being known as Samantha-Caroline instead of Sam.)

The action will most probably take place on her bed which is often of the sloshy water variety. It can be a little difficult at first to time your thrusts whilst fighting against the tide, but with practice the bed will work with you instead of against you. Sneaky men will opt for rear entry positions; push her buttocks forward and the watery momentum will propel her back again – much less work for you. Should you need to go to the bathroom because the lobster is out for revenge, but don't want to interrupt the flow, simply position a vibrator or dildo in the headboard as she continues to face away from you. You can exit to the toilet, do a crossword and still be back before she's broken sweat. During intercourse she would like you to explore all avenues of her pleasure, not just the conventional one. After all, every hero has to get caught in a tight spot. If you do not feel like breaking the law – that reliable dildo will come in handy as a stunt double.

All in all, you can count on an action-packed night that keeps you on the very edge of ecstasy until the crescendo of climax. Do remember after-play talk; like all final pages, there must be some witty one-liners.

Scene 3 **Extras**

To guarantee that you now become a loyal devotee of this woman's erotic works, you can rest assured that the follow-up to that first night will contain a larger degree of sex and violence. The more you get inside this girl's body and brain, the more complex and creative the carnal plots will become. She excels at creating mood and atmosphere and her fantasies are detailed and deviant, often centring around the master/slave scenario with her in charge. She loves you to play the passive partner so that she can inflict varying forms of punishment on you; this sometimes includes her inviting a girlfriend round for you to have sex with while she watches and gives instructions. (Don't count on receiving much sympathy from the lads on this aspect of your suffering.)

Outside of the bedroom though, her image is one of sweetness and light. On setting up home with her she will happily bake cakes for when the vicar comes to tea and only you and she will know where the cherries have been. She is an excellent housemaker and even better mother, but due to her all-or-nothing nature, expect the kids to come in batches rather than one at a time. She will support your career and may even appear to turn a blind eye to one or two of your indiscretions, although it's true to say that you'll never get to hear the talk down at her tennis club that there's a contract on your mistress's head.

Scene 4 **The Finale**

Closing chapters with this sign easily become vindictive and vicious and can end up in court. Although she will put up with a lot, there comes a point at which she is pushed over the edge and loses control, particularly if you taunt her with insults and provoke her jealousy by openly flaunting your flirtations with each and every girl you meet. With that famous Scorpion sting in the tail she is armed and dangerous and the most unpleasant enemy you could imagine. We've all heard about scorned women who slash their ex-lover's clothes with Stanley knives – well Scorpio lady is one of those, only she does it while you're still wearing them. It makes better sense to rewrite a slightly more logical ending and simply explain that you do not love her anymore, but will be her friend. She'll be mortally wounded and will conduct a full post mortem into what went wrong and why, but ultimately she will accept that maybe it would be better if she found a new leading man. Think twice before casually throwing this woman away, just like that favourite mystery novel, no matter how well you know the plot, each time you delve into it, there is always something that you hadn't seen before – perhaps the chance of a happy ending after all.

MALE
Scene 1 **The Meeting**

I sincerely hope that any female reading this guide to sex and the stars has not become at all complacent, naively believing that after seven heavenly hunks, the eighth must be a piece of cake. Mr Scorpio is many things, but piece of cake he ain't. This guy is the sexiest in the zodiac and an affair with him is the most danger-ridden ride of your life. Astrologically governed by his genitalia, he is a gynaecological Godfather and ruled by Pluto, a word synonymous with the under-world, so he is strong, silent and deadly. At his core is a sexual desire that is as unpredictable as a ticking bomb, his lifelong mission is to seek out targets, unload his deadly cargo and leave his victims deliriously devas-tated. To satisfy all his life's needs there is no risk too great, no hurdle too high, no challenge too demanding. To achieve his goals, he will do whatever is necessary but he often manages to attain a grand style of living without personally getting his hands dirty. His mesmer-ising magnetism and intensely powerful persona cause men to jump for cover and women to lie down at his feet. Most of his erotic encounters are spontaneous, sudden and short lived. He chooses quarry at random on the spur of a moment and slips away under cover of darkness not leaving so much as a calling card. Despite a cold calculating exterior, however, there is a loyal and logical heart that never forgets a favour and never forgives an injustice. He lives by a self-imposed code that is incomprehensible, yet admirable. One night of supreme sex with him is an easy ambition, indeed, just about every woman in the world is on his hit list as he is one of the few signs that can find a beautiful quality in each and any female. My recommendation to you, however, is to break down his defences, crack that carnal code and aim to be the full-time moll of this glorious gangster. It's worth selling your soul to the Devil to be his partner in crime and if you can be true to him come Hell or high water and fan the flames of his passion for the rest of eternity, you will go through life with a man who will fight to the death to protect you.

So, where do you go to find him? This is not that simple as he is not a great socialiser, cannot abide small talk and he prefers his sport to be studious rather than sweaty. There is more chance of spying him at a chess championship than a cup final. A location which is literally a good bet is a casino, as he feels at home with high rollers and gets a kick out of courting the odds. To reap the rewards of his attention you must be prepared to play with high stakes and go for broke in your appearance. Ideally, Scorpio man likes his ladies to look sexual as opposed to sexy and bold rather than brazen. He will be easy to recognise – he'll be wearing lots of black that represents his Scorpion shell and his stance will be intimidatingly confident, back upright, legs apart and head held high. For a final confirmation, just look at those eyes – they are huge, hypnotic and as deep as the ocean but reflect nothing of his thoughts, moods and emotions. Approaching him instead of one of his friends may seem as sensible as jumping out of a plane without a parachute, but remember, it's the element of danger that makes this conquest so appealing. In actual fact he will be pleasantly surprised if you make the first move – he likes women with balls. Stride purposefully towards him, look him in those eyes and ask to be his lucky charm for the evening. Being forthright will temporarily disarm him and if you gaze lower down, you will see it is most certainly not a gun in his pocket, he's genuinely happy to meet you.

Play him at his own game and present yourself as an intoxicating cocktail of mystery and secrets. There is more chance of having a long-term undercover relationship with him if you don't put all your cards on the table straight away. To hook him, you need to intrigue him and to keep him you must captivate him. For a man so complex he is amazingly susceptible to flattery so find something to praise. It's not that he falls for any old flannel, but he warms to people who tell the truth. The hardest part from now on is to keep yourself in his head and out of his bed until he has had the time to get to know you. If he explores your body on that first encounter he won't be interested in your brain so your plan should be to make him start at the top and work his way down over a reasonable period of time.

Scene 2 **The Main Event**

Whilst you are still at the stage of forging your way into his inner circle of emotions, you must try to avoid being in situations where the two of you are alone as Scorpio man cannot be trusted to stick to his part of the bargain. His testosterone levels operate on a hair trigger, sometimes independently of his brain and should an unguarded moment present itself, he might be totally incapable of not shooting up your body there and then.

When you feel that the time has come to give yourself fully to him, send a message that you're ready to go through with the whole deal. The urgency of the job in hand will be appreciated by each of you and there's no real need for the likes of a candlelit meal. If, though, you want to be traditional about it, he will be more than happy to take you for an Italian to discuss the terms of surrender. He will suggest your home as the location for love-making and this will probably be due to him having some unfinished business at his place.

There is no set pattern as to what happens next, but generally Scorpios are pouncers rather than procrastinators. He is thrilled by your surprise so even though from the minute he enters your home you know the writing's on the wall, he will still pick his moment carefully. He is at his most ruthless when you have your back to him so don't be shocked if you turn around to come face to face with a primed and poised weapon. Next he will kiss you with fearsome intensity to the point where you wonder if suffocation is to be the cause of your demise. Should you now develop a case of cold feet, it's best to put on some shoes – running shoes. This guy takes rejection badly and he's going to see this exercise through to completion with or without your cooperation. If you beg for mercy convincingly enough, he will lay off, but you can count on his return.

Scorpio's skill at the preliminaries is exemplary, his oral technique unique, he would never deliver that final blow without preparing the ground thoroughly and by the time he has calculated his precise angle for entry, you will be pleading to be put out of your misery. Prudish thoughts are the bad guys and should you have any, he will wipe them out. You should not expect him to carry contraception and in spite of the obvious gamble, he does not like employing the services of a hood. Sex with this man is not remarkable by its brutality, but by the way he turns his lover into a willing recipient of such passionate punishment. He will take you to the very limits of pain and pleasure to the point where it's impossible to tell the difference and even when he has fired into you and obliterated your senses, he will do it all again to ensure your recovery will take at least a lifetime.

The only defence you have is the knowledge that his genitals are his weak spot, take them in your palm and you'll have the upper hand. Whatever you do, don't make teasing comments about your fellatio prowess unless you can promise the goods – he will make you eat your words. The girl who perfects oral sex stands a better chance than most of having Scorpio man licked forever, so it's worth hours of practice.

To sum up: think of the best sex you ever had and then double it. This man takes you to places you have never been to before and somewhere along the way, you will realise that you've crossed a dividing line. Even if you never see him again, you'll be marked for life.

Scene 3 **Extras**

Once Mr Scorpio has found a girl who quenches his sexual thirst yet manages to keep him guessing, he is capable of extreme fidelity. Such a privileged female is then given the once-over by the family and the initiation into his life is complete. Wedding rings are not necessary to bond this union because Scorpio provides and expects a loyalty that goes beyond anything the Church has to offer. When truly happy he is not prone to playing around for kicks but he will utilise those awesome powers of persuasion to entice you into ever more deviant and perhaps sadistic activities. I'm not saying that you'll wake up to find a horse's head on your pillow but don't think a similar idea hasn't crossed his mind once or twice. He readily explores any substance or fantasy that has a pleasure potential and can himself fall prey to the excesses of drugs and drink if either promise to reach parts that normal sex can't. Keeping him sexually sated is a full-time job for his partner and as Scorpio is no right-hand man, don't think he'll sort things out for himself. If his demands are excessive, he'll have no objection to you enlisting the help of a girlfriend. Do choose your assistant carefully though, because she may turn into your arch-rival, like many of life's infamous bad guys he is alluring and addictive and women stop at nothing to have a part of his action.

Scene 4 **The Finale**

From everything you have read there is one message that should have come across loud and clear – this man must be taken seriously. Don't be fooled by his bone-dry wit and sarcastic mirth – laugh with him and he's your best buddy, laugh at him and you're history. To chip your way out of Scorpio man's heart, the tools you need to use are insults, fault-finding and mickey-taking. Very few get to see his innermost depths and if a girl is able to break his barriers and see this sacred place, the price she pays is to be kept a prisoner within it. If you attempt to break for freedom by provoking him and poking fun and contempt in his direction, he will leave your life for good as silently and coolly as he entered it. There is a twist at the end though that should make you think twice before playing mind games with him. The deadliest part of the male Scorpion lies between his legs – it's not what you're thinking, it is that famous stinging tail. One day he will be back and his desire for vengeance over you will be stronger than his lust for sex ever was. You won't know where and you won't know when, but he'll return to even the score and make you wish you'd never crossed him. To say that his revenge stings is like saying that having a tooth drilled without anaesthetic is a bit uncomfortable.

If you really can't handle his jealousy, his outbursts and furious rages or his natural suspicion of everything and everyone, then simply tell him. He'll do everything to change your mind but ultimately won't stop you leaving. All I shall say, and I'm talking from experience, is give this man a fair hearing. He does not play by the rules but to live without him is nothing short of criminal.

SAGITTARIUS

FEMALE
Scene 1 **The Meeting**

Okay then guys, you are now two-thirds of the way through your Sextrology studies and I appreciate that you could well be feeling rather tired after sampling the previous eight wonderfully wicked women. Hopefully you have paced yourself and have saved a little energy so that you can relish Sagittarius female to the full. This girl is a big experience in every way. No, I'm not referring to her build or weight because this is usually taut, muscular and fit, if perhaps slightly larger boned than other girls. What I am saying is that Sagittarius woman is ruled by Jupiter, the planet of expansion and broad horizons. She has high hopes, even taller ambitions and is always on the move – travel is a word that's always linked to this sign. She lives life to the full and covers much ground in her pursuit of friendship, passion and helping others less well off than herself, she is incredibly big-hearted. In many ways she is the Cowgirl of the zodiac; totally at peace so long as she is free to roam and enjoy each adventure as it comes along. She prefers an uncomplicated existence, is unimpressed by today's hi-tech living and often reflects wistfully on her childhood which seemed so much more straightforward. Given the choice, she would ideally love to have been born into a bygone era – perhaps the Wild West, when men were men and the sheep were scared. Should you ever have sex with her, then you're in for a bedroom bonanza, especially if you are a chap who feels uncomfortable with romance. Love-making for Sagittarius woman is a means to an end, an act to quench a physical need, just the same as eating and drinking. There are no hearts and flowers in her boudoir, simply the bare necessities needed to get the job done. These items won't include gadgets and gizmos, lotions and potions and she expects both of you to leave your emotions along with your boots outside the bedroom door. She changes lovers in the same way as cowboys changed horses – moving on to a fresh one when the old mount became exhausted and saddlesore. Such an attitude to sex can be very refreshing – she's happy to get down'n dirty without expecting an engagement ring as a reward.

So, where do you go to get roped up with this girl? Your local stables would be a good choice as Sagittarian gals have an affinity with the equine species, indeed, she is symbolised by a creature half-human, half-horse. Ignore all the ladylike goings on in the dressage ring – this female is no side-saddle rider. Like countless females before her, she knows all too well the exquisite delights that a bony set of withers can give a girl on a gallop. You need not be afraid of approaching her as she loves to make new friends and always smiles at strangers, but if you can make her laugh, your chances increase tenfold. Of all the zodiac ladies, this girl is the one whose sexual stirrings are kindled the quickest and easiest. Her passions can ignite faster than dry leaves in the desert, so you should not be shocked if she suggests a roll in the hay right there and then. She does not need to know much about you if she finds you attractive and is, in fact, quite turned on by the thought of being taken by the man with no name. Do try, though, to resist the lure of sex without sentiment because she has better things to offer if you can claim her for a longer session and if you succeed in tying her down for life, you will have struck gold. So although it's tempting to be a bandit for her body and loot her treasures on the spot, endeavour to put a price on your head and intrigue her enough to make her wait. The most passionate profits are to be had if you formulate a plan to steal her heart.

Sagittarius is a Fire sign and responds well to flattery so bolster her ego with compliments and then suggest that she accompanies you for a weekend ramble or a spot of messing about by the river. To secure her interest, tell her that it will be a group expedition – the chance to enlarge her social circle is one she will never turn down.

Scene 2 **The Main Event**

After several jaunts into the country, you will realise what a breath of fresh air this girl is – she's robust, rebellious and won't get suicidal if she breaks a nail whilst climbing a tree. For all that though, she still retains her femininity and these combined character-istics will have been playing havoc with your mascu-linity. There will come a time when you realise that a man's got to do what a man's got to do and for this you will need to separate her from the pack of regular weekend walkers. Appeal to her love of animals and mention that you have a small furry creature at home that you're sure she'd love to stroke. Unfortunately, it happens to be far more active at night-time, so could she come round that evening? Obviously, your real pet project from now on is to capture her for the whole night, so make reservations at your favourite Indian, Italian or Chinese restaurant – that love of far-off locations means she prefers foreign food and pandering to her taste buds enhances your chances of her savouring your own exotic parts.

She will know where the night is leading but as Sagittarians are thrilled by surprises, you should aim to provide one or two. When you return to your home, instead of simply taking her indoors for coffee, show her your erection in the garden. No, not that one, I'm talking about the tent you have put up next to the flower beds. There's nothing she enjoys more than the idea of sex under the stars and she'll be over the moon at your inventiveness. Furnish your temporary teepee with enough alcoholic rations to relax yourself and slow her down, remember, she is quite partial to a 'Wham, bam, thank you ma'am' encounter. Sagittarius girl is not averse to trying the odd erotic stimulant and may ask if there's a peace pipe handy. On this score you might have to disappoint her, but be a gentleman and offer something else for her to get her lips round. Oral sex is one of Sagittarius's great fortes. The fact that she talks so much means that her mouth muscles are well developed and a special trick of hers is to hum at the same time. This straight down to basics approach is sure to have you both singing the same tune instantly and you should return the compliment. If you don't, she will make her protestations very clear and very loud and the neighbours will hear how her last boyfriend was the king of cunnilingus. Unless you can convince them that this is a small African republic, it's pretty embarrassing. She likes all her intimate areas to be orally explored and the man that speaks with forked tongue has good odds of staying the distance. Her erogenous zones are around the thighs and hips and she likes to be held firmly in a manly grasp, particularly for intercourse. A word of warning here – Sagittarian women are not the world's greatest condom buyers because they prefer bareback riders. This is where you must put your foot down, because apart from anything else, these girls, like Calamity Jane, seem to attract accidents and even if you believe yourself to be firing blanks, it's not worth the risk – I can guarantee you'll be left holding the baby.

During the sex act itself there will be much movement and stopping and starting. She throws herself around like a bucking bronco and you may have to hold on tight. There is no one preferred position for this lady but she hopes that you are skilled at them all. She also expects you to know about the G-spot so if you still think that it's a breath freshener, you better do some homework. She is capable of many or multiple orgasms but they tend to be quite shallow. This, however, won't worry her, she's not a great believer in the earth-moving experience and is therefore less disappointed than some girls secretly are when they fail to reach the dizzy heights that glossy magazines say they should. What will upset her is if you instantly fall asleep after your climax. A good deal of her pleasure is derived from the *après*-sex chat and she wants to know how it was for you, mostly because she was so engrossed in her own enjoyment that she failed to notice at the time.

Scene 3 **Extras**

Sexually, with Sagittarians, what you see on that first night is by and large what you get. They don't have need of fantasies or battery-powered helpers to aid their trek towards orgasm. If a man can't deliver the goods with the tools God gave him, she will find one who can. She does have a strong sex drive though and if she is on her own when the urge strikes, she is entirely capable of doing the job herself. This is when her erotic imagination comes into play. She toys with thoughts of gynaecological examinations – not because she's turned on by doctors, but because the stirrups relate to that horsy element again. For the same reason she fancies herself as a whip-wielding madam ready to thrash her mount into submission.

The key to holding on to this lady's affections is to be her friend first and lover second. The more space you give her, the less likely she is to use it. How corrupt or depraved your mutual bedroom behaviour becomes depends on your own tenacity. She is more than willing to experiment and is also prone to exhibitionism but seldom comes up with ideas of her own. That is your department and the reason why she chooses to have sex with you as opposed to a long satisfying canter on her four-legged friend. It's worth putting your thinking cap on though, because if you dream up mind-blowing activities, generous girl that she is, she won't object to her girlfriend popping round to share in your attributes. She firmly agrees with the notion that nothing compares to sex between a man and a woman, so long as she's the one in between!

Scene 4 **The Finale**

As you may have gathered, ending a relationship with Sagittarius woman is not the hard part – it's keeping her that's tough. Hitching up with another female for some illicit sex won't provoke her anger and that takes all the fun out of being unfaithful anyway. Even if you openly flaunt a fresh filly under her nose, she's not likely to chase you out of town or hold you to ransom with emotional blackmail. Her forgiveness stems from her theory that a mere man is a helpless victim of his hormones and it is tough to argue your way out of that.

The only way to guarantee this affair drawing to a close is either to confine her to a life of domesticity, or work your way under her surprisingly thin skin and launch some below-the-belt comments about her appearance, her bedroom manner and choice of friends. She is symbolised by the Archer, so you can expect her to fire at least one parting shot. She may boast of sleeping with all your friends, knowing that it's virtually impossible for you to ditch enough pride to ask them.

There is really no need for all the typical blood and guts that mark most separations, this lovely and lusty lady won't take it badly providing you have not been an out-and-out villain. Stay friends and who knows? One day she could return and together you'll ride out into the sunset forever.

MALE
Scene 1 **The Meeting**

Would any girl who has so far done the complete tour through the preceding eight male signs believe that we only have four gorgeous astro-guys to go? What would be a serious mistake is now to apply everything you have learned on your Sextrology course to Sagittarius male. He is the Highwayman of the zodiac, living by his own rather immoral code of rules and going through life wickedly collecting unsuspecting female hearts, only to discard them when they have served his passionate purpose. You might be tempted to stay out of this guy's path altogether, but it's not that simple. He is a master of emotional disguise and on first sight comes across as disarmingly attractive – he's dashing, charming and incredibly funny. He's handsome, sporty and appears the perfect gentleman, the sort that lays his coat over a puddle so as not to dirty your shoes. Before you've realised that this is the love 'em and leave 'em type, it's too late. By then you will have surrendered to him and more than likely, let him get his hands on your valuables. The root of his troubles is that he adores the fairer sex, and can often be heard wistfully muttering, 'So many women, so little time.' Also, he is ruled by Jupiter which stops him from staying in one place for too long and finally, he is symbolised by a creature half-man and half-horse. Not only does this make him one of the better endowed signs, it also means that he covers sexual ground in breakneck speed. Before you start writing him off as a rogue and a filthy, rotten scoundrel, let me say something in his defence; basically, he does have good intentions. He always hopes that the next conquest will be 'the one', that special girl who can put an end to his life of carnal crime. Unfortunately, he has been disappointed so often that he, at a very young age, becomes cynical and lives by the motto that it is better to travel hopefully than to arrive. He finds it hard to let anybody see his real self, afraid that once he drops his cavalier facade he will be taken advantage of. Without the bravado, he feels naked and vulnerable and should he ever, on that rare occasion, fall hopelessly in love, he will not readily admit it to his friends for fear that they will accuse him of turning yellow.

Sex with him is more a matter of quantity rather than quality, so if you're a girl who likes little and often, where do you go to find him? The good news is that you need not go looking – Sagittarius male will find you, especially if you are an outdoorsy type. He opts for jobs that allow him freedom and space and should his work confine him to an office or shop, he will certainly be found in the open air during his time off. He's quite fond of animals and favours the large, energetic, canine variety. Wander past your local playing fields and you'll spot him – he's the one whose dogs look more tired than he does. I'd recommend that you leave your pussy at home and borrow a friend's Labrador. Set off for a long ramble in the nearest woods and just wait. You won't get very far before a Sagittarian male leaps out from behind a tree and ambushes you with an instantly

amorous chat-up. There is no beating about the bush
with this man's opening lines, he's blunt, direct and to
the point – tactful he's not. He'll probably inform you
that he knows of a much better way to burn off calories
so what are you both waiting for? The amazing thing is
that he's so damn attractive it will take the average
female all her will power not to stand and deliver right
there and then. If you do, it will be lusty and earthy and
his impressive weapon could make you cry out, which
will, of course, have your friend's pooch running off to
find help. Whilst the experience is sure to be exceed-
ingly pleasant, you won't have, by any stretch of the
imagination, got to see the best of him and you'll be
more than a little miffed when he meets up with you on
tomorrow's walk and enquires if he knows you from
somewhere. Your aim should be to secure his interest
by putting a value on yourself, make it appear that you
are a prized jewel for which he has to fight. By nature he
is competitive and he will find you much more of a
challenge if he thinks he has to do battle with another
male before he can steal you. Perhaps then, you should
borrow your friend's brother along with her dog for
your daily constitutional; then the chase will really be
on.

Scene 2 **The Main Event**

After several forays into the forest and assuming that
you haven't done the dirty deed with your pal's brother
now that you've got to know him so well, you should
brace yourself for a solo ramble. Sagittarius man, with
radar-like powers of detection, will sense that you are

now unprotected booty and will move in to stake his claim. Believing there to be a rival, his approach this time is sure to be a little more studied and his angle will be one of friendship. To help him along, tell him that your imaginary boyfriend is going out of town and that leaves you without a companion to a forth-coming open-air rock concert, one that you'd prefer not to attend alone. He will pull out his 'diary', otherwise known as his little black book, and will pretend to do some social juggling so that, lo and behold, yes he can just fit you in. Between you and me the only things in his diary are hundreds of telephone numbers, each with the appropriate star rating alongside, but play along with it anyway. When the big musical event arrives he will be an attentive escort and, not wanting to be disrespectful of your feminist views, will insist that you be the one to go for the beers and hamburgers.

Ideally, he would like to make love to you right there while the band plays on, as he is quite an exhibitionist at heart and is turned on by outdoor sex. Failing this, the location will probably be either of your homes, and yours is preferable as it enables him to make a quick getaway. Stimulated by lust and fuelled by the sexual beat of the night's music, you can count on Sagittarius man to have his trousers down the minute he enters your house. The element of surprise is one of his favourite tricks and when you glance at the monstrously huge beast between his legs, your reaction is not going to be so much 'what?' as 'how?' The answer will become more apparent as he sets to work purposefully undressing you and applying a skilful erotic massage as he does so. He talks dirty and plays dirty, homing in on your treasures before you've had a chance to ask if he'd like a coffee. If he wasn't so good at it, you'd have every reason to slap his face. Don't think about crying rape, his response will be 'Oh, all right then!' In actual fact, his hormones race even faster if there's a hint of taking you by force and although he'd never really do anything against your will, it wouldn't hurt to offer some token resistance. This can be easier said than done because he is supreme at administering oral sex. This sign tends to have long tongues and you can again thank his horse-like characteristics for that. For your information, his erogenous zones are around his inner thighs and lower buttocks. While you are catching your breath, try stroking or grasping these areas firmly. He won't be impressed if you produce a battery-powered gadget to spice up proceedings and will be genuinely hurt if he feels his manhood is not sufficient to satisfy you. You can explain till you're blue in the face that there is nothing a man can do to match the sensations of vibrator on clitoris – this guy belongs to the old school that it's what goes in that gets orgasms out. When all is said and done though, if any chap is going to prove that the vaginal and G-spot orgasm exists and is not a myth dreamt up by men to make us girls feel inadequate, it's him. He rapidly changes from one position to another monitoring his progress by the loudness of your ooh's and aah's. When it's all over, he wants to talk about it and then probably do it all again. After that, he'll go to the bathroom and only some time later will you notice that he's taken his clothes and the bathroom window is creaking slightly.

Scene 3 **Extras**

So, what can you look forward to in a relationship with Mr Sagittarius? Well, lots of sex, that goes without saying. He will cater to your needs at any time of the day, night, or month come to that. If you're a girl whose sex drive works at warp factor ten, you won't have much to complain about. He's experimental and loves to learn, so will buy every book or video on the market that promises to add another dimension to bedtime. If though, you start looking optimistically at rose-covered cottages and engagement rings, all he's likely to buy is a one-way plane ticket. To keep him captivated, he requires novelty and variety and if you can't stretch to threesomes or group activities, the best you can do is make an effort to be several girls in one. Obtain assorted wigs and different styles of lingerie, endeavour to swap styles so that you are alternately submissive and dominant and keep fantasies in ready supply. You will have to turn a blind eye to his roving one and do be prepared for him to get hot under the collar in the presence of ladies from exotic backgrounds – his love of travel and foreign cultures makes him very partial to dark or olive-skinned beauties. It might be worth you being the one who always goes to collect the take-away Indian or Chinese meals unless you like your spring rolls cold, soggy and spiced with a hint of suspicion.

Sagittarius man can settle down but is better at it in later life. Many girls have lovers who they describe as their best friend. Him you should view as a best friend that you can sometimes call your lover. It's a subtle distinction, but one you should remember as it saves much jealousy and many tears.

Scene 4 **The Finale**

As you might imagine, getting rid of him is the
simplest part of the process and your desire to do so
will be born out of constant doubts about his fidelity.
These men have a knack of turning easy-going women
into nags and non-possessive types into clock-
watchers. You won't like the person you have become
and neither will he. These traits alone should have
your randy Highwayman searching for a fresh mount,
but if this is not the case, then get personal. Be critical
and analytical, he hates being questioned and que-
ried. Also be as pessimistic as you can, think of a
downside to every up, adopt the philosophy that if it
can go wrong it will. Sagittarians wake up feeling that
every new day is the chance for something wonderful
to happen and you can depress him to the point of
departure by telling him it just ain't so. The final nail
in the coffin will be to keep him indoors; overwhelm
him with home repairs and refurbishments and he will
soon be doing odd jobs elsewhere. When you
separate, he will not be vindictive and will still want to
be pals which is the best possible direction your
relationship could take when you've hit a romantic
crossroads.

Hitch up with this man and you are assured fun,
companionship and lots of love-making, so give it all
you've got. At the very least, in years to come when he
flicks through that little black book, you should aim to
have been awarded the full five stars. And who knows –
one dark night he may suddenly reappear crying 'Your
body or your life!' My guess is that you'll give yourself
up just one more time.

CAPRICORN

FEMALE
Scene 1 The Meeting

I think it's fair to say that any man who so far has experienced the previous nine astro-ladies, either between the sheets, or between the pages of this book, will have discovered a lady who he is more than happy to settle down with. Well, before you make your choice, remember that there are still three to go and certainly Capricorn woman is worth the time and trouble. She is the Gold Digger of the zodiac, but before you recoil from the obvious connotations of this analogy, let me explain. Capricorn woman does go through life always hunting for the best that is on offer, but she does not expect or believe that a man alone can provide these things for her. She is an exceptionally hard worker and, being an Earth sign, cares not if she has to dirty her hands to get the rewards. To work your way into her heart though, is

133

as difficult as finding that elusive golden metal. Capricorn girls are naturally suspicious and wary of entering into a relationship. This is partly due to their ruler Saturn, but mostly caused by her having been severely let down in previous relationships. When she was young she probably made huge mistakes; she was easily tempted by fool's gold – men who appeared to have all the right ingredients but later, once the affair was tested, proved to be worthless fakes who stole her trust and self-worth. Through bitter experience she has learned to protect herself and her emotions and is now cautious and cynical. For this reason, she won't run off with the first nugget of love that comes her way, no matter how attractive or genuine it seems. She keeps her ear to the ground just in case there is something or someone more promising round the corner.

When she does finally meet that special someone who clearly demonstrates his devotion, she is the most loyal lover you could find. Should he be a little innocent or naive as is often the case with her final choice of partner, she will spend hours moulding him and shaping him – turning his basic good qualities into something with panache and style, something to be proud of. For all of this, she still protects her independence fiercely and will never hide behind your glamour or your success, she wants to be your equal and compliment your abilities, not live off the back of them. Without doubt, she is a challenge, but one worthy of undertaking as her love-making is enduring, earthy and without any inhibition.

So, where would you uncover this celestial treasure? At her place of employment would be a good start. Capricorn females are always attractive, mostly of athletic build and nearly always blonde. She prefers professions which allow her to serve, assist or beautify others and as other women feel comfortable in her company, she usually works in hair salons or establishments which promote health and fitness.

Use your powers of detection to track down a Miss Capricorn who is currently employed as a masseuse – the legitimate type. On first meeting, she won't massage your ego but will manipulate your tired aching limbs. Her skilled and nimble fingers will soon have you thinking about putting more than your well-being in her hands, but whatever you do, don't let her see your swelling interest. If you point at it, wink, then ask, 'What are you going to do about that then?', she'll reply, 'Call the manager, that's what.' Don't even think about asking for extras or she'll stick another tenner on your bill. The way to her darker recesses is through a mutual interest or similar goal so listen closely to her conversation and latch on to anything that could possibly be a common interest. All of this will take several meetings and you'll be thinking about exchanging bodily fluids long before she is thinking about exchanging phone numbers. What you must do now is make her feel important by trusting her with your valuables – no, not those valuables. Tell her that you're going away for the weekend in the country and you need someone you can count on to take care of your old, faithful pet hamster. She'll warm to that. As you leave her and walk down the street clutching a box containing Rodney – the rodent you've just purchased from the pet shop, you can confidently whistle a merry tune.

Scene 2 **The Main Event**

It's Sunday evening, you have just returned from that imaginary weekend away and you're off to Miss Capricorn's house to collect your hamster. After a short conversation during which it emerges that Rodney is quite lively and not that friendly for an old, family pet, the least you can do is invite her out for a meal to say thanks. Also, consider buying her a little present, cheap junk won't be appreciated, but something that is small and expensive or perhaps of sentimental value will go down well – you'll be hoping, of course, that she does too.

Dinner should be in elegant surroundings and she'll probably offer to pay her half. On this occasion you must insist, but let her know that it's her treat next time. After that, offer to escort her home. It's not wise to go back to your place because she'll be confused as to why the rest of your household looks quizzical when she asks you loudly how often you take Rodney out for a cuddle. Upon reaching her residence and going in for the obligatory coffee you can expect the unexpected. She is not a sign that likes being taken by surprise but she's excellent at springing some of her own. You may have talked for several hours and your hormones have reached a pitch where, yes, Rodney does actually look rather attractive, when suddenly without warning she'll tell you that you're just the sort of man she could make love to. Don't be too eager and say, 'That's lucky – I've got a packet of condoms in my pocket and the expiry date is tomorrow.' Just nod and say how flattered you are. Before you can say 'Not in front of the hamster', she will have stripped naked and will be eying up your bulge with anticipation. Let her control the pace as Capricorns like to dominate, but it is helpful to know that her thighs and her calves are areas of great erogenous potential. Your actions should be firm and forceful yet not overly experienced. The future of your sexual life together will be much more rosy if she believes she can teach you something, as she chooses sexual students as opposed to professors.

The main action will take place on her bed, it may be conventional, but comfort is her priority. Oral sex she embarks on with relish and is a skill so perfected that you feel she is going to strike gold before you've had a chance to get your tools in action. It is vital that you don't surrender your liquid assets though; although some women are very happy to take orgasm in turns and can easily be quenched by tongues and fingers, Capricorn girl thirsts for penetration. She has not led you to her treasure trove only to realise that you are just a surface worker. For intercourse you should aim to be the one that gets a view of the ceiling as she likes the superior posture as it allows you to go in deep and this is how she gets her pleasure. Her internal muscles are usually strong so there's no danger of sloppy pot holing and she does more than her share of the exertions. Once she is in place, she's there for the duration. Unlike say, Gemini girl, who changes position more times than an ice skater, this lady is unmovable. She wants you to thrust and plunge with all the determination you possess, only then can you both reap the ultimate glittering rewards. At the point of her climax she will bite and scratch and as for noise – well, it will knock Rodney off his wheel, that's for sure.

Afterwards, she quickly calms down and resumes her demure demeanour, so much so that she becomes an entirely different girl. It's as if she had sent her erotic alter-ego to do the dirty deed on her behalf. All she will want to do now is relax, smoke a cigarette and enjoy the warmth of your mutual afterglow with some interesting conversation. Perhaps, she will ask, you could chat about what you got up to during your weekend in the country?

Scene 3 **Extras**

A long-term relationship with this lusty lady is based on the simple premise of Finders – Keepers. If you manage to find, through your sensitivity and respect, a way to her heart, then she's willing to let you have a go at keeping it. Your day-to-day life together will be organised and practical. She is a superb decision-maker and runs her home and her family with meticulous precision; it can be a relief to have a girl who knows how to fix plugs, change tyres and fill in tax returns. Sexually, she is more spontaneous than the male of her sign. Whereas Capricorn man likes to circle dates in the diary for love-making, with this girl any day is a potentially sexy day. You will never know when the mood may strike her, or what that mood will be. Sometimes she will act submissively and let you take the lead, at others she can become the Mistress of Pain and inflict torturous and torrid punishments on your body. This she does more out of her love of control and power rather than for the sexual pleasure.

Capricorn girl is more broad-minded than first

appearances would indicate and her thirst for knowledge means she will try just about anything that hints at producing a new or different sensation. Mostly though, she does draw the line at having playmates come to join in the fun for a threesome – she's a touch too possessive to share you with another girl and doesn't fancy the idea of satisfying two men. The golden rule with her is, whatever you get up to, keep it to yourself. If she feels you've told the world about her sauciest secrets and that there is now a chance of other men sniffing round for a piece of the action, she will switch off from sex and leave you to polish your own baubles.

Scene 4 The Finale

Capricorn women can never truly be owned due to their need for independent security. If anything is going to threaten your relationship it may well be her career aspirations and although some male signs of the zodiac can cope with this, what if you're a guy who likes his dinner on the table as opposed to on a supermarket shelf? Simply asking her to make a choice might be enough to provoke her temper and pack her bags – after all, she'd never do that to you. Another reason for you beginning to question whether all that glistens is really gold are her famous Capricorn tantrums. She is symbolised by a mountain goat and there is no creature more stubborn that her when she digs her heels in. If you treat her job, her family and her friends as objects of ridicule, or make light of serious issues, I'm afraid the joke will be on you. She is not likely to make a scene as she exits and will philosophically accept that she has been the victim of yet another forgery – a man whose support got going when the going got tough. There will be no pleading or arguing, just a note to say she's off to them thar hills in search of fresh hope. With her she will take only what is hers, along with her pride, her disappointment and, of course, Rodney.

MALE
Scene 1 **The Meeting**

The previous nine men that you girls have encountered so far have probably left you exhilarated and exhausted. I can't promise that Capricorn man will give you a rest, but he'll certainly give you a change and that is supposed to be as good. The workings of this man's sexuality are, on the surface, quite simple. Get underneath, however, and you'll find him to be much more complex. What else could you expect from a chap who is ruled by Saturn, the planet of mystery, moodiness and the unexpected? This sign is symbolised by the Mountain Goat, a creature whose aim it is to get to the very top of the highest obstacle. It is so sure-footed and self-confident that it leaves its contemporaries far behind in its shadow and most of the other signs will not even attempt to reach the targets that he sets for himself whether personally or professionally. This then is the Mountaineer of the zodiac; an adventurer, an explorer and a man for whom the only way is up. He works hard and he plays hard and sometimes it's difficult to separate the two. He is not the sort of person to do anything he doesn't want to and so if you should get involved with him, you know that you must be quite satisfied to be by his side. This is not a man who has a partner merely because it's expected. Just like the average rock climber, the only items he takes with him in his journey onwards and upwards are the essentials – there's no excess baggage on his triumphant trail. Ambition is a key part of his make-up and to reach the summit of success he can often make life very difficult for himself. He is prepared to make great sacrifices and is capable of enduring the most extreme conditions if he has a goal in sight. Female companionship can be quite low on his list of priorities unless the female in question can do more for him than simply provide sex. He is perfectly happy to satisfy his own urges even to the point of preferring to do so because it's quicker, more efficient and he only has himself to please. Yes, you could call him selfish, that's a trait he'll readily admit to and when he begins a new affair, you could never accuse him of being dishonest. For his and his partner's security and comfort, he will go to great pains to explain that the journey together is no easy ride. He spells out the potential pitfalls and problems so clearly that you know what you're getting into. If you don't listen and believe you can make him see things from your perspective, then you only have yourself to blame if you fall into a sea of emotional despair. If you are a girl who likes to know where you stand and for that particular perch to be quite a long way up the ladder – then read on.

So, where do you find him? He is sporty and being an Earth sign, his preferences are for the muddy and macho variety such as football and rugby. He is built for comfort rather than speed and on first sight is not as agile as you'd imagine. He is strong and fearless though, so expect him to be leading the field. To attract his attention you must be good-looking or possess a special sensual appeal, as he likes the best of everything. He can be drawn to bimbos, but these are purely disposable stop-gaps which he discards like empty baked bean cans. To get roped up with him for the long haul you must display intelligence and this starts from the moment your paths cross. He's a shrewd judge of character and can rapidly discern genuine attraction from simple curiosity, so your approach must be calculated with precision. Ignore him and he won't notice you – throw yourself at him and he'll throw you back.

Once you have located your Capricorn out on the playing fields, make a point of turning up regularly but have a purpose for being there rather than to just gawp at him. He has strong humanitarian interests and does plenty for charity, so show up with a collection tin of some sort, as this greatly enhances your chances of him coming over to drop something in your slot. Over the coming weeks he will get to know you more, and he'll appear interested in everything about you and whilst this may be the case, he will also be subtly interviewing you to establish whether you really are the girl for the job. At this stage it is your turn to take the lead – he'll appreciate your pioneering spirit, but more importantly, it will hurry up the process. Capricorns are prone to the longest courtships in the zodiac, feeling that if it's worth having, it's worth waiting for.

Scene 2 **The Main Event**

You can count on enjoying several pleasant evenings of dinner or drinks before Mr Mountaineer makes his move. He is cautious and likes to think through every eventuality before going for the big one. Many times you will have raised your hopes and your hemline for such an occasion, only to be chivalrously escorted to your car and pointed in the direction of home. Then, one night he, and very soon you, will sense that this time it's different, the conditions are perfect and your Capricorn is ready to tackle your uncharted territory. As you tread that well-worn route to your vehicle, don't be surprised if a mysterious someone has let a tyre down. Before you ask, yes, he is that devious. Not one to wear his hormones on his sleeve, he will resort to taking short cuts so that he can explain your forthcoming passion as inevitable, rather than planned. There's nothing else for it, it's either his way or a walk on the highway, so as he utters those incredibly romantic words 'Are you coming home with me or what?', you know it's now or never. Prepare yourself for a long night, as your Romeo will have already ensured that the coast is clear for many hours of uninterrupted coitus. There will be no football on the telly, no pressing engagement the following morning – he's all yours.

When you arrive at his place you're sure to be impressed by its tidiness and elegance. This sign hates clutter and that goes for your clothes too, so don't tear them off in passionate abandon. He is hoping that you alone will begin the preliminaries as he really comes into his own once the pinnacle is in sight. After a drink or two he'll inform you that he's going to bed and he'd really prefer you not to sleep on the sofa – it ruins the cushions. Follow him in there and start the proceedings with kisses, his mouth is quite sensitive. Allow him to remove his own clothes (a ripped off button is a black mark for you) and then seductively peel off your own. Ideally you should be sporting stockings and suspenders and high-heeled shoes for the whole event. The Capricorn weak spot is his knees and this also makes him a leg man. His erogenous zones are down the spine and at the top of his thighs, so give these areas your best attention. He is fairly partial to oral sex and is quite proficient at it too but his best performance comes during the calorie-burning stuff. For intercourse itself you should be on top, remember, this sign likes to look up to whatever it is he's attempting to conquer. After this he is happy to experiment with many positions, always looking for the one that gives him the tightest hold. He is inquisitive of your body and will delve into every nook and cranny whilst deciding which is the most challenging to enter. Narrow crevices are his speciality and before you can protest that this is not a wise idea, that someone, namely you, may get hurt – he's in there, excavating his way to the source of your innermost pleasures. Stamina is something he possesses in great supply, as soon as he's primed and ready to go there is no stopping him from getting as much mileage out of your encounter as possible. He does tend to put his needs first, but as they are mostly concerned with giving a good account of himself, then you benefit by default. The thrill of sex for Capricorn man is more about reaching several peaks instead of tipping over the edge of the first one, so you can expect a wholly fulfilling experience. If you don't, for some strange reason, manage to attain your own ultimate euphoria, he is not likely to show too much concern and will secretly conclude that it must be a design fault on your part as opposed to any deficiency in his own equipment. In either eventuality, he will finally arrive, exhausted, at his destination making a lot of noise as he plants his flag and celebrates another victory for Capricorn men.

Scene 3 **Extras**

You will find out almost as soon as you dash for the toilet paper what your fate is to be from here. If he hands you the business card of an all-night garage and puncture repair centre, then you are sadly out in the cold. If, however, he mentions breakfast then you could have cracked it. As your sex life continues you will have to get used to making love when Capricorn man says so. He offers quality not quantity and you'll have to cope with meagre rations. Get to know him better and you will realise that he is rather kinky. Although he is not a Water sign, he does have an affinity with bathrooms and strategically placed jets of hot and cold – maybe they remind him of mountain streams. Talking of which, you may get to indulge in a golden shower, although I suspect it is more to do with Capricorn's laziness to answer the call of nature in the proper place. Then there are the masochistic tendencies to deal with. As Capricorn men get older and especially if their job is one of high power decision making, they can become fond of painful eroticism. This is where those high-heeled shoes come in useful as you walk up and down his spine leaving marks as clear as footprints in the snow.

The real benefit of life with this guy is more apparent outside the bedroom. When you get round to settling down together, he will be a very loyal mate and is extremely supportive of your career. Should you choose motherhood, then that's okay too because he loves kids and is a generous, if not strict, father. This is the man for you if you can survive against adversity and prefer success to sex.

Scene 4 The Finale

The main reason for wishing to leave a Capricorn man is usually his moods. He doesn't so much fall into a dark depression – he plummets headlong into the biggest, blackest hole of self-pity and self-doubt that you could ever imagine. Once he's in there, wrestling with these destructive demons, there is no rescuing him. As if that's not bad enough, these attacks can happen any time, any place. You may have just put the finishing touches to an important dinner party when this stubborn goat decides that he's not hungry and not in the mood for small talk. He will be off out of the door before you can stop him and your faith in him will sink as rapidly as the soufflé.

Getting him to leave for that final, solo expedition is easy. First of all, be possessive, cling to him wherever he goes as if your life depends on it – he wants to be your mate, not a Siamese twin. Secondly, insult his relatives, this is something he will not tolerate from anyone, as his family are often his safety net – the people who catch him when his high ideals come tumbling down. When it is all over, he won't be vengeful and is most likely to become your friend. Surprisingly, it is only after another man has swept you off your feet and taken you to dizzier heights that he will, at last, make a concerted effort to win your heart.

AQUARIUS

FEMALE
Scene 1 **The Meeting**

I am sure that now we are getting close to the end of your Sextrology education, with only two lovely ladies to go, many guys reading this guide will have already started to analyse the last ten fanciable females in the vain hope of deciding which is the best for them. With Aquarius woman however, it will never be you that has the privilege of making that choice, since she alone will determine who is to be her partner and cannot, like some other signs, be coerced or flattered into submission. In many ways, she is the celestial Doctor of the zodiac. This is a job she would excel at but even if she should be employed in alternative occupations, she is always ruled by a meticulous mind, is caring, conscientious and honest. At the centre of her life are her friends and her outside interests – you seldom find her at home. She is always on call to answer a social emergency, no invitation is ever too trivial or too time-consuming. She works all day, parties all night and sleeps when she's ill. Without a constant supply of companionship she'll wither and die and can sometimes be accused of getting too wrapped up in other people's affairs. If you have a problem, she'll go to great pains to offer a prognosis – advice is her speciality and it is given with or without your consent. This is not her fault though; she is symbolised by the Waterbearer – a person who provides a source of life to others. Aquarians make great sacrifices in the name of humanity, will give generous amounts to charities and would save the whale single-handedly if they could.

This is a seriously intelligent and well-organised woman, but unlike, say, Virgo or Capricorn who do everything by the book, her mind is open and flexible and she would buy any manual that promised to enhance, stimulate or broaden her horizons. Her beliefs and convictions are diverse and usually well ahead of their time and Aquarius woman has courage to defend all of them. As a lover, she'll do more than raise your pulse, once you've cracked that slightly aloof exterior, you'll experience a total inhibition bypass. Whereas many girls are content to keep fantasies locked in their heads, with her they spill out into the bedroom to be examined, dissected and explored. Her choice of sexual assistant is based on the skill they possess to aid her erotic imagination and is not founded on looks or financial status.

Given such reassuring news, I'm sure you are itching to find this female, but before you do anything rash, let me re-emphasise that the way to her heart is through her head, so would all men from the Rambo school of romance please leave now. Locating her is easy; Aquarian women are everywhere that you find people but, because of her radical views, you can cut corners by attending community meetings or a get-together of an extremist group. If anyone is going to stop that new link road being built all over the Green Belt, it's her. To get her vote you must stand out as a true campaigner. If you're not that well up on local politics, wait until someone presents a forceful point, then shout loudly against it. Even if you're talking out of your hat, she'll admire your spirit. It might actually be wise to shoot her arguments down in flames, she won't be able to resist joining you for a drink later so that you can thrash out a few things in private. Do not, under any circumstances, attempt to get her into bed on that first encounter. Just like those in medical professions, she needs to test you and although she will readily diagnose a potential friendship, it will take much time until she develops a second opinion. You may have to help her put the mockers on every new motorway or housing development north of Watford before she notices in herself the symptoms of sexual stirrings. Long before you ever notice that her temperature's gone up, she will have been busy testing her condition in the comfort of her own bed as she polishes her intimate instruments whilst picturing your face.

Scene 2 **The Main Event**

Now that Miss Aquarius has built up a head of steam, you can be confident that she will make the first move towards a rendezvous more romantic than the village hall for your next weekly meeting. To be on the safe side, this will probably be by way of an invitation to one of her many parties where there will be assorted friends to give you the once over. You need not worry if they dislike you on sight, Aquarius girl loves to be controversial and will take enormous pleasure in convincing them of your good points. First of all, of course, you need to show her your credentials and this is where you must take your turn in being the instigator. Although she is the one writing the sexual script, she expects you to be the main player. If your first proper date is indeed at a party, drag her manfully into the bathroom to show her where you've hidden the peanuts. The idea of sudden stolen passion will be very appealing and not only will she find the peanuts, she will probably lick your salty bits too.

This little nibble should just serve as an adventurous appetiser; the real main course is best saved until everyone else has gone home. Here again you must be firm – her natural need for neatness will cause her to want to do all the clearing and cleaning up before she hits the sack, so bundle all the post-party debris quickly into bin liners and bundle her into the bedroom. Once you have thrown out Scorpio man and his mate who have been in there for the last three hours, you can get down to some fun.

This girl prefers a good dash of romance in her raunch, so start with her erogenous zones which are around the calves and ankles, perhaps remove her stockings with your teeth. From here the only way is up so begin making sure and steady progress thighwards. Don't be surprised if she is not wearing any knickers and don't make any moral decisions based on this fact, nine times out of ten this is for reasons of practicality as she hates her slinky clothes to be spoiled by Visible Panty Line. You, though, being a man who hates wasted opportunities, should proceed with your oral caresses until the significant change in her vocal output suggests you have hit the right spot. Aquarian women have highly sensitive and skilled fingers that will stroke your ears, neck and face while you are otherwise engaged, she has a knack for triggering erotic responses from parts of your body that would not normally be associated with sexual pleasure. Don't worry about your big nose, she finds this an attractive asset and will suck it with relish. She is also partial to bulging biceps that she can squeeze and stroke and will be especially intrigued if you have a tattoo on this muscle. You might be surprised at the intensity with which she stares at your own particular dragon, rose or serpent, but she is merely trying to ascertain how many girls' names you have sported there previously.

Intercourse should be prolonged and varied, incorporating as many conventional and unusual positions that your mutual minds can muster. After the Peanut Incident it could be hard for the average guy to contain himself so best not to try. Her intuitive mind will tell her if you are desperately attempting to think about your tax returns to prolong the passion. Instead, let nature take its course leaving you confident of a second, lengthier performance. Simultaneous orgasms are not the main requirement of Aquarians and sometimes she'd rather take it in turns so that you both get to see each other's ecstasy separately – it's a sort of 'You show me yours and I'll show you mine'. When it is all over, she wants to discuss the entire operation; what you enjoyed and what you didn't, (which won't be much), and how you can make it even better next time. 'Next time' are the magic words you should take seriously because a long-term relationship depends on your having a supply of stimulating ideas, both for discussion and for bedtime.

Scene 3 **Extras**

There are simply not enough pages in this entire book to list all the sexual activities that Aquarian women fantasise about and attempt to put into practice. The list of what shocks her could be written on the back of a thermometer. With such a voracious sexual appetite, even the most experienced of lovers might worry that she'll have them for breakfast and spit them out before nightfall. The key to keeping her happiness and your sanity is not to come home each night with whips, ropes and rubber gloves, but is to work on joint amorous ambitions. Aquarians can derive a great deal of pleasure from talking openly and explicitly about all forms of human copulation and its variations and she'll be thrilled if you go to the trouble of setting a regular night aside simply to talk through your ideas. Outside of the bedroom, or wherever she prefers making love, you will have a smart and vivacious companion who continually amazes you with her knowledge of subjects and intuition of people. Don't think you can pin her down to marriage and maternity instantly, indeed she would rather wait until science perfected the technology to enable you to give birth. Only once she has righted as many of the world's wrongs as she feels she can, will she settle down to being a wife and mother and as you'd expect, she does both jobs excellently.

Scene 4 The Finale

There are many ways to end an affair with an Aquarian and one of the reasons for wishing to do so could be that these women can become highly strung and restless. Boredom is their life-long enemy and as soon as it starts winning the battle because all her friends have moved away or her job is no longer challenging, then it can be like living with a cat on hot bricks. Every time the phone or door bell rings she raises her hopes that it's a social call or errand of mercy, only to sink into dire depression when it turns out to be another double-glazing salesman.

Understandably, some chaps start to feel just plain inadequate. If you suggest it might be nice to have a quiet evening in with a video and an early night, she'll look at you as if you've confessed to running over her pet cat. After all, what's the good of a sizzling sex life if there is nobody around to hear about it?

Getting her to leave is easy, in fact she will notice the writing's on the wall before you've noticed the problem. Be a stay-at-home couch potato, get into a stew each time she spends money, decide that all charities are a rip-off and all vegetarians are crack-pots, eat meat! Put your name on the petition supporting the new motorway extension and, worst of all, buy leaded petrol. She will be disappointed but not devastated so don't worry about venomous retributions, it's not her style. She knows what I know – that you are the only loser.

MALE
Scene 1 **The Meeting**

With ten enticing hunks of manhood now behind you, and only two to go before we conclude your Sextrology course for the present, maybe you are feeling like a short break. Well, consider Aquarius man to be a break – a musical break. Why musical? The reason is simple: to all intents and purposes this man is the Rock Star of the zodiac. He may not be so in real life, but this is his astrological alter ego. Don't get me wrong, it's not that he needs to be constantly in the spotlight, unlike say, Leo man. No, Aquarius man is artistic, creative and light years ahead of his time. He pursues his ideologies keenly and needs a platform from which to get his message across. He also has a strong desire to give something useful to society in general. Think about his true astrological symbol, the Waterbearer – literally a giver of life. He cares enormously about the human race and does all he can to spread a little happiness, if he could do it through the power of music he would. This guy would not be a solo performer though; in life he needs to be part of a team and to have a rich diversity of friends from unusual backgrounds to help him bounce his ideas around and perhaps balance his more radical and far-out views. If he was part of a rock band, they'd be called The Non-Conformists.

His love life is far from conventional but always eventful. He attracts a good deal of female attention and not merely because he may be good looking or rich, or both. Aquarius man is irresistible due to assets that go deeper than this; he is sensitive and approachable and appreciates women for their minds much more than for their bodies and potential sexual favours. Just like the average rock star, many women can look but few get to touch for any length of time – he prefers to have lots of female friends rather than one all-encompassing relationship. Can he fall in love? Yes he can, and when he's young he does so often. It's a bit like the affair a song writer has with his compositions; he loves the one that is current at the time but when the song remains the same despite exploring every variation, then he is off in search of fresh inspiration. Eventually, he will encounter that one special girl who mystifies his mind and sates his sexuality. Then, and only then, will he stop travelling the road and contemplate a life of mortgages, nappies and a mother-in-law.

Where then, would you find this man? Head for wherever there is an intelligent gathering of people; local committees, martial arts clubs, parties, socials, the list goes on. Next, study the crowd and you'll see that there seems to be two people who are holding court to two separate discussion groups. The first group will not be able to get a word in edgeways as they listen to a loud and flamboyant speaker – that's Gemini Man. The second group will also be hanging onto every word their leader utters, but if you watch closely you will notice that he actually stops talking and listens intently to what the others are saying – this is him, Mr Aquarius. No matter what the circumstances of this first meeting and no matter what you've read in *Cosmo* about men wishing that women took the initiative, Aquarius man won't respond well if you throw your knickers at him with your phone number written on the label. If you are bright, witty and attractive he may take you outside and let you play with his instrument, but it won't be because you raised his interest, it's purely because he wants to help you and can't bear the thought of another human being in distress, sexual or otherwise.

Aquarius is an Air sign, hence that enchanting, dreamy quality, but his mind is like fertile earth, always receptive to new ideas that can grow and blossom. What you must do is plant the tiniest seed of passion in his subconscious and, over a period of time, nurture it and strengthen it so that eventually, he's thinking about planting a few seeds of his own.

Scene 2 **The Main Event**

What it pays to bear in mind about Aquarius man is that he is ruled by Uranus, the planet of sudden, unexpected changes. Because of this, you will find that one minute he's wooing you with hearts and flowers and then one day the tempo quickens and you get to glimpse all the raw sexual energy that these men possess. If he were a musician in reality, this would happen in the same way as when he sits down to write a ballad and ends up with a pumping, driving piece of pure rock. Stay alert for these signals because he is actually quite shy despite his appearance and you must be the one who releases those highly strung hormones from his head and into his bed. What you will see is that he looks at you differently and talks to you differently. When you were just one of the boys, it was okay to discuss his old partners and chosen future conquests, but now that you are to become one of the latter, he'll stop giving away his seduction secrets and start asking you subtle questions about the best sex you ever had, what made it so good and how could it have been better? Like any exceptional entertainer, he is planning the performance to end all others and for this he needs to research his audience.

Once you are confident that you are both singing the same tune and that this friendship has one foot on the stairway to heaven, you should make your overtures. Whilst you sit talking at his house or hotel room, touch his face or his lips, these areas are highly sensitive. The spine and calves are also very susceptible to erotic stimulation and you should not ignore their potential to arouse and inflame this man's passions. When the time feels right, your Aquarian will step into the lead and begin foreplay which is his favourite part of a sex session. He believes that any climax is worthless without a big build-up, so don't rush him. He adores to stroke and strum and those gifted fingers are attached to a very slow hand. Every part of your body will become instrumental in your pleasure and he is turned on by the different sounds you make as he covers each inch of flesh. His classical sexual education has taught him not merely to concentrate on your mid section – this response he is used to; what he craves is to experiment by combining what he knows with what he wants to try. He is terrifyingly intuitive about female reflexes and varies his touch frequently, alternating between light, almost imperceptible fingering to more pressured and urgent caresses.

With Aquarian men, the point where foreplay stops and intercourse begins is sometimes hard to pinpoint because he will have already explored all your most intimate areas. He is far too subtle to announce a new entry, he desires to watch your reactions as the pitch increases. It goes without saying that this guy has natural rhythm, but it might be a totally different beat to what you are familiar with, he is not afraid to take chances because this is how he learns. Try to give him as much vocal support as you can, silent appreciation will sadden him. You don't have to scream and yell and wake up the neighbours, but talk, laugh and say what feels good; remember that you are there to enjoy yourself. You will eventually reach the point where talking stops and noises of a more primitive nature fill the air, he will time his movements to suit you rather than him because your orgasmic cries are all he needs to reach his own exuberant outburst. Afterwards, you may be totally satisfied but this does not have to be the end of the show, the night is long and his talents are many. While he is regaining his senses, you could treat him to a solo performance of your own before reawakening his rapture with your oral expertise. Aquarius man takes you to a land far removed from reality; it's a place of colour and brightness mixed with deep and dark longing. Go with it, even for one night – you'll never forget or regret it.

Scene 3 Extras

Before I go on to explain what you can expect after that first night, here is as good a place as any to point out that Aquarian men fall into two types. The vast majority are the forward-thinking idealists that I've been describing. If, however, your own celestial musician is more Syd Lawrence than Sid Vicious, then you have hooked the traditional Aquarian. He may not set your adrenaline racing in the same way as his futuristic counterpart, but what he lacks in imagination is made up for by logic and family values. In terms of sexual deviancy, the only difference between these two is that traditional Aquarius fantasises about the debauched and depraved while futuristic Aquarius does it.

All Aquarians have the potential to develop fetishes, particularly those relating to bondage, submission and domination. Heavy metal equipment of handcuffs, shackles and chains all play a part. He would never intentionally hurt you, though, and is certainly happy to be on the receiving end. His flexibility means that he can be curious about bisexuality, yours or his – something he has in common with the two other Air signs. He won't insist on adding another member to the bedroom band, but if you suggest it as a bit of fun he won't offer much resistance either. In short, a sexual life with Mr Aquarius is as thrilling as you want it to be, it can only be limited by your own morals, inhibitions or laziness. I would recommend putting him at the top of your chart.

Scene 4 **The Finale**

Why on earth would you want to end your duet with this fascinating and frighteningly fanciable man? Here are a few reasons: firstly, this guy will always be a hippy at heart. Although he applies much thought and patience to practical matters of career and cash, basically he likes love on the run. He's a rolling stone that gathers no moss and the only time you will feel confident of a long-term affair is when you can look back on it as you stand together in the pension queue. Secondly, there's that creative temperament which is responsible for his uniquely inventive love-making, but also, unfortunately, his moods, his restlessness and his need for space.

To bring the curtain down is simple, it requires little more than refusing to take him seriously. Should he be fortunate enough to work in an artistic field, pour scorn and ridicule on his projects – tell him to get a proper job because his dinner will be on the table at 5.30 and in the dog by six. Insist on staying home every night to watch soap operas and when, occasionally, you do go out with his friends, let your only topic of conversation be who is doing what to whom in *Neighbours*.

He won't hate you, but he will pack his bags and hit the road. Life without him carries on, yet you'll be aware that there is something missing, like listening to a symphony performed by only half an orchestra. Never mind, you can count on him coming back to town one day and with Aquarius not being a sign to bear grudges, there's every chance of just one more erotic encore. Do all you can to avoid playing your swan song, music is the food of love and it would be a shame to starve.

PISCES

FEMALE
Scene 1 **The Meeting**

Here we are then, chaps, the very last sexy subject that completes your Sextrology studies. I know you must be feeling quite worn out after experiencing the joys of the previous eleven gorgeous girls, but don't go for a rest just yet. Pisces woman may be the final female on the list but she is every bit as intriguing as the others. This girl is the Kitten of the zodiac; innocent, playful and one hundred percent lovable, yet containing the potential to be wild, wilful and wanton. Astrologically symbolised by the sign of two fishes travelling in opposite directions, it's easy to see how she's cute and cuddly one minute, and feline and feminine the next. This is one pussy that any guy would be glad to take home. Her ruler is Neptune, planet of secrets, sensuality and enigmas, this makes her a highly intuitive woman; she seems to possess a sixth sense that allows her instinctively to understand people and situations. Because of her remarkable powers of perception, she is a sign often associated with the occult and is fascinated by mysticism and spiritualism. She would make the perfect Witch's cat due to her ability to weave wondrous spells over each and every man she meets. This sensitive sign also gets very wrapped up in the lives of her friends and there's nothing like a spot of hubble, bubble, toil and trouble in the neighbourhood to arouse her inquisitive streak and have her rushing round in the hope of helping out. An affair with her, long or short, can be heaven or it can be hell – that depends on how you treat her. Either way, what she has to offer is out of the world, in actual fact, Piscean women don't really live an earthly existence. Not for her are VAT returns and washing powders that get clothes whiter; all that practical stuff is left to the Capricorns and Virgoans of this universe. No, this girl lives in a place where damsels in distress are saved by dashing knights in silvery armour and where love will always triumph. A Piscean without a partner is like a fish without fins – going nowhere except round in circles of ever deepening despair. Because of her constant need for companionship and reassurance that she is wanted, she can make catastrophically bad decisions in her choice of men. Logic and realism are not qualities that come to her readily, instead she exists on emotion alone and puts her trust in destiny and fate.

Hopefully, you will be the man to restore her faith in happy-ever-after endings and convince her that it's worth her while to get her claws into you. To find her, you could try a local bookstore as she loves to lose herself in written romance. Alternatively, look in your nearest library – specifically the section that deals with ghosties, ghoulies and things that go bump in the night. If you quite like the idea of things going bump in the night, wander over and ask if she can suggest something for bedtime. She will notice the innuendo in your question but won't pounce on it – this girl needs wooing, she's from the old-fashioned school of champagne, candles and courtship. You will recognise this girl by her eyes, they are her most prominent feature and are often exceptionally pale or incredibly large.

When breaking the ice with her, you should strive to maintain eye contact but be friendly rather than forceful or you'll scare her away. If her psychic powers detect that you are just a dirty old Tom at heart, she will stick her nose in the air and saunter off. Don't pursue her further or she'll spit out a scathing comment for everyone to hear. If, however, she likes what she sees, she will visibly warm to you and move closer allowing you to catch the scent of her exotic personal perfume.

From this point to the bedroom is a journey of flattery and pampering, nothing quickens the rate of romance more than letting her talk about herself, only interrupt her to utter such phrases as, 'That's amazing' or 'You're an incredible woman'. Conventional compliments go down well and she'll lap up all the corny clichés you can dish out. Don't underestimate this woman, she knows you are pandering to her ego, but the way she sees it, you're gentlemanly as opposed to a caveman in your approach and for that she is prepared to reward you.

Scene 2 **The Main Event**

With your celestial kitten's curiosity piqued, you can be confident that she will make the next move. Yes, she does like the man to do the running, but now she's found you she won't want you to escape. Over the next few days or weeks there are likely to be lots of games of cat and mouse – she'll tease you and play hard to get, but on the other hand, each time you meet up it will not escape your notice that her necklines are getting lower and her skirts are getting shorter. She is likely to pop up at places where she knows you'll be, always passing it off as pure coincidence. Let her enjoy this saucy stalking act and don't spoil her fun by taking the initiative away from her. Eventually, when her hormones can no longer contain her sexual hunger, she will go for the kill. As you are leaving work, there she will be, another 'accidental' liaison. This time though, it's different; surprise, surprise, she's had a mishap and mislaid her house keys. With a pitiful expression she will tell you she has no place to go; you don't have to be Einstein to figure out that this little minx fancies some mischief. Do the only thing a nice chap like you can – offer to take care of her for a few hours. Like a lost and lonely tabby, she'll follow you home, smiling smugly to herself that her plan worked as she fiddles with the 'missing' key ring in her pocket.

At your home, and with more than a sniff of sex in the air, Pisces woman develops a flair for theatricals – maybe it's all that raunchy reading she does or those steamy soap operas she loves. Whatever the cause, she wants sex to be like it is in the movies and although we are all aware that *Basic Instinct* was more a case of clever camera angles, it doesn't stop her trying to recreate the mood and the manoeuvres. Now playing the role of sex kitten, Miss Pisces is not about to waste time. The minute you sit down on the sofa she will have yet another calamity and yes, you've guessed it, she stumbles on your carpet and topples straight on top of you. There is now a prime opportunity in your lap for you to take over; rip off her clothes *à la* Michael Douglas and smother her with kisses. Remember to wear that expression of excruciating ecstasy as she starts relieving you of your own garments and nibbles your ear.

Next comes the tricky bit, you have to get out of the chair with her legs wrapped round your waist, stand up then carry her to the bed with your trousers down round your ankles and your 'Michael' expression intact. Should the bedroom be on a different floor (which they never are in movie land) your lady will not object to continuing the action down in front of the fire. It does not matter if it's a three-bar electric job – to Pisces woman it's the roaring, crackling variety. She'll appreciate lots of attention being paid to her feet, that's her main erogenous zone, and if you don't just happen to have a bottle of chilled bubbly conveniently placed on the hearth, open the nearest can of cola and trickle the fizzy liquid over her body and lick it off in a *9½ Weeks* style. There's no need to fret about musical accompaniment, you can rely on this girl to provide loud and abandoned backing vocals. For intercourse itself, she prefers to be underneath, but then ideally loves to roll dramatically from one position to the next without, of course, allowing the main player to slip out of the action. The fact that this lady is so accident-prone should plant a doubt in your head as to whether she has taken care of the contraception. Again, this is an issue that never seems to crop up in films, but is none the less a crucial point. It might be better to withdraw from the coital proceedings and opt for an oral conclusion. Savour her delicacies first and then let her do the same to you; you'll be more than pleased by her technique and as for her – she'll look like the cat that just swallowed the cream!

Scene 3 Extras

I think it is fair to say that Pisces woman is perhaps the most obliging and understanding of signs when it comes to pleasing a man. She will literally bend over backwards to help her lucky lover live out his dreams and desires, the more confident she is of the security of your relationship, the more deviant and bizarre are her attempts to make every night seem like the first. Due to a penchant for submission, she rapidly accepts role-playing games in which she is savagely 'taken' or maybe punished for imaginary crimes. Equally, she is turned on by seriously slushy romance that consists of hours of foreplay and a sensual seduction that builds to a heart-stopping climax.

Whatever form your lovemaking takes, Pisces gets a kick out of dressing for the part. The bedroom is her stage and she'll wear the appropriate costume. From naughty schoolgirls to novice nuns; from nympho mistress to neglected housewife – all of these could be waiting for you when you come home. It might, though, be an idea to keep a check on her artistic abilities, for this sign is very prone to faking orgasms because they can't bear to let you think you have failed to satisfy them. She is really doing it to save your pride, but if she is genuinely frustrated, she may find it easier to seek fulfilment in the arms of another rather than tackle the real issue. A lesbian affair is not out of the question because she doesn't believe that this counts as infidelity. Away from the erotica, Pisces girl is an accomplished home-maker, wife and mother. Sometimes she chooses this as her full-time job so that she can turn her back on the ruthless cut and thrust of chasing a career. She does all she can to support your ambitions and cater to your personal needs, all she requires is love by the lorry load and rock-solid stability. Give it to her – she's worth it.

Scene 4 **The Finale**

Females of this sign are often accused of being nervous, neurotic and highly strung. This, unfortunately, can be the case, but it's mostly due to neglectful treatment from their partner. If these girls could learn to live their own life instead of trying to live through their lover's, there would not be so many unhappy and unstable Pisceans. They don't want to be clingy, dependent and demanding, but as a leopard can't change its spots, Piscean kittens cannot help their astrological make-up. You may reach a point in your relationship when there's trouble in paradise and pressure of work keeps you out of the home. This situation leads to tears, tantrums and cries of 'You don't love me anymore' and 'Who else are you sleeping with?' If the only person you're trying to satisfy is the mortgage man, it can get a trifle annoying.

Pisces woman then falls into a fantasy world of escapism and can turn to drink or other stimulants for comfort. Try to patch up your partnership, but if all hope and trust is gone then it's time to bail out. Do it as tactfully as is possible because a scorned Piscean resorts to emotional blackmail of the nastiest kind. Children, pets and possessions will become focal points of the drama as the fairytale disintegrates into bloody horror story. This special woman needs a special man, if that's not you, there's nothing for it. It's back to the beginning of Sextrology to find your perfect playmate.

MALE
Scene 1 **The Meeting**

So, here we are then girls, almost at the end of your Sextrology course. Don't sign off just yet though, because last, but by no means least, is Pisces man and what a mysterious and magnetic chap he is too. Pisces man is without doubt, the Magician of the zodiac, he will entice you, intrigue you and enrapture you. Astrologically symbolised by the sign of the two fishes, what you see with him is certainly not what you get. He is a master of emotional disguise thanks to his ruler, Neptune, and is unparalleled at pulling off the unexpected and the impossible. Like all Magicians, he is a man who functions best when he has a female assistant and may have several before he finds the one who understands him inside out and can give the security which he desperately craves. He won't like to admit it, but this woman is usually rather dominant and can be the driving force of a long-term partnership. With this sort of arrangement, he is free to explore each and every one of life's challenges and thrills, knowing that his lover will be there with a safety net to catch him should he come a cropper through one of his more risky ideas. Don't think that this sounds like a one-way deal though; the lucky girl who settles down with him will be rewarded by a lifetime of romance, sensitivity and sex that is out of this world.

Pisceans are natural carers and worry an abnormal amount about everybody and anybody. If he were to be a Magician in real life, he'd probably end up showing all his friends how the conjuring is done because he can't bear the thought of them losing sleep over it – also, he is hopeless at keeping secrets. Although Pisces is a sign that can easily dwell in the past, he always looks forward to what tomorrow will bring but that never seems quite as good as yesterday. If he wears spectacles, you can count on them being rose-tinted.

All of this, of course, is an exceptionally pleasant change for a girl who is thoroughly fed up with a diet of men who are all triceps and testosterone. Pisces man shed his gung-ho attitude to women along with his loincloth. What's left is a kind, generous and tender man who will fulfil your wildest fantasies and give you life made in Heaven because it's much more interesting than Earth. Where, then, to find this dreamer? His sign is usually very creative or artistic and he can often be spotted at theatres, galleries or shops that cater to those with arty ambitions. Loiter around the paint brush section for long enough and you will recognise Mr Pisces – he hates making decisions without a second opinion and is also easily influenced, so he'll be the guy who takes half an hour to choose one brush, only to put it straight back on the shelf when he notices the person next to him go for a different one altogether.

For the physical confirmation that he's your guy, look at his eyes; they will be pale and have a mesmerising liquid quality that makes you just want to dive straight in. Why not do that then? Be bold and ask if he sees anything that tickles his fancy, or perhaps he'd like some help to make a final selection. If he can't find the brush he wants, maybe he could pop over to your place and you'll show him yours? You don't have to be beautiful or a hyper-efficient Super Woman of the twentieth century as some men require. All you need to possess are a genuine and sincere personality with a hint of wickedness thrown in. From your initial and fairly forceful first encounter you should attempt to weave your own sensual spell over him on subsequent dates. He will do one-night stands, but ideally you will both find it more rewarding to make any sexual liaisons a block booking. It's fair to say that to make progress, you must be the one to quicken the pace of passion. Piscean men can be cautious about getting involved because often they have been hurt by previous lovers who took advantage of their talents and then did a disappearing act. You don't need a miracle to win his heart, but a carefully calculated strategy and a few stunts up your sleeve would not go amiss.

Scene 2 **The Main Event**

To get the best out of your first sexual experience with Mr Pisces you will need to be patient until the right location presents itself because this sign is very affected by its surroundings. Put him in a large noisy gathering of hyperactive Ariens and sarcastic Scorpions and he can become quite nervous and twitchy. Despite a calm exterior he may be irritated and agitated inside – do remember that he has perfected the art of illusion. If he is anywhere that makes him feel uncomfortable, either through not being the centre of attraction, or not being able to get his point across, he will literally be a fish out of water and to console himself he will start drinking like one. Wait until you have enjoyed a quiet and informal dinner alone together and have returned to either of your homes, a hotel room or perhaps even a deserted beach. At this point his passions should ignite quickly and they will soon need release. Don't rush though, he'll appreciate you being seductive and teasing rather than rushing to impale yourself on his magic wand at the first available opportunity. Get the show on the road with a slow striptease and play him at his own game by letting him see only as much as you want him to. Keep this up until you can detect that his interest has raised and then reveal your secrets fully. Next, you should remove his clothes as unhurriedly as your mounting hormones will allow.

When he's naked and you can see what you've got to work on, start at the bottom and travel upwards. The feet are well known to be Pisces' vulnerable and erogenous areas and he is a real sucker for a toe job, so prolong this activity combining it with an up and down stroking movement to his ankle. By now you can count on Mr Pisces to be a piece of putty except for his over-extended organ which demands attention. Cleverly now, move the action further up and, with skilled sleight of hand, grasp his growing problem. Piscean men, when romantic circumstances force them to be a solo act, are more than happy to administer their own light relief and masturbate frequently. Due to this, he has become quite fond of the sensations and will now enjoy you doing the job for him. Ask him what techniques he usually employs so that you can mimic them, he won't have any qualms about explaining his own tricks of the trade. If you happen to have one handy, try wearing a silk glove so as to maximise sensations. This man could easily find his performance coming to a premature end if you do this for too long, so stop what you're doing – you'll be missing out on his *pièce de resistance* and besides – it'll ruin your glove.

At this stage in love-play, your Piscean won't be slow in coming forward, he's keen to enter your magic circle and you'd be a fool to stop him. Naturally passive, his favourite position for intercourse is to have you on top, but after that he will add a few variations for maximum entertainment. Without question, any girl's breath will be taken away by his slow and steamy rhythm that gradually builds to a crescendo, but try not to make excessive noise. Sure, he wants to know you're having fun, but as with a real magician, he prefers gasps and sighs in all the right places instead of incessant screaming. Bear in mind you are making love, not going to a rock concert. Your own climax is enough to trigger his and when he does, he'll come and come – like a string of handerkchiefs out of a hat.

This man is more than capable of putting on several shows a night and even if his key prop is rendered sore and limp, he has absolutely no objection to pleasing you with any assortment of toys and gadgets. Afterglow is a speciality and if you have all night, he will use it to pamper you and praise you; this is no toilet paper, shower and pizza merchant. Remember that old Bette Davis movie when they are on a ship, he lights two cigarettes and passes one to her as they gaze into the night sky? He says, 'Why reach for the Moon when we have the stars?' That was Pisces man.

Scene 3 **Extras**

After that first night, it's important for the male Piscean to feel he's made a mental connection with you as well as a bodily one. If so, your relationship will develop into the stuff that airport paperbacks are made of, all grand passion, perhaps some sad or tempestuous times, but mostly a happy ending for the foreseeable future. Sexually, this guy won't come up with too many new tricks of his own but he is delighted to do almost anything you have in mind. Due to a subconscious need to be submissive he will get a real buzz out of being at your superior mercy. He doesn't pretend to be Houdini and will contentedly lie there if you feel inclined to tie him up with ropes or chains. Taken to an extreme, some of these men quite like having pain inflicted on them; he can endure physical suffering as long as there's not the emotional sort. Whatever you teach him, he will readily learn and then attempt to perfect. A happy and secure Piscean is the most compliant partner you could wish for and he'll devote his existence to keeping the romantic harmony. All he asks of you is reassurance, flattery and support. You need not bow down to him in the way that Leo man expects, merely treat him fairly and appreciatively. He has few reservations when it comes to exploring his own fantasies and will talk to you about them, one that he might not mention however, is the thought of romping with another man. The sign of the fishes is one that goes in both directions and in later life he may wrestle with his conscience as he tries to draw a veil over this part of his potential sexuality. Take away his guilt by broaching the subject, show that you care and understand – he'll love you forever.

Scene 4 **The Finale**

Ending a relationship with a Piscean is possibly more difficult than with any other sign. You are not simply pulling the curtain down on an affair, you're attacking them personally and a wounded Piscean can be something of an unknown quantity that can either become consumed with vitriol and vengeance or a basket case of despair and depression. Obviously then, you must structure your parting with caution and consideration. Why would you want to leave? Well, this sign can become a nervous mass of insecurity, never fully believing in his own abilities. If you are no-nonsense Fire sign, it can become very draining; it may seem as if you spend all your time plugging up holes in his self-confidence only for a leak to appear somewhere else. Also, Pisceans have addictive personalities, whilst this is great for your love life, it can cause complications when your man gets hooked on drugs, drink or both. The way out of this affair has to be slowly and sensibly discussed; he has to believe that he'll be much better off without you.

Ultimately though, with faults so few and a heart so big, this guy is a real catch. After experiencing the vivid variety act of the last eleven astro-men, you might just decide to give Pisces man star billing.

SEXTROLOGY QUIZ 1

There are only twelve sun signs in the zodiac and yet there are billions of people on the planet. Does this mean that each person can be shown as having the characteristics of one of these signs? Yes and no. As with all forms of behavioural analysis you need to get as full a picture of the person's character as possible. But is your subject responding to a situation according to inner nature or is he or she just having a bad day at the office?

The following quiz is hopefully not too difficult, not too easy, not too long and not too short. There are nine questions below. All you have to do is select one of the answers given beneath each question. The correct answers can be found on page 373.

1. You are in a supermarket and you come across a stranger acting in a peculiar way. This stranger is moving along the aisle in an unhurried, relaxed manner. But suddenly his trolley goes careering into a large pyramid-shaped stack of baked beans. This person is

   (a) Off his trolley.
   (b) Making his first ever trip to a supermarket.
   (c) A Taurean.

2. You are at a party. It's late and everybody is having a good time. One of the guests seems to be having a better time than anybody else and is regaling all and sundry with stories of his exploits in the business world. A rather attractive young lady comes up to him and asks if he has the time.

'Darling,' he says, 'For you I have all the time in the world.' 'Then kindly take the time to pause for breath. I think I may faint from the pleasure of hearing your voice.' The man happens to be a Leo. What sign is this woman most likely to be?

(a) Libra
(b) Gemini
(c) Cancer

3. A good place to observe people is from the strategic vantage point of a table outside a café. You watch the world go by and you can look as long as you do not hold someone's stare more than a moment. However, *you* don't follow these rules do you? You look and look and look, until your eyes are locked with his. Like an obedient servant he comes up to you and asks if you have met before. (Boy this is corny . . . but read on.) You say nothing, you don't have to. Pretty soon a conversation develops along with a new relationship. If this is not you who do you think it could be?

(a) Scorpio
(b) Virgo
(c) Aries

4. If a man was described to you as being a moody and somewhat shy character who could also be very compassionate towards family and friends you might think 'What a nice bloke.' But would you know what sun sign he was? Would you care?

Anyway, for those of you who are interested the choices are below.

(a) Cancer
(b) Sagittarius
(c) Aquarius

5. In the world of astrology there are many contradictions. This is understandable. Human nature, as they say, is prone to contradictions and some signs appear to be more capable of displaying these than others. Which sign would you say is most likely to be consistent in being inconsistent?

(a) Virgo
(b) Gemini
(c) Leo

6. Some of the signs of the zodiac have a reputation for being keen on acquiring material wealth. For some this amounts to a seeking of security, others status, still others comfort and luxury. Which one of the following sun signs is *least* likely to embody the trait above?

(a) Scorpio
(b) Aquarius
(c) Capricorn

7. A day at the beach, in the sun, on a sweltering day. Sounds great, huh? What a way to spend time. But some people just can't relax, they have to be always active, always looking to improve upon what has

already been improved upon. If this sounds like you, slow down, you may end up with an ulcer. For those of you who do not share the above trait what sign could I be describing?

(a) Pisces
(b) Aries
(c) Gemini

8. Thankfully for me and thee this quiz is almost at an end so here are a couple more questions. Let's talk about sex!! Now which one of the following signs is known to indicate the greatest sexual prowess bar none?

(a) Scorpio
(b) Taurus
(c) Aries
(d) The reader's

9. I'm reaaaaally scraping the bottom of the barrel now. There are signs where a careless remark is instantly stored away in the memory bank waiting to be retrieved at a later date for recrimination or revenge purposes. Others deal with the remark there and then and do not bear a grudge and there are signs that would not pick up on the remark in the first place. Which of the above most likely applies to Scorpio?

(a) File away for future use.
(b) Deal with remark and forget it.
(c) Too thick-skinned to notice.

SEXTROLOGY QUIZ 2

1. What is an aspect?

   (a) The position of a planet relative to another planet, as seen from Earth.
   (b) The position of a planet relative to the Moon.
   (c) The distance between the Sun and the Moon.

2. What does retrograde mean?

   (a) A term of endearment used when a partner fails to grasp the simplest concept.
   (b) The apparent periodic westward motion of a planet, as seen from Earth.
   (c) The degradation in the orbit of a comet travelling too close to the Sun.

3. What is a trine?

   (a) The sound a doorbell makes.
   (b) A third of the zodiac.
   (c) A triple toe loop executed by two skaters at the same time on the same ice rink.

4. What does 'conjunction' mean?

   (a) The attainment of a simultaneous orgasm.
   (b) Another name for a T-junction of a road.
   (c) The point at which two heavenly bodies are at their closest.

5. What are Fire signs?

   (a) The people born under this group of Sun signs who are most likely to spontaneously combust.
   (b) Leo, Libra and Taurus.
   (c) Sagittarius, Aries and Leo.

6. What does sextile mean?

   (a) The position of two heavenly bodies where they are at 60° to each other along their longitude.
   (b) A curious sexual position, where the man is upside down and the woman is the right side up.
   (c) As in (a), except the degree of longitude is 90°.

7. What does the term square mean?

   (a) An outdated slang word, meaning an unadventurous fellow.
   (b) Apparently contradictory modern slang word, meaning 'right on', as in 'Real square, man', or 'Square on, man'.
   (c) The furthest point in the orbit of two planets relative to each other.

8. What does ascendant mean?

   (a) At birth the Sun sign immediately above the horizon.
   (b) The position of the Moon at the time of birth.
   (c) In the Middle Ages a popular treatment for

impotence, whereby a high priest would invoke the powers of the planet Venus. If it worked the patient's phallus would be said to be 'in the ascendant'.

9. What is an eclipse?

   (a) The periodic blocking out of the light of the Sun by the Moon.
   (b) The reversal or deflection of a planet's orbit by close proximity of a planet, with a greater gravitational pull.
   (c) A funny foreign car.

10. How would you define opposition?

   (a) The point at which two heavenly bodies are separated by 180°.
   (b) The conflict generated by a meteorite as it approaches the Earth's outer atmosphere.
   (c) A political party currently not in power.

Sexual Compatibility

The Four Elements

The purpose of Sextrology is to teach you that with a bit of skill and some astrological insider information, just about any two signs can forge a happy life together. Suppose for a moment though, that you have not had time to read through the entire course, or, heaven forbid, you have skipped most of the chapters and have only researched your own astro-sexual characteristics. What do you do if someone extremely fanciable is sitting right next to you now, whilst on the bus or train? Don't panic – here is my brief but comprehensive guide to compatibility between the signs.

First of all you need to be aware of how the four elements react together and the chemistry they produce.

FIRE SIGNS are: Aries, Leo and Sagittarius.
EARTH SIGNS are: Taurus, Virgo and Capricorn.
AIR SIGNS are: Gemini, Libra and Aquarius.
WATER SIGNS are: Cancer, Scorpio and Pisces.

FIRE and FIRE

At the beginning of the relationship, two Fire people are an energetic, enthusiastic couple who friends see as open, friendly and generous. Behind closed doors there may well be a struggle for leadership with each having a go at getting the upper hand, but as long as this is not a serious clash of egos, there will not be a problem. Fire people are passionate and throughout the affair will mostly be found in the bedroom but can be easily tempted to stray by acting in the heat of the moment, but expect sparks to fly when the other one finds out and unleashes their temper. If both of you avoid temptation because your passion for each other is all-consuming, you will have a wonderfully exciting life so long as you do not burn out.

FIRE and EARTH

Looking at this partnership, you should consider that Earth cannot grow its best products unless it has the heat of the fiery sun, but too much intensity will scorch the Earth or too much Earth will suffocate and douse the Fire.

The best combinations of Earth and Fire give a relationship that is warm and productive, this is because the Earth partner is solid and dependable and will channel all the lively, creative ideas of the Fire person, in other words, keep their feet on the ground for them. In return, the Fire sign will bring sparks of passion into the more predictable life of the Earth sign. If one of you gets too bossy or overbearing, one of two things will happen; either Earth will completely smother Fire's enthusiasm for life, or Fire will scorch the Earth by being too hot to handle.

FIRE and AIR

There are two ways of looking at the combination of an Air sign and a Fire sign. On the one hand, the breeze of Air can cool down a hot-headed Fire person and even fan the sparks into a flaming passion or, alternatively, too much Air will blow out the Fire for good. This relationship is potentially very compatible and at its best, the Air sign will make things bright, breezy and stimulating while the Fire sign creates the passion, excitement and intrigue. Both of you share a love of thrills and spills and will always get the most from whatever you do. On the negative side though, Air can turn frosty and cool off the heat in the relationship or Fire will be so temperamental that the partnership is suffocated. All in all, an explosive mix.

FIRE and WATER

This is one of the most risky but potentially powerful combinations around and if you think about what happens literally when you mix Fire and Water, you can see why. Too much Water puts out a Fire and too much Fire evaporates the Water, but get the temperature just right and these elements produce red hot steam power. Mostly, this combination works well to begin with because you both make an effort to compromise but it is after a while when the problems begin if you're not careful. Let the Water sign have too much their own way and they will drown Fire's passionate enthusiasm. If the Fire sign gets too big for their boots, then Water will be heated to boiling point and will explode. Fortunately, if you're clever, the sparks will be so big in the bedroom that you simply don't have time to squabble.

EARTH and EARTH

Earth signs together provide a very strong, reliable basis of a partnership. Earth and Earth is characterised by plenty of hard work and physical activity. You both need your lives to be structured so you know where you're going and you also like routine. Each of you is dependable and reliable and this relationship is set to last for a long time, as neither of you would be prepared to risk upsetting the applecart for cheap thrills. Together you are likely to be successful and financially well off, partly because you are ambitious and partly because material things are important to you. The only problem that you might face is that after a time you become a little set in your ways and a touch old-fashioned. Keeping up the excitement in the bedroom will get round this problem.

EARTH and AIR

In this partnership, the gentle breeze created by the Air person can give a new lease of life to the solid Earth sign, but if Air is too strong, then a tornado blows up and destroys everything. This relationship can be very beneficial to both of you if you manage to avoid the pitfalls. It will work well so long as you tolerate each other's differences of opinion. In the very worst case, the Earth partner will be a little too plodding and predictable for the excitable Air person, or on the other hand, the Air partner will be too lightweight and unreliable for Earth. At best, however, Earth will keep Air on the straight and narrow and Air will breathe new excitement into Earth, particularly in the bedroom.

EARTH and WATER

The combination of a Water sign with an Earth sign can give a relationship that is refreshing and powerful, and it is probably one of the most mutually beneficial mixes of the elements. Earth is practical enough to channel the creative ideas of Water and Water will refresh and give new thoughts and perspectives to Earth's more solid nature. If we had to look for potential problems though, it could be that Water will swamp Earth and erode the relationship with too many hair-brained schemes and high ideals, or the more straightforward Earth partner will tread all over the sensitive Water and stem the flow of its creative personality.

AIR and AIR

Air couples thrive on all forms of travel and communication. You love variety, new ideas and gadgets which makes for great fun in the bedroom and a very unusual home. As you both love talking so much you will be intellectually stimulated as well as physically and you will spend lots of time discussing and debating issues that you have in common. What must be taken into account is that you two need a sense of freedom in your lives and neither would want to tie down, or be tied down by, the other. Air men in particular can take a long time to make a firm commitment and even when they are in love will not always show it. Providing you are both tolerant of each other and give each other plenty of scope, you will enjoy a lively and loving life without too much danger of the relationship blowing itself out.

AIR and WATER

Although individually, Air and Water are both vital for life, there can be times when if you put them together, a very stormy partnership exists as Air and Water are the causes of clouds, fog and storms. However, you two can also make refreshing lively ripples of excitement and have a relationship that is jam-packed with fun. The Air person can whip Water into a frenzy and you won't be able to keep your hands off each other. Problems only arise when the Water sign gets too intense and clinging which quickly puts a dampener on Air's freedom-loving spirit, or alternatively, Air might become a bit too lightweight for Water's depth of character.

WATER and WATER

Partnership-wise, you are both sensitive and emotional and will have lots of feeling for each other that runs very deep. You are characterised by your caring, loving natures and both of you are very fond of your home which will always be warm and welcoming. All Water signs tend to love peace and harmony within a relationship and so when a potential argument arises, one of you will always go with the flow and back down to please your mate. In most cases, Water signs will share the same dreams and high ideals but the one negative side can be that you have a tendency to be a bit too wet from time to time if neither of you has the get-up-and-go to tackle life's everyday problems.

ARIES COMPATIBILITY

ARIES/ARIES

As an Arien female is as strong-willed as her mate, she'll make him happiest by understanding and supporting his dreams and drives and, likewise, he must respect hers. If both of you are working for the same goal and have the same sense of adventure in the bedroom, the Aries/Aries mix will be secure and passionate – perhaps one of the strongest combinations going.

This relationship can suffer from one of two failings; either he will be so involved in his own interests that his partner feels unloved. Or she will be the career type who believes she should not just do as well as her mate, but better. The constant competitiveness could be the kiss of death to this union.

ARIES/TAURUS

Taurus likes to plan for long sessions of passion whereas Aries prefers impulsive sex and does not much care about the location. To maintain the harmony, there has to be quite a lot of compromise, but a wilful Arien can teach Taurus to be a little quicker off the mark and Taurus can demonstrate the benefits of slow sexual love-making. Aries has rather shocking fantasies that can frighten the more conservative Bull so it is best to introduce them a step at a time. It's surprising how quickly Taurus will start to enjoy the sport. On the home front, both signs love building a home as well as spending time on their careers so this match can be very materialistic and profitable.

ARIES/GEMINI

Both these signs are full of energy and invention and a relationship will be totally without conformity or even direction. Fantasies between these two are wild and wacky with sex being for fun rather than an expression of emotion. If anything, Gemini is more restless than Aries so the Ram has to take the stabilising role without tying the Twin down too much. Sexually, both are totally uninhibited, so there are no end of thrills and novelties and discussing fantasies poses no problem. Infidelity is the biggest threat to this partnership because eventually one or both can't help but test out their bedroom skills with another eager admirer. Financially, this pair should not be short of cash – Gemini has the ideas and Aries puts them into action.

ARIES/CANCER

The adventurous Aries can view Cancer as a bit of a stick in the mud, but wise Rams let the Crab take the role of teacher which is something they enjoy. Although Aries' fantasies are often much more advanced than Cancer's, it is worth suggesting some deviant desires and then letting Cancer think it was all their idea. Coming on too strong to a Crab is sure to have them scuttling away to safety. Cancer insists on taking the lead in the home with Aries seldom getting any credit for their share of domestic duties. This relationship usually works best when each has a clear idea of their roles. Aries tends to bring home the bacon, while Cancer is happiest in the kitchen cooking it.

ARIES/LEO

When this fiery twosome set up home together, they don't just keep up with the Joneses, they are streets ahead of them. Their mutual lust for luxury and desire for all things expensive makes this a magnificent and material-loving match. Behind those quality curtains, however, fur flies on a regular basis. Both speak their minds with no holds barred and the sound of shattering china is not an uncommon one for the neighbours. What they are good at is making up in bed and some of the best sex will follow a furious flare-up. They are equally experimental and inquisitive about new games and techniques and are also able to laugh at themselves. This intense affair and firm friendship can last for many successful years.

ARIES/VIRGO

Initially, Aries admires Virgo's calm unruffled manner and Virgo is impressed by Aries' go-getting, fearless ambition. Providing both signs remember that it was this that first attracted them, all will be well. Unfortunately these very qualities can be the ones that start to irritate and grate on the other. The Ram will always be trying to speed up Virgo whilst Virgo gets exasperated by Aries' lack of patience. For this union to last, Aries must be allowed to take the lead and to treat the responsibility that comes with it very seriously. Without a doubt, the intimate side of the relationship has to be worked on as their drives and deviances are poles apart.

ARIES/LIBRA

A very compatible and fulfilling partnership perhaps lasting a lifetime is the outcome of this coupling. Both adore all forms of sexual pleasure and while Libra brings a touch of grace and refinement to the bedroom, Aries' present is spontaneity and surprise. Fantasies run riot between them and a friendly competition can ensue with each trying to dream up the most outrageous erotic activity. Potential pitfalls arise when life throws them a crisis, as they don't merely make a drama out of it, but a full theatrical production. Neither copes with stress that well over long periods and either could be tempted to exit stage left in search of escapism by way of an affair.

ARIES/SCORPIO

There will always be power struggles within this arrangement, but mutual respect prevents them from becoming a threat. In many ways, this characteristic can be perfect and a feeling of 'Us against the world' ensures a strong bond and considerable monetary success. Chemistry is what draws them together and a sizzling, sometimes sordid, sex life is the cement. The bond will only be broken if Aries abuses Scorpio's loyalty or if Scorpio's intense and extreme emotions crack Aries' spirit. Jealousy is enemy number one. When this relationship works it goes where angels fear to tread but with understanding it is nothing short of heavenly.

ARIES/SAGITTARIUS

Archers are always looking for greener grass and are one of the hardest signs to pin down. Aries, however, has a better than average chance of achieving this. These two Fire signs share many goals and career targets and are prepared to take more risks with their security than most other couples. Playing with high stakes often brings rich rewards and it's not likely that they will be hard up for cash in later years. Both are prone to impulsive affairs yet this is not the main cause of disagreements or break-ups. Should they split, it will probably be because they hardly see each other due to their tremendous social commitments.

ARIES/CAPRICORN

Capricorn only realises just what a fortuitous match this can be once it's over. In the early days of a relationship, the Goat has better things to do than spend afternoons in bed and prefers to use sex as an outlet rather than a pastime. Invariably, Aries loses patience before the real benefits of the partnership become apparent. This is a shame because both are motivated and energetic individuals who can move mountains together if they combine their strong wills. Aries might have to literally tie Capricorn to the bed to get sexual satisfaction and with perseverance, Capricorn starts to like it.

ARIES/AQUARIUS

These signs are entirely different characters but have an intense fascination for each other. Aries is captivated by the complex and imaginative Aquarian mind and the Waterbearer lusts after the Arien body and is stirred by their intense sexuality. Aries is the driving force of the relationship but Aquarius's intuition will steer it in the right direction. Home life will be happy as both know how to strike the right balance of work and play. Lots of leisure time is spent in the bedroom conjuring up ways to keep love-making varied. There is seldom the chance of illicit affairs wrecking the relationship as this generous duo prefers to bring new lovers home to share!

ARIES/PISCES

Aries is aggressive and Pisces is passive, so there is a strong chance of lasting compatibility if both are content to live by these astrological rules. As the union progresses through, Pisces may begin to emulate Aries and fight for supremacy by making rash decisions which they then will refuse to take responsibility for, obviously infuriating Aries. Equally, the Ram can take the Fish for granted, always expecting to get their own way without question. Sexually there is a lot of mileage in this match with Pisces being able to soften Aries' edges by injecting romance and daydreams into the Ram's heart. With plenty of communication, this double act is a cracker.

TAURUS COMPATIBILITY

TAURUS/ARIES

With Taurus being the foreplay expert and Aries being the master of the main event, you would assume this to be a well-balanced combination. To be honest, this can be a good match if Taurus takes the time to listen to what Aries really wants from sex and Aries is prepared to put up with the Taurean stubbornness to try new things. The early coupling will be both fun and sexually gratifying, but to stand the test of time, Aries' erotic impulsiveness to explore all forms of intimate fantasies and deviant tendencies might be a little too much for Taurus to take in the long run. Often, however, this highly ambitious pair are too busy making money to address the sexual discrepancies.

TAURUS/TAURUS

For this combination to work, a common goal is the answer. Sexually the male Bull is attractive and friendly to other ladies and can also be too earthy and practical for the sentimental Taurean female to find true happiness in the longevity of a relationship. An affair tends to be a lot of fun because the general Taurean traits are similar and mutual business and leisure interests will keep this union alive and well, especially if it is a joint working venture when Taurus/Taurus becomes a formidable partnership. When sensually locking horns in the bedroom, providing fantasies are shared equally, there could be enough stamina and sexual desires to last a lifetime.

TAURUS/GEMINI

The notorious Taurean art of seduction is sure to intrigue changeable Gemini into at least a successful sexual affair, but for the pairing to survive a lifetime Taurus may find Gemini's thirst for new adventures outside of the relationship a threat to its own necessary need for security. It has been known for this unlikely match to make it into old age together and when it does the alliance has a love/hate format, which at times will be volatile. Sexually, if Gemini's passion for abstract fantasies and the latest gadgets for bettering orgasms doesn't put Taurus off and if Taurus is a willing sex pupil, this liaison should go far.

TAURUS/CANCER

Both Taurus and Cancer are 'Mills & Boon' connoisseurs because they have a mutual love of romance. The Taurean stability and reliability should cope with Cancer's moods and offer the security which Cancer needs to sustain love. It's only the Bull's brooding and daydreaming and the Crab's constant battle with confidence and procrastination that could lead to a breakdown in the relationship. Sexually, although Cancer can have a deep, intense and fragile sensuality to start with, Taurus should overcome this with a seductive charm and sensitivity that will leave Cancer panting for more, and then the erotic scene will be set for a lifetime of sexual adventure.

TAURUS/LEO

Leo's proud and often arrogant ways could prove too much for Taurus to cope with even in a brief fling. For this unusual pair to go the full nine yards, Taurus must keep Leo well supplied with loyal physical love and heaps of affection and Leo must show the corresponding amount of appreciation. When it comes to sex, Leo will need to set the pace, but also the Taurean art of seduction should keep Leo's head in a spin. Together once they are in tune, the Lion and Bull should find passion and erotica something to share equally, for they both have plenty of stamina and fertile imagination to support a long and sexy union.

TAURUS/VIRGO

There are two ways of looking at the Bull and Virgin compatibility; both are materialistic, practical, admire efficiency and are lovers of the home, so this match can work very well. On the other hand, Taurus can be too selfish, stubborn and untidy, which is liable to bring out the scathing overly critical Virgoan traits in abundance and the relationship will be doomed before it really gets going. Sexually, the bonding could be just as difficult and a sexual compromise may be needed. For Taurus is likely to want more from sex than Virgo, both in quantity and variety, but if they look to grow together and take it step by step, it could be one of the strongest sexual unions the zodiac has seen.

TAURUS/LIBRA

Given the right circumstances these two can really hit it off, not just in the short term, but for a lifetime. Libra will offer an emotional excitement and a warm security that settles and comforts Taurus, whereas Taurus should compliment Libra by being logical in helping to make those important decisions. They both have a love of the finer things in life, so setting up a home together is something they will get a lot of happiness from. Sexually, Libra has a very erotic and instinctive bent for theatricals in the bedroom and they both are experts in foreplay, so anything can happen in this intimate relationship as they take it in turn to take the sexual lead.

TAURUS/SCORPIO

Tolerance will be the key word in this pairing, for Scorpio won't accept the stubborn, plodding and moody ways of Taurus and the sign of the Bull is likely to find Scorpio's wrath and domineering attitude too intense to handle. Now if tolerance is exercised to the full, the personable characteristics of both signs can forge a harmonious union, but they will have to work at it. When it comes to passion this couple's bedroom is sure to be a hot bed of very erotic fantasies. The Taurean stamina and foreplay expertise will complement Scorpio's comprehensive knowledge of anatomy and sexual tricks to the point of no return. All in all, a great sexual match and possibly a happy partnership.

TAURUS/SAGITTARIUS

The Sagittarian need for many friends and their ability unemotionally to mix sex with social life will make Taurus run for security in another sign's arms. Taurus, on the other hand, is sure to try and tie the Archer down, which is the basis for many confrontations. For it to work, both will need to compromise by seeing the other point of view and making constant allowances for the very differing personalities. One thing they have in common is a mutual love of sex and lust. Both should share the lead in the bedroom and will have a joint staying power. Their fantasies are quite diverse, with Sagittarius loving sex in the great outdoors and Taurus opening up new amorous adventures around the home. Either way the intimacy will never be dull.

TAURUS/CAPRICORN

With Taurus being an emotion hoover and a hopeless romantic, he or she will be dismayed to find Capricorn quite the opposite, so to make this unusual twosome work, both will need to find a happy medium and stick to it rigorously, especially for a long-term partnership. When it comes to sex, Capricorn can have a secret sadistic side that could make Taurus feel uneasy in the bedroom, but nonetheless intrigued. Also, the Taurean foreplay expertise will be lost on Capricorn, because they don't need much warming up. The main course though can be very satisfying over a long period, providing a compromise is sought between emotion and lust.

TAURUS/AQUARIUS

Taurus could well be too demanding for Aquarius who tends to want a lively mental rapport as the main element, so from the start both signs' needs are poles apart. Now as opposites can attract, this union can work especially in a brief affair. Both need to re-arrange their individual requirements and meet each other half way, and if they can settle down together this way, then it could go the distance. Sexually, these two have a wonderful erotic imagination and providing neither is too forceful, the sexual world is their oyster. It's an unusual match to say the least, but contrary to popular belief it can work well, in the right circumstances and will depend on their individual rising signs.

TAURUS/PISCES

Pisces is an incurable romantic and Taurus should find this trait a perfect compliment to its own sensitive needs. Both require constant security to feel loved and contented and this is likely to flow in both directions in uncontrollable amounts. If Taurus can keep the stubborn and moody side repressed and Pisces can tone down its persecution complex, this partnership should stand the test of time. To make the sexual side work, Taurus should take the lead on most occasions and guide Pisces gently through the intimacy game. Fantasies are sure to play a key part, but Pisces will need to feel very secure before being able to really let go and enjoy what the Bull can offer.

GEMINI COMPATIBILITY

GEMINI/ARIES

Change and variety are the two key aspects of life that these signs live for, so it's not surprising that Gemini and Aries could enjoy a brief fling or a long-term partnership together. Both signs are easily bored and Gemini may suffer from bouts of restlessness, but Aries should help Gemini keep its feet on terra firma. Sexually, these two are sure to go from A to Z in terms of outrageous fantasies before they start on ever more deviant practices. Once they have worked through them, they will start rewriting the sex manuals with their own erotic and creative sexual thinking.

GEMINI/TAURUS

Gemini's continual waywardness and extreme bouts of flirting should make Taurus run a mile. Also, the possessive and jealous streak in Taurus is sure to put too much constraint on Gemini culminating in many confrontations. For this match to work, and it will be very hard, Gemini will need to offer Taurus constant security and reassurance. Taurus in turn should compensate by giving Gemini the freedom to chase its dreams and ideals and tone down the moodiness and stubborn side to its nature. Sexually, Taurus will have to work at bringing variety to the bedroom and Gemini should try to be less demanding and more romantic, and in this way there may just be a chance for them to work it out together.

GEMINI/GEMINI

What a versatile match these two could turn out to be! Both love adventure, are generally intelligent and need constant stimulation. There's never a dull moment when two Geminians get it together and it's this that could lead to a sticking point – they are sure to be always trying to outdo each other and this may lead to some fierce verbal battles. The good news is, neither tends to hold a grudge and the fight is forgotten the second it is over. Sexually, this innovative hot bed of passion won't cool down until hell freezes over, and as long as they don't exhaust all the sexual permutations they should have a long, erotic and torrid relationship to enjoy.

GEMINI/CANCER

Cupid has orchestrated some amazing combinations, but he will need to be a miracle worker to make this match viable. Cancer is too soft and sensitive for

Gemini's sharp tongue and Gemini is too restless and changeable to keep Cancer happy. As always though, opposites can attract, so if Gemini can be more of a home-loving person and offer Cancer some security and if Cancer can keep its moody and insecure feelings on hold, then there is a chance, even if it is slight. Sexually, if Cancer feels appreciated and Gemini displays affection and warmth instead of technique, they can find middle ground in the bedroom, or wherever they make love.

GEMINI/LEO

The Twin and Lion should have many things in common as both love life in the fast lane, especially when out on the town together and these two have an insatiable quest for new adventures. So it is not unusual for Gemini to really hit it off with Leo. The only problem may occur when both want to star in the limelight and it is here where they must seek a compromise to stop the fur flying. Sexually, their strong sensual personalities should make for an orgasmic time. Both will enjoy taking the lead, although Gemini may have the monopoly on fantasies, which is not necessarily one of Leo's fortes. In time though, Leo could spring a few erotic surprises of its own as Leos hate to be outdone.

GEMINI/VIRGO

Without doubt, Virgo's unending ability to criticise Gemini's unpredictability should prove to be the cause of World War Three. It is very hard for these two to find common ground, because each one's traits are vastly different. If this union is to work, Gemini has to be more stable and commit to the relationship lock, stock, and barrel. Virgo, for its part, needs to be more open, less restricting and see life with Gemini without the typical Virgoan blinkers. This way there is a chance for their romantic survival. Sexually, Gemini will need to coax Virgo slowly, but once Virgo feels secure and loved the sensual fun and games are sure to begin in earnest.

GEMINI/LIBRA

Libra's impulsive love of life is certain to attract Gemini's curiosity and from there it is pretty much plain sailing and a relationship between these two should stand the test of time. The negative traits of Gemini and Libra won't cause too much of a problem, because their desires and ambitions in life are almost the same. Sexually, there is bound to be much procrastination as to who does what to whom first, but they will never be short on erotic ideas as both try to outmanoeuvre each other by way of dreaming up the most outlandish of fantasies. This match is set to be full of promise and imagination that could bring a new meaning to sex!

GEMINI/SCORPIO

Scorpio could prove to be too jealous and headstrong for Gemini to feel comfortable in a long-term union and Gemini's fickle persona is likely to bring out the worst in

Scorpio. Certainly this pairing has the chemistry for an interesting short haul, but both will have to work exceptionally hard in the compromise department to make it go the distance. Sexually, in the first instance there is sure to be lots of raw physical attraction and sex could be more for pleasure-seeking purposes than romantic ones. These two have the recipe for great no-holds-barred imaginative sex, but they will need to communicate their feelings continually to keep the intimate spark alive.

GEMINI/SAGITTARIUS

As neither sign is particularly possessive or demanding in a relationship, there's a chance they may hit it off and stay together, especially as they also don't wear their hearts on their sleeves and are not overly emotional. The downside that is Gemini's self-doubting complex nature will be at loggerheads with Sagittarius's live-and-let-live open views of life. So in order to achieve lasting love, both should learn to compensate for each other's needs and understand their differing temperaments. Sexually, if Gemini doesn't criticise the Archer's sexual ability, then they should be able to make whoopee for eternity as they can learn to grow passionately together.

GEMINI/CAPRICORN

Gemini's need for stimulation and variety could prove too much for the Capricorn single-mindedness. Also, Gemini needs affection and reassurance from a mate and Capricorn is more the unemotional type who perceives career and financial gains to be more important than physical requirements. If they can come to terms with these monumental differences then it's more than possible a durable relationship will ensue, although a brief fling is more likely. Sexually, both have a bent for the unusual and if Capricorn can cope with and learn from Gemini's outlandish bedroom behaviour, they'll rewrite the text books and create their own joy of sex.

GEMINI/AQUARIUS

Although love won't always run smoothly between these two, they have a basic mutual understanding of what keeps the other happy. Both signs' traits should be complementary and this is the ingredient to keep a successful relationship rolling on into old age, where even as pensioners, their thirst for new adventure together will keep them in the bedroom and out of the potting shed. Sexually, their inventive minds work overtime and some of the fantasies are certain to be outrageous and futuristic. Without doubt Gemini and Aquarius are a super-sensual and erotic match where nothing is likely to be left to the imagination. Most of all, they'll be firm friends.

GEMINI/PISCES

Pisces' insecure temperament and constant search for security and reassurance is likely to make Gemini move on rather quickly after a brief fling. Gemini, on the other hand, has rebellious ways, is constantly searching for new thrills and needs an emotionally strong partner to keep them in check, probably too difficult a task for sensitive Pisces to rise to. Now, for love to conquer all, Pisces must be more trusting and Gemini should never give cause for Pisces not to be. Sexually, again Pisces requires stability to flourish, but once gained and if Gemini really understands what makes Pisces tick, these two should have quite a naughty and adventurous intimate life together.

CANCER
COMPATIBILITY

CANCER/ARIES

Cancer's tendencies towards possessiveness and over-protectiveness together with its moody and jealous nature is sure to make this partnership extremely hard going as Aries require space to breathe. Aries for its part will upset Cancer by making a drama out of every crisis and always thirsting for adventure. This union can work, but both sides will have to settle for a happy medium by being sensitive and understanding of each other's personality. Sexually, at first there could be an almost obsessive attraction, but conservative Cancer needs reassurance to be more deviant and to play a part in those erotic Arien fantasies.

CANCER/TAURUS

The great thing about this relationship is neither partner needs outside interests to be happy together and these two have a deep understanding of what makes each other tick. Taurus will keep Cancer's moody nature at bay by looking after its troubles and Cancer's sensitive imagination should more than please Taurus. Sexually, they are on a par with each other. Both will share the lead and bring variety to the bedroom. In the right circumstances their passion could inspire some pretty outrageous fantasies and their intimate lives should never become boring or lose their romantic qualities.

CANCER/GEMINI

Gemini's adventure-seeking, fickle and flirtatious attitude could bring out Cancer's inborn insecurity to the point where the relationship breaks down irrevocably. Cancer's love of the home and tendency to prefer the quiet life is the opposite of Gemini's non-stop whirlwind need for activity. As always, opposites can attract and both signs will need to meet in the middle and compromise if this partnership is to last into old age. Sexually, an affair could produce quite a torrid and sensual pairing, but over a longer duration, Cancer will need to keep Gemini stimulated and meet it halfway in terms of erotic imagination so that boredom never enters into Gemini's mind.

CANCER/CANCER

The emotional problems that will result from these two sharing a life together are sure to be too much for either to handle. Although they are physically attracted to one another and an affair is certain to bring both much pleasure, a more permanent fixture is very unlikely, unless one is dominant and the other naturally passive. If so, this could actually work quite well. Sexually, there may be friction at first as to who takes the lead, but once the intricacies are sorted out, these two undoubtedly should have a lot of very sensitive and sensual fun together. This might not be a sexual union of quantity, but one of fulfilment whenever between the sheets.

CANCER/LEO

If Cancer can pander to Leo's need for admiration and also complement its sexual prowess, then Leo will give much in return by being a stabilising influence and helping Cancer through its moodiness and insecurity. They are both very affectionate signs and should be sensitive to the other's needs, so this relationship could well stand the test of time. Sexually, they share a passion for the more sensual side of sex, rather than wild exotic fantasies. Of course there will be some naughtier games to play in the bedroom, but both are really happier enjoying sex in a more 'Mills & Boon' style with bundles of romance thrown in as opposed to mere physical thrills.

CANCER/VIRGO

Now, these two stand a very good chance of making it to old age together if they approach this partnership slowly and intelligently. Cancer may be a little more emotional than reserved Virgo, but with Virgo's practical view of all things, these lovers should complement each other well, especially through their mutual love of the home. Sexually, Cancer will need to lead shy Virgo for quite some time and Virgo should find Cancer's sensitivity reassuring enough to relax into inventive sex. In time, their quiet desires for more outrageous fantasies should keep the spark alive and well in the bedroom and their ambitious natures will keep the bank balance more than healthy.

CANCER/LIBRA

Here, Cancer's basic insecure temperament is likely to drive Libra away in the same way as Libra's emotional detachment could cause Cancer to feel unloved. Looking at the positive side, Libra could support and help Cancer through the unpredictable moody periods, whilst Cancer's sensitivity and practicality should aid Libra's inability to formulate decisions and also be beneficial to its quest for constant harmony, so this partnership can work well in the right circumstances. Sexually, they are both passionate, affectionate and sensual, which is the pattern their sex life together will follow. Once Libra gains Cancer's confidence they are likely to try anything once and twice if they both find it pleasurable.

CANCER/SCORPIO

Scorpio's possessiveness and strength within a relationship will make Cancer a very happy Crab indeed and Cancer's loyalty and sensitive nature is sure to pleasure Scorpio. So as you can imagine not much can go wrong with this pairing, as they will be fine in an affair and a marriage could be made in heaven if they are both true to their sign. Sexually, Scorpio might scorch Cancer with its intense passion, but Cancer won't mind too much as long as it feels loved and secure. Providing Scorpio introduces certain sexual preferences and fantasies slowly, Cancer will turn out to become a wonderfully imaginative sexual playmate as well as a partner.

CANCER/SAGITTARIUS

As these two signs have opposite desires and ambitions, there isn't a great chance of it working. Cancer is too inflexible and won't comprehend Sagittarius's need for freedom and adventure, whereas the Archer will find Cancer's unforgiving nature too hard to swallow. If this union is to work, especially in the long term, then they both need to decide together which compromises are necessary and stick to them. It no doubt will be hard, but it can work with effort. Sexually, Sagittarius will bring a breezy sensual charm to the bedroom and Cancer's need for being wooed will be nicely complemented. For sex to be permanently fulfilling, Cancer needs to be more adventurous and take the lead to stop Sagittarius's low boredom threshold being reached.

CANCER/CAPRICORN

Unemotional Capricorn is certain to find Cancer's vulnerable ego a problem to handle, in the same way as Cancer will find it difficult to deal with Capricorn's obsessional nature in placing work or business endeavours before a relationship. Capricorn's lazy and stubborn streak could also try the Crab's patience. In a nutshell, these two need to work out a lot of fundamental differences to go for the long haul, but it can happen. Sexually, there is naturally a strong physical attraction and if they can work on this inbuilt magnetism and Cancer feels secure, then they could explore all forms of erotic pleasures from the most romantic to the most bizarre form of fantasies.

CANCER/AQUARIUS

This is a combination where many adjustments on both sides are necessary for it to work. Basically both want entirely different things from a partnership. Cancer, for example, needs a mate to be home-loving, sensitive and provide overdoses of affection, whereas Aquarius needs freedom, adventure and space to be creative with its innovative ideas. This union can, however, sometimes work given the right circumstances and compatible rising signs. Sexually, Aquarians normally want to make love to the mind first and then the body so if the Waterbearer lives up to its reputation and treats Cancer as an intellectual equal, Cancer may be prepared to work harder at the relationship.

CANCER/PISCES

Any fights between these two are likely to be resolved in bed as both Cancer and Pisces were made for each other. There might, indeed, be a touch too much sensitivity, but their unique mutual desires to be loved and wanted should give each the security to formulate a long and contented relationship. Sexually, Cancer is more likely to take the lead at first, but Pisces won't be too long in showing Cancer a new trick or two. As both signs should feel totally at peace and in harmony, they could go on to play some very adventurous and erotic games together. As the relationship evolves, both partners will want to give more to the other, where almost anything sexual is possible.

LEO COMPATIBILITY

LEO/ARIES

The only real problem for this very compatible union is that Aries has a compulsion to lead from the front and Leo being the ruler of the jungle wants to do exactly the same. Providing these two can share the power amicably, or one is naturally submissive through their ascendant, then there is no reason why they can't settle down into old age together. Sexually, there is an instant attraction as both adore sex and a whole range of erotica. Aries at times may be a little wide of Leo's mark by virtue of its exotic fantasies and carnal tastes for the bizarre, but Leo won't want to be seen as a prude and will indulge Aries and probably enjoy the experience.

LEO/TAURUS

Leo's arrogant and proud nature should prove too much for stubborn and practical Taurus. They both want to have their say first and when this isn't possible, one or two of the afore-mentioned traits are sure to be the cause of many confrontations. Opposites can attract though and if these two can work at their differences, which is a big hurdle to overcome, they could reap a happy life together. Sexually, they'll enjoy an affectionate intimate relationship where Leo is more than satisfied by the Taurean expertise with foreplay and lasting stamina and Taurus will find satisfaction from Leo's desire to please its mate. The fantasies won't be wild and deviant, but there will be plenty of them.

LEO/GEMINI

This pairing can go the distance although their relationship is likely to be stormy to say the least. It will be one of those love to hate routines, but where love can conquer all. Both will be continually stimulated and fascinated by the other, especially mentally and Gemini's clever ability with words and general affable nature is sure to take the decibel level out of Leo's roar. Sexually, they should have plenty of erotic fun in the bedroom. Leo will probably take the lead at first, but after exhausting its intimate repertoire will let Gemini take over, eventually bringing more diversity and variance to the bedroom and life in general.

LEO/CANCER

Cancer will need a lot of reassurance and security from Leo and, in turn, Leo requires total commitment of love and some hero worship thrown in for good measure from Cancer. If so, this relationship will be very workable all round. One thing they both have in common is the love of home and domestic life, and this will give them something to build together and children can bond the union forever. When it comes to sex, Leo will be in its element in teaching conservative Cancer new ways to get the most from passionate love-making. Providing Leo doesn't go too fast for Cancer at the outset, they should go on to explore many forms of erotic fantasies and in the long run Cancer may just surprise Leo.

LEO/LEO

Although this mix doesn't always work, when it does, it is a very powerful combination providing one can take a back seat from time to time and let the other make decisions. There is no shortage of hearts and flowers between these two and they will enjoy building a regal palace together ready for their cubs to enter. Both are very family-orientated and take pride in establishing a solid home life. Sexually, there could be a power play in the bedroom, but more in a fun and humorous sense rather than serious competition. Both are likely to spring some very erotic and romantic surprises and life between the sheets will never be dull.

LEO/VIRGO

The problem with this match is that Virgo won't want to be dominated and Leo can't help but do anything else, so there will be friction right from the start. Another bone of contention is Virgo's continual tendency to be critical of a partner and this is the kiss of death to Leo who loves praise and flattery. Leo's arrogance could be enough to turn Virgo into a nun or monk at bedtime, or at least run for cover. For this partnership to work, a serious compromise is needed on both parts and it has been known to happen, but not often. Sexually, Leo needs to lead Virgo slowly, but given time and patience Leo will find Virgo to be a very willing pupil, who eventually could turn the sexual tables on Leo and introduce some unexpected fantasies of its own.

LEO/LIBRA

Libra's love of the finer things in life and tendency for theatricals in the bedroom is certain to make Leo very happy. Leo in return will stabilise Libra and help with decisions and other awkward areas of Libra's existence. All Leo requires in return are reasonable amounts of homage throughout the relationship, especially in the bedroom. Sexually, Leo is more direct in its approach whereas Libra tends to play elaborate erotic games. One thing is for sure, neither will get bored with their bedroom antics and in time Libra could become the initiator with Leo being a big submissive pussy cat.

LEO/SCORPIO

Scorpio's possessiveness won't be met with Leo's approval and a fight for supremacy will ensure many confrontations between these two. If the balance of power can be sorted out at the beginning and Leo is prepared to take the back seat as well as putting up with a general lack of worshipping from Scorpio, then this relationship can really work well. The place it should really happen is in the bedroom, as both signs are very sexual and it is here where they can learn to share the lead role. Their sexual attraction is immense and electrifying, so they should forge a special chemistry that will be torrid, passionate and extremely erotic.

LEO/SAGITTARIUS

These two passionate and extrovert personalities have a mutual love of adventure and friendship. I say friendship, as this union is likely to be set up that way. They could live together in an open relationship which is more the Archer's way of thinking, but equally Leo is one of the few signs capable of extracting loyalty from Sagittarius. Sexually, the Archer will allow Leo to take the lead through many an erotic and passionate experience. The great outdoors is the sexual playground of Sagittarius, so Leo can expect the unexpected when out for a simple stroll with the Archer and that may include other people witnessing the sexy fun too.

231

LEO/CAPRICORN

Leo will find Capricorn to be short on emotion, especially where romance and affection are concerned. Capricorn, in contrast, is sure to find Leo's demanding nature too much to take. So this partnership will have to evolve slowly with many compromises sought if it is to work in the long term or even for a brief fling. One thing is certain, Leo's arrogance and Capricorn's moodiness will make for a rocky passage no matter how hard they try to be compatible. Sexually though, Capricorn's deviant tendencies don't offend Leo, so they could explore some very bizarre fantasies and have an exceptionally passionate love life indeed.

LEO/AQUARIUS

Aquarius will need to tone down its verbal bluntness if this pairing is to work, as it would shake the confidence of Leo to the point of no return. There are many reasons why this union won't last, but equally so, there are as many justifications for an enduring relationship. It will depend on the individuals and what is in their rising signs. When it comes to sex, Aquarius will need to revise its unorthodox approach and bizarre fantasies, but Leo would do well to let the Aquarian imagination take the lead from time to time. Leo also will teach Aquarius how to put the passion into love-making and make the simple fantasies more sexually fulfilling.

LEO/PISCES

These two zodiac signs are more takers than givers, so right from the start a relationship is likely to get off on the wrong foot. The typical Piscean sensitivity and insecurity may bring out Leo's maternal or paternal instincts, but Leo is sure to get fed up with this after a while. On the other hand, Leo's ambitions and sense of adventure could drive introverted Pisces crazy. For it to work, both signs will need to meet each other halfway and if Leo can give Pisces long-term stability and if Pisces offers the respect Leo merits and desires, then it could just go the distance. Sexually, Leo will need to coax Pisces into the pleasures of fantasies and will also enjoy Pisces being the submissive partner, so in the bedroom it could really work well.

VIRGO
COMPATIBILITY

VIRGO/ARIES

The differences here are that Virgo loves stimulating talk, whereas Aries adores stimulating adventure. Also Virgo finds the Arien traits of making a drama out of a crisis and excessive impatience very disconcerting. By the same token, Aries finds Virgo's critical and analytical nature difficult to comprehend. This match will only work if both signs meet each other halfway and show tolerance for the other's shortcomings. Sexually, Aries should keep the pace slow to start with so Virgo can adjust to the rampant Arien needs. Also, if Aries strives for success outside the bedroom, Virgo will endeavour to provide romantic fulfilment and rewards.

VIRGO/TAURUS

Virgo should get along with Taurus in most areas of a relationship. The Taurean practicality, efficiency and materialistic nature will bring out the best in Virgo. This match should go the distance providing Taurus doesn't provoke the typical Virgoan tendency to be overly critical. These two will set up quite a home together and any offspring are likely to get a very balanced and intelligent upbringing. Sexually, Virgo will prove to be a willing partner to start with, which should cater to the initial Taurean lust. After that and as the relationship matures, the need to get it right will become important for both sides making their sex lives both fulfilling and exciting.

VIRGO/GEMINI

Gemini's constant thirst for excitement and activity away from the home is a major turn off to Virgo. Gemini sees Virgo's domineering and critical nature a major handicap, so these two will have to find common ground if they are to stand a chance of a lasting relationship. Sexually, they should initially thrive on lust as neither is too sensitive or over-romantically inclined. In the long term with Gemini needing constant variety and Virgo unsure as what to do next, Gemini will need to exercise control and be innovative with fantasies and erotic ideas. If Virgo really loves Gemini and allows it freedom, Gemini will make the effort to provide security.

VIRGO/CANCER

Cancer will find all the security and attention it needs to be happy in a relationship with Virgo and Virgo sees Cancer's dependency the perfect answer to its overly protective nature. These two complement each other very well as Cancer's imagination stimulates Virgo and Cancer's willingness to please brings Virgo's affections to the surface. Sexually, given time they will learn together and share the lead equally. In terms of how erotic and passionate the love-making will become, it is down to the individuals, but I would suspect as each year goes by their sex lives will mature with no holds barred, so long as it is all good clean, not too deviant, fun.

VIRGO/LEO

Virgo's critical nature will be the kiss of death for Leo in a relationship, so this trait needs to be kept well and truly hidden. The other downside is that Virgo has a practical down-to-earth approach, whereas Leo naturally has an optimistic and expansive disposition, which makes them opposites. As total extremes can attract each other, this combination can work occasionally, so there is a chance they could hit it off and go the distance. Sexually, if Virgo feels secure and loved then Leo can take charge. There may be a difference in sex drives to start with, but Virgo in the long run won't want to miss out and will want to do its share too, so the signs are good for a contented sex life.

VIRGO/VIRGO

These two should get on like a house on fire. They will, no doubt, criticise each other constantly, but the fact that they strive for the same goals and adore a neat, orderly and subtle lifestyle means that this is the basis of a long and contented relationship. They are sure to have the tidiest home in the universe and will sit up all night, often preferring intellectual conversation to sex itself while they put the world's wrongs to right. Sexually, at first it will be the blind leading the blind, but in time they'll work at it and make a successful sexual combination that could become quite adventurous through curiosity alone.

VIRGO/LIBRA

Libra will need to give up its indiscretions forever if it is to enter into a relationship with Virgo. Virgo will have to keep criticisms to a minimum or risk undermining Libra's self-confidence. These two are going to have to make a lot of sacrifices if this union is to last and it may be that it will only be okay if they both have compatible rising signs because of their extremely differing complexities of character. Sexually, Virgo needs to demonstrate sensitivity and sensuality to make Libra feel sexy and desirable. If this happens and both keep an open mind there could be a lot of erotic fun to be had.

VIRGO/SCORPIO

It has always amazed me how these two can be so compatible, but it does work and has worked on numerous occasions. Even so, there does have to be a compromise, in as much as Scorpio will need to keep its aggression stifled and Virgo should never criticise Scorpio, or it risks facing the famous sting in the tail. Intellectually they have a lot in common and share the same causes to fight so if they meet halfway with their differing natures, the partnership should go from strength to strength. Sexually, Virgo needs an asbestos suit to cope with Scorpio's burning passion at first, but once signed there will be no looking back and after that it is sex, sex, sex, all the way . . .

VIRGO/SAGITTARIUS

Virgo will find it really hard to attain the security it needs in a relationship with Sagittarius. The Archer, on the other hand, sees Virgo's tidy and organised nature too hard to handle in the short or long term. With Sagittarius being sporty, happy-go-lucky and a lover of the great outdoors and Virgo being a home body and a connoisseur of intellectual conversation, you would think I'm mad in saying that these two can work out their differences but the truth is they can! It is very rare but stranger things have happened. Sexually, they need to compromise in this department too, but if they can reach an understanding, their sex lives together can be as energetic and erotic as any other relationship – or even better.

VIRGO/CAPRICORN

Virgo really understands Capricorn's desire to work hard and formulate success, in fact as a business partnership this is almost unbeatable. The only real problem here is that Capricorn is lazy around the home and that infuriates Virgo past the point of control. They do share many common interests, especially regarding humanitarian problems and the finer things in life. Sexually, both love it, but neither see it as the major crux of the relationship and in the same way neither are too emotional. Despite all I have just mentioned, they will forge a very earthy and sometimes unusual sex life together with both ultimately sharing the lead equally.

VIRGO/AQUARIUS

Aquarius is too melodramatic for Virgo's liking and also has rather erratic tendencies in the bedroom which Virgo fails to comprehend. Virgo, on the other hand, can't offer the real zest and excitement that Aquarius needs from a long-term partner. Aquarius is very creative and Virgo is essentially practical and logical, so their thinking is worlds apart. If these two can find common ground and settle their differences, it can flourish in isolated incidents. Sexually, Aquarius needs to be patient whilst Virgo adapts to the Waterbearer's sexual preferences and desires. Once Virgo feels loved and is contented, it could just pull out a few surprises of its own.

VIRGO/PISCES

The Piscean insecurity and constant need for reassurance are a real headache for Virgo. Virgo wants to help, but after a short while will think it futile to go any further. Pisces, for its part, sees Virgo as being too unemotional and reserved to seek pleasure from a relationship. So for this union to become a harmonious partnership for all time, they will need to accept each other's characteristics and make allowances for them. This way it does stand a chance, especially if Virgo saves its criticism for someone else. Sexually, Virgo gets a rare chance here to be the dominant partner and lead Pisces on whatever erotic escapade Virgo desires. Pisces will soon catch up though and in time they both should enjoy a rich and stimulating sex life together.

LIBRA COMPATIBILITY

LIBRA/ARIES

The Libran procrastination and inability to meet life's adversities head-on will be seen as a weakness by Aries, in the same way as Libra sees the Arien fieriness and aggressiveness a threat to their quest for harmony. They also perceive Aries' tendency to make a drama out of a crisis to be a waste of energy and time. Without doubt these two are drawn together even though their personalities can be poles apart. Certainly an affair is breathtaking, but to go the distance they need to work hard on their differences. Sexually, the bedroom sees many an erotic theatrical fantasy, as their tastes for sexual adventure and variety are almost non-stop and that may include deviant nights with an extra person to make up the numbers.

LIBRA/TAURUS

Libra can't help flirting with other people; it's just their nature and most of the time it's harmless unless Libra feels neglected. The Taurean jealousy knows no bounds in this situation and many unnecessary confrontations will ensue. On the plus side, however, Libra is mostly considerate and understanding, so this will help keep the Bull's temper and stubbornness under control. If Taurus can cope with Libra's fickleness then these two could enjoy a lifetime together. Sexually, they really are physically in tune. Taurus has a flair for foreplay and a sexual stamina to boot while Libra loves romance and dramatised fantasies, so they are unlikely to get bored in the bedroom, or anywhere else they make love.

LIBRA/GEMINI

Once these two meet it's fascinating to watch how they wear their emotions on their sleeves and overdose each other with affection. As you can imagine the Libra/Gemini pairing is almost as perfect as it comes, providing both are true to their signs. Gemini bolsters Libra's confidence and Libra keeps Gemini's dark and moody twin side hidden through care and understanding, so Libra's quest for constant harmony is intact. Sexually, they are very in tune with one another. Both are bored easily, so this intimate relationship will cover much ground as they strive to find new and exciting ways to please each other erotically.

LIBRA/CANCER

Thrifty Cancer finds Libra's extravagance too much to cope with and outgoing Libra will be at loggerheads with Cancer over its conservative desire to stay at home for peace and quiet. As Cancer needs constant reassurance and Libra can appear to be shallow with its emotions, you could be forgiven for thinking hell will freeze over before these two can grow old together. The truth is they can, but with a lot of compromising and soul-searching. Sexually, their relationship may be a little tame at first by Libra's standards, but once Cancer feels loved and secure, the Crab could spring some erotic surprises on Libra, and then the world is their sexual oyster.

LIBRA/LEO

This is a super partnership providing their egos don't clash. If so, the Scales will have to give way to regal Leo, but, to be honest, Libra secretly won't mind Leo being masterly regardless of the gender situation. With Leo needing passion and Libra being demonstrative all will be well with this union for a lifetime and then some. Sexually, they should share the same sex drive and will go all out to bring pleasure and variety to the bedroom. Sex to them is a never-ending erotic game with very few rules and no referee. This could be a match made in heaven where both sides score.

LIBRA/VIRGO

Orderly, neat and tidy Virgo is more concerned with its career and righting the world's wrongs than being involved in a mind-blowing sexual relationship with Libra. Virgo finds Libra's extravagance and indecision unforgivable and Libra will run to another's arms as soon as Virgo starts with the criticism and nagging. To make a life together it helps to have compatible rising signs. Sexually, Libra needs to coax Virgo and understand that Virgo does really love sex and passion, but it's not a priority. Virgo, given time to recognise Libra's devotion and undying love, will learn quickly from it and become just as adventurous and sensual as it is. It's worth the effort and patience.

LIBRA/LIBRA

Watching these two make a serious decision together will take as long as getting a straight answer from a politician. They have so much in common it actually makes a life-long partnership quite difficult. Once the whirlwind romance slows and the erotic passion burns down, they will have to apply extreme practicality to their relationship to make it work, or their tendency to indulge in affairs could take over as they look for new excitement. When this union is successful though, they seem to be joined at the hip in a state of contentment. Sexually, they have equal amounts of passion, imagination and stamina and if boredom does set in they only have themselves to blame.

LIBRA/SCORPIO

This is your typical love/hate relationship as Libra can't help itself from being flirtatious and Scorpio's possessiveness and jealousy are likely to arm its stinging tail and painfully bring Libra down to earth. Their making up in bed though will more than ease Libra's pain and wounded pride. For this relationship really to stand the test of time, Scorpio needs to dominate and Libra initially must cooperate in all areas. When Scorpio feels in control, then the balance of power can be moderated on a fairer basis. Sexually, once Libra has sampled the famous Scorpionic erotica, Libra should be hooked on this sexually charged demon; like a love junkie, it can't wait for its next fantastic fix.

LIBRA/SAGITTARIUS

Libra will have a tough job to keep the Archer pinned down, especially when trying to set up a home. Sagittarius loves to be on the move and sees a home merely as a place to change clothes and sleep. Other than that these two signs share many things in common; they love adventure, the great outdoors and have low boredom thresholds which need continual stimulation. So if Sagittarius is prepared to enter fully into a committed relationship with Libra, it should be an exciting and contented partnership. Sexually, for them variety is the spice of life and in this area they are very well suited indeed. Both may have an occasional secret sexual affair, they can't help themselves, but a solution could be to invite others to join the fun.

LIBRA/CAPRICORN

Libra will love Capricorn's capacity for making money and Capricorn has a strong attraction to Libra's sensual nature, but that really is the good news. In most other areas they are pretty much opposites. Libra loves socialising and flirting, Capricorn is more sober and prefers more intellectual stimulation. Libra can be lazy and Capricorn is a workaholic so no change here, and the list goes on. This is another case where although unusual it can work well and be durable, but compatible rising signs and compromises are necessary. Sexually, they get along fine at first, but over a lifetime, Capricorn needs to be more inventive to keep up with Libra, but Libra will indulge Capricorn in its deviant requests.

LIBRA/AQUARIUS

This is a wonderful match, perhaps the best Libra can make. Libra finds Aquarius continually stimulating and admires the Waterbearer's leadership qualities and creative futuristic thinking. Aquarius adores the Libran sensuality and penchant for the theatricals both in and out of the bedroom. They love socialising and also appreciate the need for individual space from time to time, even if it means a quick hormone release by way of a one-off sexual affair. Neither is overly jealous and both can eventually forgive the odd indiscretion. Sexually, they are connoisseurs of erotic drama and are extremely and sensually inventive, and on more than one occasion someone may be invited to watch their uninhibited performances.

LIBRA/PISCES

The lack of Piscean leadership prowess is likely to upset Libra because Libra likes a partner to make the big decisions. They do, however, have much in common; Libra will adore the Piscean sensitivity and genteel make-up and Pisces is enthralled by Libra's creativity, especially in the bedroom. If this relationship is to last a lifetime, Pisces needs to understand Libra's need for space and its own identity and Libra, for its part, should keep its shallow emotions hidden and give Pisces the constant reassurance it requires. Sexually, at first it will take on a 'Mills & Boon' existence until Libra gets fed up, then the meatier fantasies take over. If Pisces feels confident and loved it will be a ready and willing partner for Libra.

SCORPIO
COMPATIBILITY

SCORPIO/ARIES

This is another one of the zodiac combinations that many astrologers say does not work, especially in the long term. I can tell you different, for I am an Aries and my partner is a Scorpio. The relationship is one of power, enthusiasm and ambition which is shared equally between the signs. Aries can be a little flighty for Scorpio's possessive nature and a few other idiosyncrasies do come into the equation, but there is a common drive towards mutual goals and with some minor compromises and fine-tuning a lasting and durable relationship can be enjoyed. Sexually, it starts off hot and the temperature rises from there as these two will try almost anything once and twice if they like it.

SCORPIO/TAURUS

These two are really quite similar in many ways, they share traits of being proud, stubborn and domineering and it is this mirror imaging that causes many problems within the relationship. Their differences are mostly centred around money and laziness. Taurus loves to spend cash on luxuries and can often suffer from the 'can't be bothered' syndrome, whereas Scorpio is generally very thrifty and tends to be the 'Do it now' type of workaholic. For this match to go the distance, Scorpio needs to be the leader and Taurus should enjoy being second-in-command and support the Scorpionic effort. They have the perfect blend in their sexual natures to keep the erotic fires burning for a lifetime.

SCORPIO/GEMINI

Scorpio has difficulty in accepting Gemini's continually changing flights of fancy and juggling of many projects at one time. Gemini finds it hard to understand the intense Scorpion determination in dealing with singular activities rather than the plural. There are several other notable differences, but these two have a way of intriguing each other to the point where they are prepared to iron out the problems together and settle down to a long-term union. Sexually, they both naturally have a mutual love of erotic pleasures and sensual fun. Scorpio is bound to lead from the front at first and when new ideas and fantasies need injecting, Gemini takes over. One thing is for sure, their carnal desire will never lose lustre or be less than orgasmic.

SCORPIO/CANCER

Conservative Cancer is one of Scorpio's natural partners. They are both Water signs, so have much in common and Scorpio supplies Cancer with the constant security it needs to sustain contentment within a relationship. With Cancer being fiercely loyal, the Scorpio possessiveness and jealousy should never pose a problem. The only note for concern is the Crab's ability to be extremely moody evoking the typical stubborn traits of Scorpio, and when this happens the fur could really fly. The making up will be quite spectacular and is most likely to take place beneath the sheets, because sexually they can be one of the most erotic and intense partnerships around.

SCORPIO/LEO

Although passion for life is a common denominator, there are numerous differences to be understood by these two if they are to have a successful lifelong relationship. Both signs lack patience, especially the emotional kind, so there is a strong likelihood of many confrontations. Also, both like to be in control and there is only room for one leader within this partnership. Providing Scorpio gives respect to Leo and Leo doesn't provoke the Scorpio jealousy, all could be well. Sexually, they are on par with each other, where fantasies and unusual pleasures should be forthcoming from both sides. The ongoing physical attraction and quest for success could last a lifetime.

SCORPIO/VIRGO

When these two have a war of words you would want to be within the exclusion zone, for it will be explosive to say the least. Virgo's critical nature tends to make Scorpio feel under pressure to defend its actions logically, which makes the situation worse. So, for it to work well, Virgo needs to meet Scorpio more than half way. In these circumstances Scorpio will make the necessary adjustments to ensure Virgo is happy and contented. Sexually, Scorpio will have to teach Virgo to begin with, but Virgo is sure to be a willing pupil and in time will show Scorpio that it doesn't have the monopoly regarding fantasies and the pursuit of pleasure.

SCORPIO/LIBRA

The evidence of Libra's often shallow emotions is more than likely to bring out the famed Scorpio sting in the tail, something that is not advisable. The Libran love of luxury and its lazy nature might also be a stumbling block for thrifty, hard-working Scorpio and to be honest there are many other grey areas to consider. Now this partnership can work often in the form of an on/off affair quite successfully and may stand the test of time. It will all be about compromises and Scorpio being in control. Sexually, providing Libra is wise and doesn't stray, all will be well. They have a wonderful sparky chemistry and a mutual addiction for decadently deviant thrills, so there is never room for boredom to set in.

SCORPIO/SCORPIO

Asbestos suits are necessary when these two power houses get it together. The upshot of it all, though, is that they really are too much alike with both the positive and negative side of their personalities. For this union to work, one will need to be submissive and this is where compatible rising signs might be the decider along with serious concessions from both sides. Sexually, the physical attraction is immeasurable and the intensity of their love-making could melt the ice caps in Antarctica. It's a case of erotic fantasies, deviance, perverse activities, the list goes on and on – get the picture?

SCORPIO/SAGITTARIUS

Scorpio is a homebody, whereas the Archer loves to be in the great outdoors. They do, however, have a mutual love of sport and exotic holiday travel so it is not all bad. Sagittarius will have to be totally loyal which is difficult for it and Scorpio needs to keep its jealous and possessive nature toned down by giving the Archer some freedom. Sexually, after Sagittarius has captured Scorpio's mind, Scorpio will take over and intensely passionate sex will ensue. Their sex life could turn out to be quite bizarre when the Sagittarian desires to bring others into their love play. This may intrigue rather than offend Scorpio. A potentially very strange pairing.

SCORPIO/CAPRICORN

Capricorn has sex when there is nothing better to do and for Scorpio there is never anything better to do than have sex. In fact, Capricorn can prefer masturbation because there is no pressure to please the other person and it has even been known for Capricorn to fake orgasms during self-relief if time is against it. As you can guess, this is a difficult relationship both sexually and practically. For this to go the distance, both need to meet each other halfway when compromising. So long as Scorpio is in charge and Capricorn understands this situation, then they have a reasonable chance of happiness together. Ultimately, it could be the arrival of children that binds them closer.

SCORPIO/AQUARIUS

Scorpio's main interests are mostly linked to its home and sex life, whereas Aquarius loves to be free to pursue many and varied projects, especially the creative ones that involve travel, music or art. The result is that if Aquarius can get Scorpio to be involved in its social scene and artistic enterprises, then there is hope that these two can forge a life together, especially if Aquarius is clever in letting Scorpio feel in charge. Sexually, there should never be a dull moment in or out of the bedroom and their love-making is certainly going to be inventive, especially where Aquarius is concerned. If Scorpio can hack it, the odd orgy is not totally out of the question – that will pleasure Aquarius!

SCORPIO/PISCES

Many experts say that this is the perfect match, but I am afraid it is sometimes one of the most volatile, take Richard Burton and Elizabeth Taylor for example. Although Scorpio enjoys it at first, the Piscean dependency and clinginess become more of a pressure than a pleasure. If Pisces feels 1 per cent less loved than usual or imagines injury, then it can be venomous through insecurity, which is something Scorpio can't tolerate. After all is said and done, these two may stand a good chance of a long-lasting relationship, but there must be constant communication and understanding. Sexually, Scorpio is intensely passionate and Pisces can be very imaginative and sensual, so the recipe for carnal compatibility is very good indeed.

SAGITTARIUS COMPATIBILITY

SAGITTARIUS/ARIES

These two Fire signs have an infinity with one another for they share many interests. In an affair or a long-term partnership together they seek constant adventure and crave excitement. At times, though, there are sure to be some very heated moments as their sparky natures and impatient temperaments are the cause of much friction, but fortunately any confrontations are short-lived. This couple are certain to have many outside interests and a large social circle of friends to enjoy. Sexually, their attitude is to try almost anything once and twice if they like it and their erotic endeavours won't be confined to the bedroom. Don't be too surprised if either introduces a friend to the intimate proceedings for extra pleasure.

259

SAGITTARIUS/TAURUS

The Archer won't be pleased when Taurus tries to restrict its freedom by dominance. Taurus, on the other hand, will find it hard to comprehend the typical Sagittarian low-key emotions, for Taurus is a romantic sign and Sagittarius is more interested in friendship and impulsive desires. Another huge difference is that Taurus is a home-loving person and the Archer is more concerned with events away from its dwelling. So for this union to work, both will need to meet each other halfway and Sagittarius will have to keep its philandering nature under wraps. Sexually, they should try to understand their differing needs and pander to each other's desires. One thing is for sure, their sex life together will be unconventional.

SAGITTARIUS/GEMINI

If these two are ever in one place long enough to forge a partnership it will be an amazing feat. In many ways they are very much alike, in fact almost too similar to share a life together. They balance many projects at a time, they love one-off affairs, are not overly emotional and only use a home for practical purposes. When these two get together, life will be lived in the fast lane, the relationship is sure to be action-packed and full of fun and if they can devise a plan to keep it that way, then they could spend a lifetime together. Sexually, as emotions and jealousy don't play much of a part, both will concentrate on pleasing the other in the most bizarre ways possible and with these two, anything is possible.

SAGITTARIUS/CANCER

The Sagittarian free spirit and love of the great outdoors will drive sensitive and home-loving Cancer to despair. Cancer needs security and stability just as much as it requires air and water to sustain life and Sagittarius will really only want to be Cancer's friend for it is not emotionally charged in the way that Cancer is. For this to work in the long term, major compromises are necessary and, to be honest, compatible rising signs will be a big factor in their working out their differences. Sex is the one area where they could get on well, providing Cancer feels loved and wanted. If this is the case, then Cancer could spring some erotic surprises of its own on an unsuspecting Sagittarius.

SAGITTARIUS/LEO

Leo has the right blend of emotions to help Sagittarius settle down to a relationship. They are mentally in tune and have so much in common. Their natural respect for each other makes it easy for them to become friends first, then later, after realising how much they like each other, they become lovers who are able to enjoy a long-term union, seeking out adventure and making light of life's adversities together. Sexually, they are super partners, as both love to give pleasure as well as receive it. A lifetime of erotic adventure is likely to ensue, providing Sagittarius can curb its lust for illicit encounters and Leo is prepared to take a back seat now and again.

SAGITTARIUS/VIRGO

Complex and studious Virgo is the exact opposite of free and easy Sagittarius. Virgo is a home-lover and has to run its life in an orderly, neat fashion, whereas Sagittarius has no real interest in a domestic life and loves to balance many projects in a disorganised way. If love is to conquer all, Virgo will need to curb its critical nature and meet Sagittarius more than halfway in terms of compromise. It is a very unlikely match, but in rare circumstances it has been known to work, especially if the rising signs are compatible. Sexually, Sagittarius will have to lead Virgo at first, but fortunately Virgo is a quick learner and should become quite adventurous over a period of time.

SAGITTARIUS/LIBRA

Without doubt, discerning Libra will bring out the best in Sagittarius and their relationship is likely to be a match made in heaven. They have much in common and very little reason to fight. Their partnership will be as much about being friends as well as partners in love and they are sure to have a large social circle and varied outside solo interests. Sexually, they are both prone to shallow emotions and can tolerate one-off affairs if they don't threaten to encroach on the union. Together their erotic flair for excitement knows no bounds and the odd *ménage à trois* could play a part along with many other deviant fantasies.

SAGITTARIUS/SCORPIO

Scorpio's ardent possessiveness, jealousy and dominant nature are a major dampener on the Archer's happy-go-lucky attitude to life. Scorpio is intensely passionate and loyal, whereas Sagittarius is not deeply emotional and is prone to affairs, so they really are poles apart in personalities. Now as opposites have a tendency to attract, so these two signs can work out their differences – just! It will never be a harmonious relationship and a supply of flak jackets and steel helmets is wise, but the positive sides will be exciting and adventurous. Sexually, they should be compatible and when the Scorpionic passions subside temporarily, the Archer will inject some erotic excitement of its own.

SAGITTARIUS/SAGITTARIUS

What a combination! You've heard the saying 'the left hand doesn't know what the right hand is doing', well, these two Archers will actually enjoy a relationship that works in that way. Both will be up to so many things at the same time, confusion will rule, but at least it's exciting. The only real problem for the Sagittarian match is that they can be too independent and restless to spend a lifetime together, but if their friendship and love are strong, then they could go the distance in an unconventional manner. There may be brief affairs on both sides – they can't help it, and their sex life is likely to be so adventurous that it becomes bizarre and very deviant, all in the name of sexual adventure.

SAGITTARIUS/CAPRICORN

Capricorn is likely to be offended by the blunt and frank Sagittarian tongue, especially when the cautious Goat tries to put the brakes on free-spirited Sagittarius. Capricorn is dependable and extremely cautious, whereas Sagittarius is impulsive and, at times, careless, so these two are in many ways at loggerheads with one another. To make this work both need to exert patience (a tough job) and seek compromises. Similar to the Virgoan match, it's very unlikely these two could go the distance, but it is not totally out of the question. Sexually, they can hit it off, but Capricorn may be too lazy for the Archer's liking, which sends Sagittarius off for a quick affair, just for the hell of it. They need to work very hard to enjoy great sex.

SAGITTARIUS/AQUARIUS

Together these two are set to enjoy a lifetime of adventure and excitement. Aquarius tends to keep Sagittarius's feet firmly on the ground and Sagittarius is the ideal person to help Aquarius with its creative and artistic flair. Neither are the jealous or dominant type and both are capable of the odd unintentional brief fling, which neither sign sees as a threat to the relationship. Sexually, their love-making is more fun and flirty rather than passionately emotional. It will be full of eroticism and imaginative fantasies, where the possible inclusion of a mutual friend or third party is just another sexual form of fun and games to them.

SAGITTARIUS/PISCES

Pisces is similar to Cancer in that it needs constant reassurance and stability in a relationship. Both challenges are almost impossible for Sagittarius to cope with, or supply in depth. This relationship will be more of a love/hate routine and there are sure to be many upsets and confrontations, mostly from the insecure Piscean side. If this partnership is to work, Sagittarius will have to make many sacrifices and Pisces needs to be stronger both mentally and emotionally, then it stands a good chance of going the distance. Sexually, providing Pisces can overcome the problems mentioned, the sex between these two can get quite outrageous, and in fact Pisces can use sex as a form of escapism and be very erotically deviant.

CAPRICORN COMPATIBILITY

CAPRICORN/ARIES

Thrifty Capricorn likes to conserve its hard-earned cash, whereas Aries is more frivolous in its spending. Also Aries is quite gregarious and enjoys a large circle of friends and Capricorn is more the stay at home or career type, so not much time for the social scene. The key to this relationship lasting is who will make the decisions as both want to be the boss. Can Aries keep its fiery and impatient nature harnessed? And will Capricorn abstain from its moody and stubborn outbursts? The answer? Well, it will depend on you, the individual. Sexually, Aries has a bent for erotic adventure and Capricorn adores dominant and deviant fantasies, so these two could really get into anything that brings pleasure.

267

CAPRICORN/TAURUS

A powerful blend of common ambitions and interests is offered when these two Earth signs enter into a relationship together. Both put high values on financial security, loyalty and building a stylish home together, but the downside is that they both can be very moody and stubborn, so when the fur flies it does so in style. Sexually, there is never a dull moment, as both seem to bring out the darker sexuality of each other, where decadence and deviance can play a huge part. The missionary position to the most outlandish perversion are all part of their sexual make-up, and together they may just reveal all.

CAPRICORN/GEMINI

Gemini permanently lives life in the fast lane and overtakes more opportunities than it sees. By contrast Capricorn is content in travelling at a much more cautious pace so that nothing is overlooked, especially regarding career matters. Impulsive Gemini is very excitable, adores flirting, is an expert orator and loves to hold court, whereas Capricorn is down-to-earth, faithful and prefers solitude, so these two have a lot of compromises to make if they are to spend a lifetime together. Sexually, they are chalk and cheese, so one has to bow to the other, and probably Capricorn will give way because it is the easiest option and requires less effort.

CAPRICORN/CANCER

Shy, moody and sensitive Cancer will have difficulty in understanding Capricorn for in many ways they are complete opposites. Capricorn can be mean with its emotions and spends more time on its career, which leaves Cancer feeling lonely and dejected. If the two can meet halfway and Cancer can be more independent and emotionally strong, then this partnership could stand the test of time – it's a long shot but it is possible. Sexually, Capricorn will enjoy teaching Cancer and the Crab is a willing pupil. Given time and if Cancer feels secure, then the roles will be reversed, because Cancer can be one of the most sensual signs of the zodiac when in the right relationship.

CAPRICORN/LEO

The Jungle Lion and the Mountain Goat doesn't sound very promising, does it? To all intents and purposes it isn't. They are poles apart in almost every area, Capricorn is generally unemotional, unimaginative, plodding, moody, stubborn and at times lazy. Leo can be proud, arrogant, emotional, imaginative and gregarious, so as you can see, these two will have a hard time in forming a relationship and I suspect it will be compatible rising signs that help this unusual partnership become a long-term one. Sexually, Leo needs Capricorn to be more demonstrative with affection during their love-making and Capricorn has deeper deviant sexual tastes that don't tickle Leo's fancy. This is another area they both need to discuss to make it work.

CAPRICORN/VIRGO

These two can be in their element by just making money together for their career is the main focus of their life. Both are very similar in as much as they are well organised, dependable, conservative and have a great understanding of what each other needs. Neither is the jealous type unless really provoked and their negative sides of being overly critical and moody are not likely to surface that often because they are pretty much in tune with each other. Sex for them is not the be-all. They tend to have lesser sex drives, so quality is more important than quantity. Given time though, they can be as risqué and deviant as the rest of the zodiac signs.

CAPRICORN/LIBRA

Libra tends to captivate Capricorn at first, but after a short time Libra finds Capricorn's moody and stubborn nature too stifling for its liking. Capricorn, for its part, sees Libra as being self-centred and possessing shallow emotions and could seek an affair to reaffirm its confidence. Libra will do likewise, so turning a blind eye could be the key to saving the partnership. These two really need to work hard in keeping their relationship afloat and it requires a deep understanding from both sides to spend a lifetime together. Sexually, once the initial magnetic chemistry evaporates and both have exhausted their sexual repertoires, they will either have more serious affairs or will look for new ways of making sex exciting again.

CAPRICORN/SCORPIO

One of the few signs that really understands Capricorn is Scorpio, especially concerning the Goat's attitude towards career and financial goals. In this relationship, Scorpio is destined to be the dominant partner, even though Capricorn is strong-willed. There will be times when the Capricorn moodiness and stubborn nature arouse the famed Scorpio temper, but rows are short-lived and quickly forgotten, leaving this partnership truly to stand the test of time. Sexually, Scorpio is immensely passionate and Capricorn strives to be. With their imaginative and often deviant sexual chemistry they could scorch the space shuttle heat shield – get the picture?

CAPRICORN/SAGITTARIUS

Stay-at-home Capricorn finds little in common with fancy-free Sagittarius. Capricorn is conservative, frugal with money and has a cautious outlook on all matters. In contrast, Sagittarius shirks responsibility, is extravagant and will always gamble on the short odds. For these two to have a durable and successful relationship both will need to change their ways dramatically and, of course, have compatible rising signs. Sexually, Sagittarius is a Martini person, any time anywhere, whereas Capricorn chooses the time and place carefully. Despite this, Capricorn is intrigued by the Archer's adventurous sexuality and they are likely to explore all forms of fantasies from the extreme to the bizarre.

CAPRICORN/CAPRICORN

When a war of words is sparked between these two it could be weeks before they communicate again, as their natural moody and stubborn natures leave them saying 'it is his or her fault, so he or she can apologise'. The truth is that they are almost too alike to make a go of it, but stranger things have happened and they can settle down together and enjoy a long, happy yet sedate relationship. Sexually, it will be sex, sex, sex all the way for the first six months, but as the initial chemistry wears off they become stuck for innovative and imaginative ideas. This is when their natural flair for deviance should be allowed to surface and sex can then become more experimental.

CAPRICORN/AQUARIUS

Aquarius will really want to be Capricorn's friend and this will be confusing for the poor Mountain Goat, because there is a strong initial attraction. Aquarius is an unconventional free spirit who needs solitude from time to time and home-loving Capricorn is orthodox to say the least and is more into companionship. Although there are many differences, they can forge a strong union that could last a lifetime. It is Capricorn who needs to accommodate Aquarius, not the other way round if this relationship is to last, but in the long run the Goat will be glad it did. Sexually, once Capricorn gets used to the Aquarian erotic outlandishness between the sheets and sheds its staid views anything can happen and with Aquarius it normally does.

CAPRICORN/PISCES

Although these two are very different, they do actually get on very well. The Piscean trait of continually seeking reassurance bolsters Capricorn's ego, for it can be the dominant partner without too much of a fight. They also appeal to each other's emotional requirements, which tones down their respective negative sides, creating harmony and peace within the relationship. There should be nothing to stop both signs attaining old age together unless Pisces feel threatened or unloved. Sexually, Capricorn leads and the willing Pisces follows. When Capricorn runs out of ideas Pisces takes over and can be even more raunchy than Capricorn as Pisces loves escapism through sex and other stimulants.

AQUARIUS COMPATIBILITY

AQUARIUS/ARIES

The only area where there could be problems within this relationship is if one tries to dominate the other outside of the bedroom or even in their sexual playground. These two really do have many things in common. Aries will help Aquarius put its creative thinking into operation and Aquarius tones down the Arien impatient fiery nature. It goes without saying that this partnership could easily turn into a life-long union. Sexually, both are erotically inventive and adore all forms of sex. Aries tends to be the forceful one, but Aquarius stretches the imaginative Arien mind and introduces fantasies that could include friends or bizarre gadgets. Wow!

AQUARIUS/TAURUS

Aquarius wants to be the Bull's best friend, but Taurus wants a lover and mate. Both tend to travel on parallel lines and never really understand the other's needs. Home-loving Taurus is put out by the Waterbearer's frenetic pursuit of outside activities, which leads to confrontations and brings out the stubborn Taurean nature. For this union to work both signs have to meet each other halfway and harness their negative traits, then the relationship stands a good chance of going the distance. Sexually, once Taurus understands the unusual Aquarian views on eroticism they can make some wonderful sexual music together in which the song never remains the same.

AQUARIUS/GEMINI

What a great team, both have strengths where the other has weaknesses, so naturally complement each other. They have no real use of a home as they are out and about all the time pursuing their many varied interests and career projects. Aquarius stabilises the Geminian twin personalities and Gemini supports the Waterbearer's innovative ideas by putting them into action. Not much can go wrong with this relationship, even the odd indiscretion by either shouldn't pose a problem to the long-term security, as they see it as par for the course in the need for variety. Sexually, Aquarius dominates Gemini much to the Twin's pleasure. There is almost nothing these two won't stop at to reap erotic and sensual pleasures.

AQUARIUS/CANCER

Clinging Cancer is too sensitive and insecure for Aquarius and the Waterbearer's continual search for adventure outside of the home brings out moody resentment from Cancer who feels unloved and unwanted. For this match to work, Aquarius has to supply Cancer with continual affection, warmth and reassurance and Cancer in return should offer Aquarius space and freedom for its creative thinking. This way it can work in the long term but will depend on the individuals. Sexually, Cancer is very passionate and Aquarius has more of a casual attitude. Once the Crab sees the future is secure, then it will view things Aquarius's way and will leave Aquarius breathless with its no-holds-barred eroticism.

AQUARIUS/LEO

Leo is more interested in the physical side of the relationship, whereas Aquarius adores mental stimulation and intellect. Aquarius won't bow to Leo and resents being dominated, so these independent signs have difficulty from the start. Now, providing Leo makes allowances for the creative Aquarian personality and Aquarius panders to Leo's regal make-up, with their many shared outdoor interests they could forge a permanent union. It might be unconventional, but it works well. Sexually, both are demonstrative in differing ways, the unique, erotic, Aquarian fantasies combined with Leo's passion should make for an innovative and compelling sex life.

AQUARIUS/VIRGO

Virgo's overly critical nature is brought out in style as Aquarius exercises its need for stimulation and variety from life. Intellectually they are on par with each other and a relationship formed on this basis could work very well and be durable. Otherwise there are too many differences in their personality profiles to find common ground. Sexually, neither is too passionate and contrary to popular belief Virgo can excel in the bedroom providing Aquarius is patient and takes things one step at a time, giving Virgo a chance to understand what is required and that there is more to sex than the missionary position. After that it could be Virgo springing erotic surprises on Aquarius.

AQUARIUS/LIBRA

The Aquarian friendly disposition warms Libra's heart and lower regions and from the first meeting there's likely to be a very strong attraction, both physical and mental. Both signs adore the arts and are creatively imaginative. Neither is jealous and can overlook the odd one-off affair and these two signs appreciate luxury and spending money for the pleasure it brings. As you've probably guessed, the Aquarian and Libran relationship is as good as it can get and should last a lifetime. Sexually, it is theatricals, way out fantasies and erotic sensitivity and that's just the first night! These two could progress onto the bizarre, such as orgies and partner swapping all in the name of variety and pursuit of erotic pleasures.

AQUARIUS/SCORPIO

Possessive and jealous Scorpio will not tolerate the Aquarian free and easy attitude towards sex and infidelity, all hell will break loose. Scorpio is dominant and aggressive and this drives easy-going Aquarius into the arms of a friend. The upshot is that they are poles apart and have very little in the way of common ground. However, opposites can attract and Scorpio, if really in love, can be the chameleon of the zodiac and adopt Aquarius's principles thus giving the relationship a good chance of survival. Sexually, Scorpio will need to tone down its intense passion, but will enjoy the Aquarian creative and erotic imagination and from there it is steamy unconventional sexual fun and plenty of it.

AQUARIUS/SAGITTARIUS

This vibrant and outgoing pair could be one of those matches made in heaven for they are similar in almost every way. They love a wide and varied social scene and have numerous friends who are very important to them. The only blot on the landscape is that both can be brutally frank, so their rare quarrels will be a huge battle of words. Neither is jealous so will not worry if the other has a brief fling. In fact these two are not overly emotional and could well invite friends or even strangers to share some of their erotic fantasies. Sexually, a wonderful mix of spontaneity along with elaborate lengthy and imaginative fantasies are typical of them both, and when one is lost for ideas the other steps in and takes over.

AQUARIUS/CAPRICORN

Cautious and conservative Capricorn is not an ideal match for free-spirited Aquarius and they have very little in common. Aquarius would rather be Capricorn's friend first, lover second and to be honest that's the best chance this relationship has of surviving. If Capricorn can cope with this arrangement, then all will be fine. It gives Aquarius the space it needs to be creative and pursue its arty projects. It in turn will allow Capricorn to spend as much time as necessary in achieving its career ambitions. A partnership of this nature also helps keep both signs' disruptive and negative traits firmly under control. Sexually, they can get on for both adore sex for the pleasure it brings and for them variety is the spice of life and spicy it will be.

AQUARIUS/AQUARIUS

This is probably the best mix of the same two elements. Whereas the other signs that mirror image each other find it difficult when the going gets tough, these two are too sensible and rational to be affected. Jealousy plays no part in this relationship and both turn a blind eye to any indiscretions. In fact the other may want to join in for the hell of it. Obviously this partnership is set to be harmonious and last a lifetime. Sexually, never a dull moment, both are incredibly inventive and stimulate each other mentally and physically – the perfect blend for a sexual union. No stone is left unturned in their pursuit of ever-increasing erotic pleasures.

AQUARIUS/PISCES

An emotional tug of war will take place with Pisces doing most of the tugging. Aquarius finds it hard to cope with the draining effect clinging Pisces creates in wanting continual reassurances of love. Aquarius needs space and freedom like it needs air and water, but Pisces won't understand and is likely to enter into a long-term illicit affair. Compatible rising signs are necessary here and Pisces has to be stronger both emotionally and mentally, and only then will this relationship stand a good chance. Sexually, both are sensitive, but Aquarius needs to stick to the basics until Pisces gains confidence. After that Pisces can be very decadent and use deviance as escapism, as it can also do with alcohol.

PISCES COMPATIBILITY

PISCES/ARIES

Pisces takes heart from Aries being the dominant partner and will gain the security it needs to sustain love. Aries sees Pisces as a sensitive, caring person, but can become impatient with the way Pisces seeks reassurance all of the time, and it can be emotionally draining. For this relationship to go the distance, Pisces has to be more in command of its emotions and be stronger willed. Aries, for its part, needs to keep its fiery and blunt nature under wraps and have a better understanding of the Piscean personality. Sexually, Aries leads the way and Pisces follows willingly at first and if Pisces feels truly loved its erotic potential will become unlocked and a passionate, sensual sex life will ensue.

PISCES/TAURUS

Providing Taurus isn't negligent of the typical Piscean emotions by being down to earth and matter of fact and if Pisces can be more confident within the relationship, this alliance of love could last a lifetime. They have many common interests, such as building a home, rearing children, enjoying food and drink and of course, passion. Sexually, both are equal and adore sensuality. Taurus will lead from the front, but Pisces is quick to play a more dominant part too, especially if Pisces is confident the relationship is heading for the long term. In fact, Pisces can become quite decadent and deviant once the initial Taurean sexual repertoire has been depleted.

PISCES/GEMINI

Pisces feels uncomfortable with Gemini because Gemini is too changeable in its make-up. A complex personality such as Gemini has difficulty in accepting Pisces' lack of confidence and need for constant reassurance, for Gemini has more important projects to hand than having to sort out its partner's emotions. Another cruel reality is that Gemini can be very thoughtless and Pisces is often self-centred, so for this union to stand the test of time, both have to make an enormous effort to understand what makes the other tick and make allowances. Sexually, Gemini intrigues Pisces at first, but Pisces needs more and has to be quite dominant and sexually enterprising in keeping Gemini happy and content.

PISCES/CANCER

These two are so busy trying to seek mutual reassurance that before they know it, they are hooked and dependent on each other. Both are very sensitive, caring and ultra-emotional, so in reality they are compatible in every way. Providing these Water signs don't drown in their insecurities when arguments occur, all will be well and a long and happy relationship could be enjoyed by both signs. Sexually, Cancer is quite demanding and Pisces revels in that, but in time they become equal in sharing the lead and fresh activities are brought by each in to the bedroom. If problems do occur, one needs to accept the role of decision-maker.

PISCES/LEO

Leo is offended by the Piscean drain on its emotions, Leo's standpoint is; 'If I say I love you, then I mean it.' Being asked continually to prove devotion makes Leo shy away, probably into another's arms. These two have a real difficulty in coming to terms with the other's complex personality, so there is a need for compatible rising signs if they are to stand a chance of making it into old age together. Sexually, Leo rules the bedroom and Pisces enjoys playing the subservient subject. Providing Pisces panders to the royal Leo ego, a great sex life can be born. Given time, Leo will lay back purring while Pisces perfects its passionate skills.

PISCES/VIRGO

Pisces tends to act on impulse, whereas Virgo plans thing meticulously and is logically practical. Pisces wears its emotions on its sleeves and Virgo is a dark horse who rarely shows weakness or sensitivity. As you can imagine, these two are poles apart in almost every way. Virgo, though, is good at helping lost causes and might just see Pisces as one to take on. If this is the case, then there is a chance that a relationship could work, especially if Pisces can identify with Virgo's reserved conservative nature and be more emotionally sound itself. Sexually, Pisces has to be the dominant partner at first as Virgo seeks confidence in its erotic prowess, but after that they become settled into a more basic routine.

PISCES/LIBRA

Although both are extravagant with money, neither have the real impetus to secure the necessary income. Libra's shallow emotions tend to have Pisces diving into its personal murky pool, not really knowing what to do. By this time Libra has found someone else. To all intents and purposes they don't stand a chance of even having a successful fling together, but stranger things have happened and if the rising signs are compatible, there is always a chance, even if a remote one. Sexually, they do have a big physical attraction which may help to bolster the relationship further. Pisces needs to be very creative to capture Libra's love of sexual theatricals and Libra should be more demonstrative and affectionate.

PISCES/SCORPIO

Providing Pisces doesn't provoke Scorpio's jealous and possessive nature, or spend the Scorpion's cash unwisely, then these two should go on to have a very contented life together. Scorpio provides all the security Pisces constantly requires and Pisces gains confidence in Scorpio's fiercely protective ways, so much so that Pisces feels it has met a match made in heaven – and it has. Sexually, Scorpio is the dominant one and Pisces loves to be taken and amorously abused. In time though, Pisces can spring a few erotic surprises of its own, especially with fantasies that revolve around escapism through deviance and often sadism.

PISCES/SAGITTARIUS

Independent and adventurous Sagittarius has no time for cautious and overly sensitive Pisces unless Pisces wants only to be the Archer's friend. If Pisces can survive in a relationship based this way then all will be well. Restless Sagittarius can't understand why Pisces is always tugging at its heart strings in search of reassurance and Pisces fails to see why the Archer isn't more free with its affections, so never the twain do meet. In other words, serious compromises, compatible rising signs and a small miracle are needed for long-term romance. Sexually, great at first, but Sagittarius needs to express itself fully and unless Pisces can cope, sex goes downhill from there.

PISCES/CAPRICORN

These two need each other in the same way a fish needs water. Pisces brings romance into Capricorn's practical orderly life and Capricorn, in being dominant and protective, gives Pisces the reassurance and stability it requires to be happy and contented. The negative disruptive traits of these compatible signs tend to stay under the surface, so that arguments are few and far between and when they occur they are over and forgotten about quickly. Sexually, Capricorn knows how to make Pisces feel sexy and desirable and is the dominant sexual partner. However, Pisces can become extremely responsive and teach Capricorn a trick or two.

PISCES/AQUARIUS

Independent Aquarius wonders what all the fuss is about when it asks for space to pursue its many creative solo projects. Pisces also can't turn a blind eye to the Waterbearer's occasional indiscretions. Pisces won't get much in the way of reassurance and equally could be forced into an affair because it feels abandoned and unloved. Both will need to be not that typical of their zodiac signs to make this relationship work; it has been known, but is a rarity by any stretch of the imagination. Sexually, they can really stimulate each other and if the partnership does find common ground, their sex life together can become very unusual to the point of deviance, danger and decadence. This appeals to the Pisces escapist fantasies.

PISCES/PISCES

Both will put a huge drain on the other's emotional resources and with neither being the dominant type this relationship could end up like a ship without a rudder. Having said that, if they can stabilise their alliance by constantly praising each other, they have so many things in common that it could end up the best match in the zodiac. Sexually, their mutual understanding of their intimate needs soon gets their sex life off the ground sensually and sensitively. As time goes by, they can become engrossed and intrigued by behaviour that includes most forms of depravity. It's a case of try it once and twice if we like it and we'll take some drugs and alcohol for good measure.

SEXTROLOGY QUIZ 3

Question: Can you tell how typical someone is of their star sign by what they like to do in bed?

Answer: Not always, but you'll have a lot of fun finding out. Especially if you do not take it too seriously.

Try this quiz for size on your partner.

1. **GEMINI**
    Does your lover enjoy trying out new and outrageous positions with you?

    (a) Yes but he/she has delusions of grandeur and you both end up in a heap on the floor.
    (b) Absolutely not. In fact suggesting anything other than the missionary position is likely to result in tears.
    (c) Yes, but sometimes you are in two minds about it.

2. **LEO**
    How does your partner react after a climax?

    (a) Immediately gets off you, rolls over and falls sound asleep.
    (b) Goes to the bedroom window, looks up at the moon and makes wolf noises.
    (c) Neither of the above.

3. **SCORPIO**
    How experimental is your partner?

(a) There are no limits as long as both partners are willing.

(b) 'Experimental? You mean there's more than one way to do this?'

(c) Some interest, but your partner would prefer to wait for a more appropriate moment, like a long way in the future.

4. ARIES
    Does your partner wake up full of beans and ready for sex?

    (a) It's hard enough waking up in the morning without the pressure of needing to perform.

    (b) Sex in the morning is great but does it have to be today?

    (c) No.

5. TAURUS
    Sexual technique, does your partner have any?

    (a) No.

    (b) Think of a jackhammer. Things look pretty good until it runs out of juice.

    (c) He/she is the most wonderful sexual athlete.

6. CAPRICORN
    How would your partner react to your suggestion of a 'quickie' just before going out?

    (a) You must be mad. The taxi will be here any minute.

    (b) Is that all you can think about?

(c) OK . . . the taxi can wait.

7. **AQUARIUS**
Your partner suggests that a spot of wife swap-ping might spice up your sex life. How would you react?

(a) He/she must be joking.
(b) Say you're all for it knowing your partner does not have the bottle to go through with it.
(c) Tentatively agree and hope that the suggestion will die a natural death.

8. **LIBRA**
Your partner accuses you of 'faking it'. What would you say?

(a) Subtly make the point that it is quality not quantity that counts.
(b) Deny it.
(c) Ignore the accusation and launch a counter-attack.

9. **PISCES**
It's Sunday morning. No work. No kids. No clean-ing. So what do you do? Your partner suggests some nookie. Do you . . .

(a) Readily agree?
(b) Agree on the condition that afterwards you get breakfast in bed?
(c) Agree on the condition that afterwards you both go to church?

10. CANCER
In the throes of passion you call your lover by the name of a previous partner. How does your current partner react?

(a) Does he/she remind you of the story of Lorena Bobbitt and the consequences thereof?
(b) Immediately go into a deep and undignified sulk?
(c) Suggest that the previous partner pops round for tea and crumpets?

11. SAGITTARIUS
You indicate that it might be interesting if your lover were to dress up in your clothing.

(a) Your partner is all for it (anything for a laugh).
(b) Your partner is lukewarm about the idea but not totally dismissive.
(c) He/she agrees, but only if there is a cuddle in it.

12. VIRGO
In a lighter moment you suggest that you must purchase a chastity belt for your Virgoan partner. What is her reaction?

(a) Shock! Horror!
(b) A suggestion of an uncanny resemblance to a pig of questionable parentage.
(c) Immediate agreement, with the proviso that you must wear the male equivalent.

SEXTROLOGY QUIZ 4

1. Not all charts made by astrologers are personality/
    birth chart. Can you name another from the
    options below?

    (a) Missionary.
    (b) Horary.
    (c) Visionary.

2. If you correctly guessed what an aspect was in a
    previous quiz you probably know what its
    significance is. If so, read on. A beneficial aspect
    is:

    (a) Optimism.
    (b) A square.
    (c) A trine.

3. A well-known personality trait of a Scorpio is:

    (a) A distinct lack of libido.
    (b) A wishy-washy outlook on life.
    (c) A search for control over one's destiny.

4. Capricorns are most likely to be found:

    (a) In the army.
    (b) In a bank.
    (c) Working as a foreign aid worker.

5. The planet Jupiter is:

(a) The planet that is fourth placed from the Sun (distance wise).

(b) Known in astrology as a fortunate planet.

(c) The name of a well-known cartoon character.

6. A New Moon is a good day to:

(a) Retreat and retrench.

(b) Make new resolutions (i.e., give up smoking).

(c) Do nothing.

7. When Saturn is in transit through your chart, you should:

(a) Ignore it.

(b) Panic.

(c) Accept it is not particularly propitious, but, forewarned is forearmed.

8. If an old flame re-enters your life, it is most likely that:

(a) Venus is in retrograde.

(b) Pluto is in Cancer.

(c) You can't believe your luck.

9. When Mars is in Leo, this is generally:

(a) Negative.

(b) Positive.

(c) Neutral.

10. When the Moon is close to the ascendant at birth, the subject's early experiences are likely to be:

    (a) Of particular significance in shaping adult behaviour.
    (b) Of no significance whatsoever.
    (c) Of minor significance.

The Complete Year Ahead

ARIES 1995

As 1995 dawns we start your year with Uranus and Neptune moving into Capricorn. This planetary action will be a long-term transition lasting until 1997, but the influences will be periodical. With it will come much confusion in your love life as your relationships will go through periods of change and uncertainty. You may be forgiven for thinking that this is all bad news, Aries, but I am pleased to say it isn't. You are a sign that thrives on challenges and with that, changes are inevitable. Some will be for the better and some for the worse, it will all depend on how you react to the varying situations.

The best way to ease into the New Year is to stay away from emotional issues until the middle of January and allow time for creative Pluto and fortunate Jupiter to enter Sagittarius. To be honest, this is when your romantic fortunes will start to take shape in earnest; rampant Ariens will really be able to get a grip on affairs of the heart and determine how the rest of the year will flow. The decisions you make during mid-January concerning your partner must be upheld no matter how tempting the diversions may be. Gut feelings and your famed intuition will be marred by the presence of Uranus and Neptune, so base your thinking more on logic, rather than emotional inclinations.

A celestial movement on 14 January could change the course of the year because love planet Venus will move into conjunction with Pluto bringing a new dimension into your romantic picture. You will have a strong attraction to someone you come into contact with on the 16th which makes your love and social life very torrid and turbulent. The Full Moon in Cancer with Uranus, again on the 16th, could make you realise that a certain person or situation is no longer necessary to your life, so you may end a relationship that has declined and died. If this becomes true for you, then make sure you don't get caught on the rebound. Remember, Uranus and Neptune will be confusing your highly charged emotions, so even if a new suitor is ready, willing and available – give yourself breathing space.

From 23 January, impulsive Mars will re-enter Leo giving your energy banks a boost and your confidence will be at its peak. This planetary movement will have a profound effect on your skills of tact and understanding, which will enable you to get the results you want without facing any confrontations head-on which is more your usual style. Don't be surprised if your sex life sees you taking on a more authoritative role than usual (if that's possible) and fantasies of the 'Just do as you're told!' type will be more prevalent, so keep your handcuffs handy!

With the onset of February, Saturn will enter Pisces around the 10th and will stay there until the 28th. This will be a somewhat restrictive period for Ariens; travel plans that were made for Valentine's Day will be re-shuffled due to unforeseen events, so it would be wise to stay closer to home. If you and your loved one live apart from each other, then let him or her do the journeying, as there will be less chance of your naughty arrangements going wrong. A word of warning for the last quarter of February – a person you think is a trusted friend could shockingly turn out to be a wolf in sheep's clothing, so keep an eye on anyone behaving out of character and don't take a lover for granted. This rival has sexual designs on your mate and if you don't heed this advice you could find out when it is too late.

Just as the March weather is unpredictable, unfortunately your love life will be the same. The love planet Venus will be in conjunction with both of the emotional planets, Uranus and Neptune. This will be a rather negative phase when romance will be neglected, especially by you, Aries. Certain events up to 20 March will be very confusing for you and in consequence, these feelings of uncertainty will keep your normally active hormones hidden under a blanket of stress. Be careful not to vent your famed fieriness on your loved one around the 13th, as he or she might read into these outbursts a message that you no longer care, or that you have found a new lover. Either way it could lead to a permanent breakdown of your relationship.

Once you reach 21 March, the life-giving Sun will enter your own sign of Aries and to make the picture even brighter, there will be a New Moon also in Aries. All the negativity from early March will disappear as quickly as it arrived in your life. For the next ten days you will feel energised and your sex drive will be very much on the up, much to the pleasure of all concerned.

The early part of April will be affected by the Sun's relationship with Mars. This is a great combination to aid your pursuit of someone whom you've had your eye on for some time. If you are working on a joint venture, you may find that you are thrown together in a creative sideline and this will have much success. Inevitably with your minds in tune, it is only a matter of very little time before bodies follow suit. You are likely to share in a spontaneous burst of lust anytime from 23 April until 17 May when Venus in Aries will enhance all aspects of passionate spontaneity.

The middle of May until 21 July will run along quite nicely – new relationships will bond well and existing long-term unions will be more relaxing, so expect to get fit with lots of horizontal jogging. Also expect a fantasy of yours involving the open air to be fulfilled. Your summer holiday could be the time, so let your hair down – your audience awaits! Speaking of vacations, try to ensure that you take them before 21 July, or after 8 September, for in the intervening period, Mars will be in Libra, which will cause you to feel under extreme physical pressure and this in turn will cause a lot of conflict in your relationship. If you can keep your love life on an even keel until 17 September, Venus will oust Mars and move into Libra restoring the balance of harmony once again. In fact this is a very positive period for all Arien lovers and a phase when you could rekindle a union that has long passed its sell-by date. Surprisingly, you will be glad that you gave it a second chance, as affairs will be plain sailing until the middle of November.

The final phase of the year will be helped along by Mars and Pluto in Sagittarius. This will be quite an energetic time for you, Aries, when you are likely to involve yourself in some unusual sexual practices due to the strong urge to explore and experiment which is a typical by-product of this planetary line up. You know what you want and how you want it, so go for it, Aries, your most deviant desires could come true.

Finally, on to Christmas, this will be a reassuring and fulfilling period all round with you rediscovering the joys of family life. I should just add that December is a fertile month for female Rams, so if you don't want the permanent pleasures of life with little ones, don't linger under the mistletoe for too long!

TAURUS 1995

Your romantic year will get off the ground almost as soon as the last verse of 'Auld Lang Syne' has drifted away for another year. New Year's Day will see a New Moon in Capricorn and although this is generally associated with productivity in business affairs, in this instance it will also be very helpful to your amorous aspirations. You will feel an inner strength which will provide the confidence needed to make important decisions regarding the direction of your love life for 1995. Watch out for 7 January when Venus, the planet of love and also your ruler, is in conjunction with obsessional Pluto. To add to this, both planets will be in smouldering Scorpio, so it shouldn't come as a shock when I tell you that it will be a time of sexual impulsiveness. Your erotic magnetism is likely to bring out the green-eyed monster in the people you associate with, for they will resent you being the centre of attention. Affairs that stem from lust are on the cards during this period and Bulls would do well to think before hankering for increasingly greener grass.

As of 23 January you will go through an awkward period as disruptive Mars enters proud Leo. This is likely to affect you until early April, so for the following two months you will need to put your brain in gear before operating your vocal chords. All relationships will be somewhat fraught, whether they be work-, family- or romance-orientated. The daily grind of life's frustrations will lead to many an argument and whatever you try will be seemingly met by resistance from those around you. Don't be too surprised if by the middle of Spring, some of you Taureans will have decided to sample singledom again.

However, 2 April sees emotional Uranus moving into eccentric Aquarius which will bring all sorts of volatile influences to the forefront. More than a fair share of mental stress and pressure will plague you, but happily there will also be some thrilling developments causing some alterations for the better. In fact if you understand the necessity for changes, you will benefit more from them. New relationships are starred to be very harmonious and long-lasting as are Spring marriages.

When the life-giving Sun enters Taurus on 20 April you will find that for the next thirty days or so you feel much stronger and confident in all you do. A sense of security will be another powerful confidence-booster for you to enjoy. You are not necessarily prone to feelings of insecurity, but you do need to feel loved and wanted along with the rest of us and this reassurance you crave will be available in abundance.

A bevy of contrasting lunar movements from 21

May involving the Sun, Pluto and Mars will cause some power struggles and conflict mostly in your working life, and if you are involved romantically with someone from your business environment, then the path of true love will become temporarily rocky. Around early June, try not to let your famed stubbornness spoil what has been and will be a good thing, or a little misunderstanding will turn into a full-blown confrontation which may take a long time to resolve. Remember you only have to wait until 11 June when Venus enters in Taurus, for feelings of good-will towards others to prevail and the previous strife and turmoil will give way to affection and tranquillity. All Taureans will feel both inwardly and outwardly attractive. In fact you will be a veritable honey pot to members of the opposite sex so if you are looking for a new mate, this period of your year could be very productive; an early summer holiday might not be a bad move.

What will be an added bonus is that from 26 May until 21 July, Mars will occupy Virgo. During these weeks your work will tend to preoccupy a lot of your previously spare time and bring extra funds into the kitty. The even better news is that you will feel incredibly energised throughout these two months and whatever you turn your hand to will give the rewards you deserve and inevitably your sex drive will be spurred on by the success you create for yourself. The only word of warning I would offer here is if you have booked a holiday between the end of May and 21 July; you may well find the distraction of your commitments back home jeopardising the romantic escapism you desire when away with your loved one. Do fight your Taurean tendency to take your work on holiday with you and endeavour to treat yourself and your mate to the rest you need.

If holidaying between the 21 May and 20 August, you can expect your sex drive to move up a gear and the added influences of the sun, sand, sea and surf could lead you into exploring some risqué territory with your partner. Or if you are single, then a torrid holiday romance could make your past sexual encounters seem like child's play. The outcome of this potentially hormone-busting vacation could bring the sound of little hoofs in May 1996, so if you don't want to increase your herd, then take the appropriate precautions or learn the local lingo for 'No'.

From 21 to 24 August some very challenging situations will be revealed. Most relationships will see an upheaval dispelling the usual harmony. You may want your partnership to move in a certain direction that you see as being better, but your loved one is likely to have different ideas, so unfortunately power struggles are very high on the agenda. This will be a particularly difficult time, not helped by a distractingly attractive stranger arriving on the scene and distorting the picture further. Don't forget, when true love doesn't run smoothly for Bulls, there's a slight chance of being led by the nose into an affair and in this case it will be lust rather than logic calling the shots. Be warned! Be wise! And above all be thankful that there will only be a few days of temptation for you to tussle with.

Once that tricky period is out of the way and the Sun and Venus both enter Virgo on 24 August, you will find that peace and quiet once again prevail within your life. During the next couple of weeks you will pretty much be able to get your own way with your existing soulmate or a new lover and the way to do this is to turn on your famed charm. From the middle of September to 20 October, your relationship could be put under threat by the influences of Mars and Pluto both being in Scorpio. Jealousy will be the cause when an outsider appears to be making a play for either you or your mate, and either way keep a close eye on this person's intentions.

As late October arrives, the Sun and Venus take up residence in sexy Scorpio and your union of love will become strengthened and many a Taurean can expect a steamy period of sensual awareness. Be prepared for some very out of the ordinary eroticism when your wildest fantasies stand more than a chance of being fulfilled, especially around 3 November when your passion will be at a peak.

For December, the transition of the Sun, Mercury, Venus, Mars, Uranus and Neptune all in Capricorn makes this festive Month one to remember with many loose ends suddenly coming together and providing explanations for some of the year's puzzles. There is nothing to mar your Christmas and New Year celebrations – not even the most wayward work's party or interfering in-law. You will definitely be making love and not war as that familiar old chorus strikes up again to toast the beginning of another year, but what about after that? . . . Well, that's another story!

GEMINI 1995

You Gemini, it's true, have many assets – you are
charismatic, charming and cultured and have the gift of
the gab, but these attributes do not necessarily make
you the easiest of zodiac signs to live with. 1995,
however, throws a lifeline to your long-suffering mate
or any potential new partner. Opportune Jupiter and
creative Pluto occupy Sagittarius all year and provide a
great array of stabilising influences to assist in each and
every partnership. A major key to fulfilment in 1995 is
in learning to grow within your relationships, perhaps
with help from someone else who is close to you and
who has been a supportive shoulder to cry on through
last year's ups and downs. In other words, take advice
and learn from your mistakes.

From as early as 7 January, the planetary trends will
start to create strong romantic influences, for example,
the love planet Venus is in conjunction with expansive

and opportune Jupiter. This delightful celestial two-some will help you to be luckier in love and for the following two weeks life with your loved one should be the best it's been for some time. Financial affairs are equally well starred and if you are involved in a business venture with your other half, then expect there to be good dividends which have a knock-on effect in the bedroom. One word of warning, though; don't take gambles with your relationship or your premises no matter how tempting the alternatives seem to be, either way you could come very unstuck.

As good and bad fortunes seem to travel in cycles, so will your year and between 2 and 15 February, when Mercury is retrograde in Aquarius, comes a time when communications feel somewhat strained through silly misunderstandings on both sides. Don't expect Valentine's Day to be special unless you and your loved one make a real effort to see the other's perspective. The problem may well be that you both are involved in many external activities and not allowing enough time to be supportive of each other's needs, so inevitably either one or both of you could feel a touch used and abused.

Once past 15 February, life will gradually pick up, pressures will ease and with Saturn in Pisces, emotional stability will once again return. An honest heart to heart on the 17th will be revealing, yet enlightening. The only real hurdle you will have to endure at this time is a formal family get-together, something you Geminians try to avoid like the plague unless, of course, you get the chance to hold court. One close relative in particular is hell-bent on making life difficult for you and you may have a sneaky suspicion as to who this is. Subtle diplomacy will triumph in this instance and this is a skill you should work on, for it will stand you in good stead for many of the year's confrontations.

With March under way you will need to keep a close watch on your hormones, because obsessional Pluto in Sagittarius is likely to cause a spur of the moment attraction – the real danger zone is to be found around the third quarter of this month and the risk is increased if you are planning a trip away for this period. You are not normally averse to the odd affair, but usually it is for better reasons than mere lust. Do carefully consider the consequences of reckless action as there may be more strings attached to this illicit romp than meets the eye. The other aspect of this lunar transition is that, given time, your regular sexual relationship is destined to change for the better.

From early April until the 22nd, a series of sexual power plays between you and your partner are, if you let them, going to reveal some critical psychological blocks that have in the past kept your erotic ambitions in the closet, but some very frank talking about what you both want from sex will pave the way to conjuring up some new and exciting fantasies together; even more reason not to succumb to outside temptations.

June provides profitable spin-offs from April and there are two bonuses for you to enjoy. Firstly, Uranus in Aquarius will send influences that suit you down to the ground. Through April's frankness, your partnership will become more liberated and understanding. Together you both will take on a free-spirited view and any practices you previously saw as comfortable are now likely to be deemed as old-fashioned and inhibited. Second, until nearly the end of June, the life-giving Sun will be in your own sign of Gemini. Through this period your confidence will be at its highest and people will see you as an exceptional, intelligent, witty and admirable person. If you are looking for a new relationship, then this will be the best time to impress a potential playmate.

Getting away from romance for a minute, you stand to do pretty well in your money-making aspirations. Finances shouldn't be a problem as the people who make the decisions will recognise you for the high flyer you are. Needless to say, your self-esteem will swell greatly and this could drive you to seek more from others too. Don't be too hard on those who fail to match up.

July and August herald a very active social life and any holiday taken during these months should turn out to be both interesting and different, the two words that are the basis of your existence. The next eight weeks will be advantageous if you are single but don't want to remain so. Venus in Gemini will make you completely irresistible, so don't be too surprised if you meet your match around 26 August in the strangest of circumstances; what appears to be nothing more than a friendship could easily blossom into an erotic entanglement.

A feeling of extra physical well-being is likely to be the product of energetic Mars in Libra during September and this in turn will make you work harder and longer. The result of this industriousness will be good for your career, but will take its toll on your relationship. If you don't make time to be with your loved one, then you can expect some disgruntlement that is reminiscent of February's problems. In fact, you could find yourself going through a rocky patch during the last week of September and if you leave your relationship to stagnate, then being single again is not out of the question.

October sees both single and attached Twins in the spotlight thanks to a blend of luck and judgement and with the Sun and Venus in Libra, your ego will be vigorously massaged along with other parts of your body. Your communication skills are the foundation of all personal and professional success during this important month.

Compromise, Gemini, is something you hate to do and for portions of November this will be the biggest thorn in your side. You will have to take a back seat to your partner in many ways, but to be fair to him or her, you have had the lion's share of decision-making for most of the year and if you don't allow for this change in the seating arrangement, you can expect more fireworks than 5 November brings.

A final, festive word of caution goes out to singles – an exceptionally generous gift from an admirer could turn your head, so do investigate this saucy Santa's motives before turning down the bedcovers.

CANCER 1995

From the start of 1995 you will probably be giving more
serious thought to your future as you will feel the need
to create a more secure environment for yourself and
family. This aim will be helped by rewarding Saturn
being in Pisces for the whole of the year and strong
attempts at responsibility and reliability will be the
recipe for your success.

From 1 to 20 January your quest for stability will be
instigated by a meeting with someone who could have a
profound effect on you, both in a business and emotional sphere. It's not guaranteed that you will enter
into an affair with this person, but you are sure to give it
more than a fleeting thought. All of this will be the
effect of the Sun being in Capricorn promoting influences that will put an emphasis on new partnerships, as
going it alone could seem too daunting for you. And 16
January is a key date, one when you are likely to see a

change in your circumstances. The Full Moon in opposition with emotionally unstable Uranus could cause you to rethink which way your present personal relationship is heading. Don't be surprised if you decide to be single again, for during this period you won't be afraid of changes, no matter how drastic they seem.

The positive turmoil of January is sure to leave you feeling in the middle of no man's land as far as your personal life is concerned and it will be a member of the fairer sex that will ultimately help you put things into perspective during February. This attraction, aided by the love planet Venus occupying Capricorn, could become special and even if you are female yourself, a sexual affair with this soul mate is not out of the question. It could shock you, Cancer, but you are one of the few zodiac signs who can deal emotionally with such an intricate liaison.

You would be right in thinking that the first two months of 1995 offer enough excitement to last a year, but through bitter experience you have learned that nothing is ever straightforward in this life. March, moreover the 6th, will have a more balancing effect on you, as the likelihood is that you will be offered more responsibility at your place of business, which in turn promises extra cash. The other good or bad news, depending how you view it, is that a new addition could be on the way, so if you are unprepared, you will have some serious thinking to do, but if you are keen to dabble with dirty nappies, then a Sagittarian baby in December should make your Christmas even more complete.

April, or at least until the 20th, looks as though it will be quite an emotional month for Crabs to endure. The

Sun in Aries is going to offer a mixture of restless, reckless feelings and you will go through some very awkward moments which make you anxious and impatient. The only way through April is to wear a bold, brave face and look any adversities straight between the eyes, and this game of bluff can be fortuitous in any negotiations you undertake. Your personal relationship will be peacefully harmonious through the middle to end of April, as Venus in Pisces will let your caring side shine through and, more importantly, give you time to repay those who have supported you.

May and the first three weeks of June let you enjoy a relaxing breather; no real miracles or maelstroms will shake you off course and mainly the purpose of this time is to allow you the freedom to analyse the first third of 1995 and push ahead unhindered with your personal goals for the rest of the year. Use this interlude wisely and some of your best strategies will be devised.

The pleasing aspects of the last week of June and the start of July cause a more confident mood. Projects you have started during the past two months should now start to show some dividends on the business front and if you have entered into a new relationship, you should see signs that it is going in the direction you hoped for and that long-term commitment is on the cards. All of this will be due to Venus being in your own sign of Cancer, making you more forthright and motivated and again actuating some changes in your lifestyle or circumstances for the better. From the middle to end of July, the celestial transition I have just mentioned will also be responsible for your social life picking up, as will your personal magnetism, so if you are single, it is a great time to find a new partner, which, incidentally will probably turn out to be an Arien or Scorpion. Either way, a union with one of these two will leave you breathless, confused and dallying with fantasies you have never previously had the courage even to talk about.

Now as the July sun fades away into August, a huge bevy of planetary movements swirl into your chart. The Sun in Cancer being in opposition with Uranus and Neptune, whilst they in turn are in Capricorn is all as complex as it sounds and is the reason why you might not know whether you are on your head or your heels. Well, throughout August you can expect to have to choose between your personal needs and the more unpredictable or impractical demands of your relationship. This could sound like an impossible task, but basically the reality is that you are going to put your partnership under the microscope, dissect the potential sources of conflict and perhaps begin to experiment more. This should open up some wonderful possibilities and fend off the threat of either of you succumbing to holiday flirtations.

All of this paves the way for September and up until 20 October, when sexually you are much more forceful and electrifying. Whether newly attached or married, between these dates your hormones are likely to rule your head and erotic exploration of fantasies leads this to be possibly the most sexually liberating period of your life. You have to thank sexy Mars being in impulsive Scorpio for these naughty yet nice six weeks, but you should also be warned that between 18 and 21 October, Mars will be in conjunction with Pluto whilst they are both in Scorpio promoting an obsessional period when you are feeling strong and perhaps aggressive. Certainly you may feel the need to confront someone in order to show them what's what, but don't be shocked if it turns into a provocative steamy affair with him or her.

With everything due to happen this year, especially during the last eight weeks you will be pleased to know that November is a consolidation month, when you can take time out. In fact you will probably need a rest to give your hormones time to recover. Providing you haven't played around when you shouldn't, November will be plain sailing and quite uneventful.

Finally, on to December, and you can expect your energy levels to be partially depleted, but that won't cause you too much concern as it is the festive season and Venus along with Mars in Capricorn will focus your attention on family demands and desires. The company of others will be very enjoyable and offers stimulation of the mental kind as well as physical – what more could a Crab want for Christmas? Nothing except a happy 1996 . . . but more of that next year.

LEO 1995

Overall you are destined to have a very upbeat year with only a few grey areas to look out for, thanks to expansive Jupiter and power-hungry Pluto affecting your fifth solar house of pleasure and entertainment. Throughout the twelve months you will reap the rewards of a new-found sense of freedom and optimism, especially when taking on big projects or challenges. Around 8 January the overall view of your relationship is looking good as it travels through a more contented phase, so if you had any doubts during late 1994 that your partnership might not stand the test of time, you should see signs that the feelings of love are once again blossoming. By spending some quality time together around the 15th, the influences of the love planets Venus and Jupiter both in Sagittarius will help settle any uncertainty there may have been during the winter months.

If you are attached, then February could be a tricky month for you to get through. The problem is that you are very likely to be attracted to or even captivated by someone you meet, either in your place of work, or a club you frequent. The Sun in Aquarius could bring out the proud and narcissistic part of your nature and you will have a difficult time turning down this person's obvious sexual desires for you. Now, as you are not renowned for having affairs unless you are unhappy with your relationship, it will depend on your personal circumstances as to how far you succumb to temptation. My advice is that if you are single, go for it Leo, but if you are spoken for then resist the temptation and reap the rewards of fidelity, especially on Valentine's Day.

All through March you will need to be on your mettle which is caused by there being the first stage of a lengthy transition of Pluto in Sagittarius, but the real long-term effects of this lunar passage won't start in earnest until 1996. The essence of it all is that you'll be able to take advantage of a new-found capacity to deal with big challenges, especially business ones. Throughout the following four weeks work could play a big part in any relationship you are committed to, because although you may have to put more time and energy into achieving the goals you set yourself, your partner is sure to appreciate your efforts and around the 20th onwards, you could be pampered in a way that should have you purring with content.

April and May are two of the more dynamic months to take advantage of, as the Sun in Aries will heighten your natural sense of poise and increase your self-confidence. Now if you are single, this is a great month for finding a new mate to roam with. The most likely place to find this person is at a sporting event, where your driving ambition and leadership prowess result in you giving off a magnetic sexual aura. This is also a period when many a Leo will tie the knot and a marriage during April or May should be a long and contented one.

As June begins, your good fortune will have a temporary setback. On 9 June Uranus will retrograde back into Capricorn and although this is a situation that will affect you more from January 1996, you should be ready for the unexpected as exciting people start to enter your world. If you don't keep on your toes you could miss out on some excellent opportunities. The real negative side to this planetary transition is instability or upset that could hinder not only your love life but your work as well. Try to understand that changes are normally for the better and by resisting the necessity for change, you'll only make life more difficult for yourself.

Something you have probably been held back by for, believe it or not, eleven years, is the long-term motion of Pluto in Scorpio. I am pleased to say that as July ends so will this transition, but you could still feel your personal power is under threat. To turn the negative influences into a positive feature, you will need to be quietly determined without being noticeably obsessive. In other words don't make a drama out of a crisis, but do be ready to act when necessary.

With holidays now being taken all through the year, you personally will get the best results from travelling during August. After the trials of June and July you will be pleased to know you are still lord and master of your jungle, especially as this month is going to be a super time for romance with a capital 'R'. Singles may find a summer holiday tryst turning into something more permanent. Should you be in a relationship, the summer sun could well be the reason for the patter of little paws in May of 1996. All of this will be because of the delightful influences that the Sun, Mercury and Venus are instigating in your first house. The only note for caution is between 20 and 24 August, when the Sun and Venus square Pluto. You might feel threatened or jealous over something trivial, try to see it as just that or you could spoil an excellent month – and I promise you it will pass quickly.

Strange as it may seem, you could determine the outcome of September for yourself. It all depends on how you react around 20 August. If you take my advice and act rationally, it should be a quiet month when you will be able to sit back and think through how to make the rest of 1995 and your relationship more contented and successful. But if on the other hand, you react arrogantly and let things get out of control, then you can expect this to be an indifferent month when you spend much of your energy trying, unsuccessfully, to make amends.

The first two weeks of October should see you forging ahead with a creative project and your partner will have been instrumental in getting it off the ground. Unfortunately this month and your enterprising spirit may be marred on the 16th to the 20th by Mars being in conjunction with Pluto, whilst both are in Scorpio. During this period you are likely to feel drained and your Pluto-induced obsessional working attitude is almost certain to bring out your normally hidden aggression. Be careful not to let these emotional areas affect your home life or you could find yourself wallowing in self-pity and your loved one seeing you in a different light. The rest of October after the 20th should pan out well and also provide an influx of extra cash from an unexpected source.

Well, that is the last of any real bad news, the rest of the year will be plain sailing as it was for the first quarter of 1995. November will be full of feelings of optimism, freedom to forge ahead and, more importantly, a large dose of romance, thanks to Venus, Mars, Jupiter and Pluto all in Sagittarius. Apart from your career ticking over nicely, your relationship will be on the up as well, and if single you are destined to find some new thrills with a new mate.

Sexually, both November and December are months when anything can happen, so it will depend on what you want from sex. It could be as risqué and erotic as you and your partner's imagination will let it, especially during late December because the Sun in Sagittarius is sure to create a surge in libido that will stay with you until the New Year. This is possibly the best astrological present you could want.

VIRGO

Patience is going to be your key word during 1995 and you will also achieve more than you imagine if you learn to be less rigid with others. There will be many challenges for you to face over the coming months and from time to time you will feel as if the barriers in your way are too big to climb, but you of all the zodiac signs are best equipped to deal with such adversities, especially with your outstanding powers of reasoning and the ability to be logical in an emotional crisis.

At the start of 1995 you will feel strong, confident and your health will be the best it's been for some time. In fact you should be able to tackle any problem with enhanced personal initiative thanks to the Sun in Capricorn and Mars in Virgo being supportive to all you do. There are, however, a few days in January, namely the 15th to the 23rd when you are sure to be at loggerheads with the person closest to you. This hiccup results from

331

a quirky mixture of planetary movements that cause you to be obsessive about your work and this in turn will temporarily drain your energy, making you moody and non-committal. You would do well to avoid being drawn into battles or power struggles with your loved one during this tempestuous period, or it could have a further reaching affect on your relationship.

The whole of February is destined to be a better month for you as your fifth house of pleasure is occupied by Venus. Both your social and love life are going to be featured highly throughout these weeks and you will get a lot of satisfaction from spending more time with your partner. Another good reason for February being a bright month is that a woman will be invaluable in helping your career take off in the direction you ultimately want it to go. All of this should set up your Valentine's Day nicely and, if single, you can expect to be admired from afar by a person who is, without your knowing, getting progressively closer to you.

I'm afraid you will have to put March down to being one of those months as the Sun puts a bearing on your seventh house of marriage and partnerships, which is then subject to disruptive influences of trouble-making planet Saturn. Any relationship you are involved in could prove troublesome and you will need to look at the situation very seriously. You may feel too restricted being with your current lover even if you have been together for many years and if so, the Full Moon on the 17th will induce you to make some necessary changes, one of which could result in you considering a trial separation.

The stellar patterns influencing April will be something of a foretaste of 1996. These lunar persuasions will be more evident next year, but you are likely to find that the whole of this month is a testing period. You could feel rather dominated and pressured by your partner and if you are to salvage the month and your romantic alliance, then you definitely need to keep calm and cool, as well as setting realistic objectives for you and your partnership.

As soon as May arrives, however, you should notice that the stresses of March and April will evaporate quickly, almost as if they never existed. The Sun in Taurus will increase your social life no end and if you are single then it is a very good month to capture a new heart. Surprisingly, you may also find love blossoming with an old friend or companion of many years standing. Married Virgins are going to gain by the influences of your eleventh house of luck and a windfall or win is on the cards. Get the best out of May by spending some quality time with your mate to talk honestly about anything that is bothering you.

Don't expect too much from June, other than pleasant signs that your bank balance is going to be boosted. You will have Venus in Taurus plus your sheer tenacious efforts to thank for this monetary gain. Your social calender will be fairly full for this month and surprising developments surrounding this could let you know who your real friends are.

July will bring a delightful mixture of excitement and luck for you to enjoy as your first house of individuality and bodily appearance is positively influenced by Mars. Your health may have shown signs of deteriorating over prior weeks, but after the first few days of July you should feel energised and strong enough to tackle any long-standing problem where solutions have previously been eluding you. The only blot on the landscape for July is around the 10th to the 15th, when unrewarding Saturn creates havoc in your twelfth house of troubles. You may find that delays or physical danger can result from you being too self-willed or aggressive.

Your life will become much more orderly in August as the Sun and Venus occupy your own sign of Virgo. Control will be your key word and you should endeavour to be in the driving seat in all you do. Any relationship you are involved in, or one that is instigated during August, is going to be highlighted in a positive way, especially around the 26th when the New Moon in Virgo gets your imagination working overtime and takes the routine out of romance.

For September and October you will have to get used to taking second best and accepting situations that are less than ideal. The problem is Virgo, you of all the zodiac signs tend to demand higher standards than the rest of us in every sphere, so whereas the events of this month are perfectly acceptable to everybody else, they just won't do for you. With this in mind you can expect some more obstacles and limitations to restrict your constant quest for perfection, ultimately affecting both your love and business life.

Now, November is going to be an active period for you, especially so for your home life owing to Venus, Mars and Jupiter's conjunction in Sagittarius. This month will see you dragged along in the fast lane and this won't suit you too well because when pushed along you tend to make mistakes. There are likely to be many ups and downs as far as your relationship is concerned and you would do well to keep your overly critical side hidden, or you might find even the most easygoing partner flaring up and retaliating. If single, be wary of a new potential playmate who intrigues, but scares you a little. This person is not all he or she seems and by striking up a relationship you could be biting off more than you can chew. The sexual fireworks could easily dazzle you and lead you into thinking about a long-term romance, but it will be a false sense of security and one that could leave you scarred.

Finally, on to December and probably your best month of the year, sounds like a lager commercial, doesn't it? Well jovial I may be, but December is certainly intoxicating. The Sun, Mercury (your ruler), Venus and Mars are a heady mix that affect your house of marriage and partnerships making any established relationship more practical and purposeful. There will be more lighthearted moments too which have perhaps been lacking and there won't be any adverse lunar activity to spoil your Christmas. Single Virgins may not be so for every long because a magic meeting could happen beneath the mistletoe and this festive stranger is set to be around long after the decorations have been packed away.

LIBRA 1995

From the beginning of January you should be feeling that you are finally in control of your own destiny. There will be more courage in your convictions which enables you to overcome the barriers that hemmed you in throughout 1994. With communicative Mercury firmly in Aquarius, you could make some exciting contacts through writing and receiving letters. If dealt with intelligently throughout the year, some of these powerful people will assist you in achieving your personal goals and ambitions. January will also be a busy time for your social life, as you are sure to be in demand by friends and a special loved one. The note of discontent for January surfaces around the 17th, when there is a Full Moon in Cancer. Be very careful someone isn't deceiving you then, either in business affairs or your personal life. Either way you will need to be practical and realistic to uncover the truth and the whole situation is bound to unsettle you temporarily. One thing is definite, you must not make any serious decisions at this time, or if you really have to, ensure you think through all possible consequences carefully.

It's not often that anything is ever really plain sailing for you, is it, Libra? Well, I am pleased to say February will be just that and a very lively month as well. The Sun in your fifth house of pleasure is likely to play havoc with your hormones and it is destined to be a very experimental time when you could explore some adventurous fantasies with your lover. The key to getting the most out of your sexual relationship will be in giving your mate the security he or she needs, and once you have done this your partner will have the willingness to try almost any exotic idea you have, even if it is somewhat deviant. Looking quickly at the business front, you should trust any creative urges you have as they could bring in more money than some of your practical schemes.

The enjoyment continues into March, due to romantic Venus stimulating inventive Aquarius. Creativity is still the key word and you are sure to succeed in anything that is innovative. Apply this to your love life too – single Scales could find that perfect person around the 15th as your persona will attract many people from varying backgrounds. Your quest for extra sexual excitement knows no bounds, so don't be surprised if you end up in bed with a member of your own sex. He or she is likely to be a good friend of many years' standing and it will be an unusual circumstance which leads to this naughty and novel fun.

Apart from you being the butt of an April fool's prank on the 1st, the rest of April is going to be influenced by the Sun and Mercury in your seventh house of marriage and partnerships. For the harmony to continue within your relationship you will need to consider others in your plans, especially your loved one's family. There are going to be one or two important decisions to make in your work or business sphere and it will be your love partner who eases you off the fence and into action.

Throughout May, your fifth house entertains changeable Uranus. Although you tend to resist any sudden changes, your best move is to recognise the need for opening up new possibilities, because the Full Moon in April saw the end of one personal phase and the start of another which will become increasingly apparent during the following weeks. This trend is actually set to last for ten years so pay attention and read the signs!

June may see you going on a course to improve your current financial situation and if you study hard, it will. Now you are not normally the most loyal of zodiac signs, are you, Libra? Well, with this busy and fast-moving month, temptation is definitely going to be put in your path, perhaps from a Fire sign. Obviously if you are single, then this is going to be great news for you, but if you are attached you will find it hard to avoid someone who has designs on your body. This is going to be a difficult choice to make so, if in doubt, play for time and weigh up the pros and cons or you will tumble into a predicament from which there is no easy escape.

July is the best month to take summer holidays, especially if you are single, for it will be a flirtatious few weeks. The other reason is that loving Venus is going to be highlighted in your ninth house of travel, so there is no better time to get away from it all. Whether single or attached, sex will play a big part all through July and there will be a few 1996 Arien babies to remind Librans of this vacation.

The activity of Mars in your own sign during August is certain to sustain your energy levels for the entire month. You might find that your relationship is going to suffer through your love of sport and outdoor pursuits. It will be a case of those at home feeling neglected yet you will wonder what all the fuss is about. Try to save a little time for your loved one or keep the peace by at least including him or her, even if it is only as a spectator.

Although the early part of September is going to fall a touch flat, from the 16th when Venus enters your first house of individuality, you will find your social life picking up dramatically. Mid-September onwards is a delightful time for you as your financial standing is going from strength to strength and this is likely to induce some impulse spending on the luxuries you continually crave. The month is also going to hold social and romantic possibilities regardless of your personal circumstances, so, whether single or attached, you are destined for a lot of fun.

You could be forgiven for wondering if there is going to be a bad spell for you to endure this year; to be honest, the answer is no! October is full of positive influences as the Sun in Libra helps you to attract people who appreciate your unparalleled natural charm. It would seem no matter what you want to try, whether it is a new outrageous sexual act, or an unexplored form of money-making, others will want to follow suit, so don't be worried if you are treated like a god during October – enjoy it while it lasts.

Moving on to November, you are going to have to increase the pace of your life to accommodate hectic job or career developments. Venus, Mars and opportune Jupiter are all loudly expressing themselves in Sagittarius, which is a marvellous planetary line-up for you to take advantage of. There may be one or two areas that worry you though and you will need to be forceful with someone, possibly your boss, if you are to achieve a long-term goal. One thing is guaranteed, if you let November slip through your hands without achieving anything, you will live to regret it.

After a brilliant year, all you must guard against is complacency and believing that you can't put a foot wrong in December. A mini financial crisis could give you a jolt so don't charge too many Christmas pressies to your credit card. Have a frugal festive season and save your pennies. You will need them for a New Year's Eve proposal that links love with a journey. Without giving too much away, it's fair to say that your motto for 1996 will be 'Have romance, will travel!'

SCORPIO 1995

Last year was special for you because Jupiter was expanding your horizons from November 1993 to November 1994. Now that Jupiter has departed you could feel as though your crutches have been removed, leaving you in limbo land. This means January 1995 will be, to all intents and purposes, a month for you to put the important areas of your life into perspective. The Sun, Uranus and Neptune in Capricorn, together with Pluto and Saturn in Pisces are a wonderful mix of planetary influences, in as much as they will help you to sort your financial matters out and balance the books. It isn't going to be a particularly romantic month, for your thinking is more likely to be concentrated on matters relating to your work and business affairs.

To get the best out of February you would be wise to let others step into the limelight in your place of work. This way you can quietly sit back and analyse which path you want your career to follow. If you don't, the Full Moon in Leo whilst in conjunction with Mars on the 15th could force you into making decisions that you normally would give more thought to. You may also find yourself embroiled in conflict regarding your career, so give your natural Scorpion intuition a chance to work some magic for you. As far as love goes, you can expect quite a peaceful month as your partner will probably play the supportive role in understanding that he or she has to take a back seat whilst you ponder and set your strategies for the rest of the year.

The onset of March is destined to be much more light-hearted and sociable, the Sun shining in your fifth house of pleasure will see to that. Any creative or artistic talent you have could boost your bank balance, but more importantly it is sure to bring out the best in you. Now that the pressures of the first two months have passed, you should feel much more relaxed and affectionate towards the people who matter the most to you.

In April your pleasure house again is going to be inspired by loving Venus, so you can expect the whole month to be full of charm and romance. Now don't worry if you are single at the start of April because the chances are you won't be by the beginning of May. You are destined to meet someone in an arty location, such as the theatre, a concert or cinema and he or she could well turn out to be a permanent part of your programme. Something that will be more of a feature during 1996 and the rest of the decade is also going to affect you during most of May. Out of the blue you may be forced to make some changes. If you are aware of this possibility you should be able to take these events in your stride, or even better, anticipate them before they happen. What will be a great asset to you is the influence of the Sun in your seventh house of marriage and relationships. Your partner will have a strong stabilising effect on you, which emotionally steers you through the inevitable turmoil which comes your way. Another important aspect of May will be on the 14th when the Full Moon is in your own sign of Scorpio symbolising the end of a personal phase. It is more than possible that this Lunar transition will leave you feeling stressed and anxious, yet offering no apparent reason for this. I can assure you it will pass as quickly as it appeared and normality will resume.

June contains few upsets and is a time to reflect and regroup. For singles, this is another period when you could find that rare, special person to share your life. The likelihood is you know him or her well, but never thought the friendship would blossom into a love match. Attached Scorpions can anticipate some very passionate clinches that won't be constrained to conventional activities. You may be in for a sexy surprise that takes even your breath away.

If you are holidaying this year, July is the best month for doing so. There is a wonderful mixture of the love planet Venus and the life-giving Sun in your ninth house of travel. Whatever your marital status may be, you are destined to have a romantic vacation. Back home your career is shaping up nicely and there are some pleasing aspects to look forward to in the coming months, so you should feel relaxed regarding your financial position. Also your health is showing no ill effect from the recent trials and tribulations, so all is well in that department. All of this plus the celestial equation already mentioned will put you in the mood for love and unadulterated sex, so you and your partner can expect a lot of sexercising, not just whilst away, but all through July.

You are likely to be spurred on by your ambitions during August for it will be a time to start realising your goals after all the hard work you have put in. Rightly so, you will probably feel that you should take the centre stage because of your achievements, but this could be overshadowed by an associate who is naturally more flamboyant than you are, probably a Leo. Remember the old proverb about the tortoise and the hare, for in the long run you will be the tortoise and will have your day and the last laugh.

The combination of Mars in Scorpio during September is a very powerful planetary blend and will affect you in two ways. First, your single-mindedness and steely determination will return with a vengeance. Whatever you put your mind to should show results with immediate effect. One thing is for sure, woe betide anyone who gets on your wrong side through default or stupidity, because your deadly sting is now fully armed and operational again. Second, your hormones are going to work overtime and you will be feeling extra horny all month. Your sexual urges will be at their strongest for the year, which could lead to all sorts of erotic or deviant encounters with your lover and an impulsive phase towards the end of the month could see you taking part in group sex or sleeping with your own gender!

Don't expect October to be much different from September, for Venus in Scorpio is going to make you seem larger than life and it is another amorous sexual month to provide you with pleasure. If single you will go through a phase when you are at your most desirable in the eyes of others and although you feel exceptionally sexy, you still will need to keep your intimate liaisons on a meaningful basis, as you are not a sign who can enjoy superficial sex unless it's for a very good reason.

Being a deep and perceptive person, November sees you feeling more in control of your destiny and the Sun and Mercury in Scorpio will help you gain more power for yourself, which you can use to whatever advantage you deem necessary.

December is for winding down and looking forward to the coming festivities. Nothing much will happen on the work front except tidying up the smaller projects you previously put on the back burner. Relationship-wise, you are set to have a terrific Christmas and New Year to set you up nicely for 1996. If you are single you may find that you end up in a friend's bed and an experimental time is had by all. Don't expect it to last because Christmas has a habit of creating bizarre liaisons, which ultimately end on New Year's Day. Still, it'll be good while it lasts!

SAGITTARIUS 1995

This will be your Jupiter year and you should take full advantage of it, as this very special celestial pattern only occurs once every twelve years. The accent for the next twelve months is on travel, expanding knowledge and broadening horizons. You can be optimistic about your ambitions, especially with the added bonus of creative Pluto in your first house, which will give you the confidence to decide what is and isn't necessary in your life. By the time 1996 arrives you should have achieved many things to make your long-term future secure.

So to kick this great epoch into action, January is pretty much a fun month for you, when socialising and getting out and about to new places will release your strong sense of freedom. Look out for the 16th, when you could be lucky with your financial endeavours, but if attached make sure you include your mate in your extra curriculum activities or he or she may feel neglected and unloved.

The whole of February is very much influenced by Pluto in your own sign of Sagittarius, and you can expect some difficult yet ultimately life-transforming realisations or experiences. Certainly your morals or philosophies will be tested, possibly to the edge of breaking point. Now all of this probably sounds heavy-going and in some ways it is, but it is an extremely beneficial period when you will make some decisions that will affect you for many years to come. It might also mean the end of a relationship that has become stagnated and run to the end of its course.

Around 6 March you may feel somewhat restricted by social obligations, or codes of conduct, which in turn will call for you to have more responsibility in terms of your public image. Jupiter in Sagittarius, square Pisces is a decidedly positive, yet awkward planetary transition, which could help you to curb your over-optimism and make you realistic in setting your goals. This won't be a particularly romantic month for you, not because you will have troubles in that department – they happened during February. It's more a case of sowing the seeds for long-term financial security, which inadvertently will benefit any relationship you are involved in.

Now the events of the last three months should set you up nicely for April. Powerful Mars in Leo bolsters your ego and makes you proud of yourself. It also should help you to be fearless in all you attempt, especially if it involves creativity. One thing is for sure, physically you'll feel strong and ready to tackle any task, no matter how difficult and from around the middle of April life in general will lighten up thanks to the Sun in

Aries. Travel and romance are joined at the hip so to speak and if you are single, you should use this combination as you could meet someone who intrigues you and entices you to go all the way. Only one note of caution, with such positive planetary action this month you could appear to people as being unintentionally narcissistic, so be confident and dynamic, but be careful not to overdo it.

With your pleasure house stimulated by Venus, May is looking to be filled with romance for both single and attached Sagittarians. If you are single and looking for a mate, then he or she will not be hard to find. With your confidence brimming over, shyness is something you won't suffer from, in fact you will not be slow in going forward if you get my drift. This is also a month when you could finally succumb to marriage if you have been in a relationship for some time. I know you being a Sagittarian means that you find the possibility of getting hitched mind-boggling, but as it is your Jupiter year, this could be one of the changes that will offer you and a special someone guaranteed stability for the future.

If you don't expect too much from June, you won't be disappointed. This month is mostly concerned with your love life, in a similar way to May. There may be an element of hostility during the middle of the month if you tend to dominate your partner too much. But by giving him or her more freedom of choice and room to express their feelings regarding how your union could mature, you should find that all will be well and it will be a contented period for you both to enjoy.

From as early as 2 July, good news from your business endeavours is sure to add a little extra feeling of excitement that everything is going to plan. This could be somewhat marred by your continual desire to be in the great outdoors with friends and sporting companions. To get the best from July you will need to make some choices regarding your social life. With Venus in Gemini the accent again is on your love life and if you have not got one, the likelihood is you will have before the next four weeks are over. Put some excitement back in your relationship and involve your mate in all you do, for you will be more than compensated by some outrageous and erotic love-making.

Now if you are taking a holiday this year, the last few days of July and the whole of August are the best time for a summer adventure. Wherever you go and what-ever you do, the Sun and Venus in your ninth house of travel will bestow some magic on your trip, even if it is only a long weekend excursion to Blackpool, but I would bet money that you are destined for a faraway shore in the sun. Either way, August should be a happy and loving month.

September and October are periods when Jupiter in your first house of personality will be still bringing some beneficial influences, but no major boosts or threats are likely to occur. My advice is to relax, let the projects you have put in motion over the past months come to fruition and prepare for the end of the year when the ball really starts rolling down your path of good fortune.

As November draws in, Venus, Mars, Pluto and, of course, Jupiter are all in Sagittarius making you dynamic, attractive and far-sighted. Endless amounts of opportunities appear during this month, so look for and make the most of them, for this is probably your best period of the year. You could also feel quite hedonistic and be susceptible to an affair. If single then no problem, but you would be wise to keep your loving for your loved one if you are attached. It is almost certain to wreck all the good you have done earlier in 1995 if you fall victim to the temptation.

Your roller coaster of good fortune will start in earnest during December when you should be able to take control and chase your dreams with some measure of success for your efforts. One thing is for sure, you must not rest on your laurels thinking you have done enough in taking advantage of your Jupiter year – you haven't and you should take all you can out of this celestial line-up. Some time around the 15th, you should look into the investment field and take advice from someone you trust, because the dates from the 21st to the 23rd are super days to speculate with your hard-earned pennies. Okay, that's enough about finances! What about love do I hear you say? Well, that is also going to play a big part during your Christmas, as Venus in Sagittarius will see to that. Basically you are destined for lots of pressies, passion and potential intrigue. Happy Christmas, Sagittarius and I promise you it will be!

CAPRICORN 1995

There are a few interesting planetary transitions to set the scene for January; first, the New Moon in Capricorn on the 1st should help you to get a recent idea off the ground and the chances are it will be financially gratifying. Second, Mercury in conjunction with Neptune in your first house of personality is likely to get your imagination working overtime regarding some areas which have been a constant worry, and the solutions you conjure up undoubtedly will improve your present situation. Now lastly, the Sun in Capricorn should make you feel in control of personal matters and the people close to you will respect your authority, or at least your dynamic thinking. The only bone of contention for January is on the 16th, when the Full Moon in Cancer being opposite Uranus and Neptune, creates a set of difficult changes which may have to be acted upon. Surprise events could force you to take a different approach to a relationship problem. The chances are you may need to find more space or freedom, which could mean the end of either your romantic or business partnership.

You should find February to be a more light-hearted month. For you to really make some headway with your career, it is important you meet new and influential contacts. You know where to go, but you need to exercise a strong self-discipline to turn your cautious nature into go-getting entrepreneurial flair. Creativity is not generally one of your fortes, but with the Moon in conjunction with Venus, Uranus and Neptune whilst in your first house, you could have a potent blend of inspiration together with an artistic bent which could see you making a change or an addition to your usual line of business.

The events of March won't affect you too much. In fact it is a time when nothing good or bad is likely to happen, especially within your chosen career. As there isn't much you can do to increase your bank balance for the next four weeks, why not concentrate your efforts on your family, friends, or partner if you have one? Whatever your personal situation, you are sure to have neglected your private life over the past few months, so use this period to enhance your social circle.

Without doubt, April will be a challenging time, and you have the Sun in Aries to thank for that. In forging ahead with your ambitions you will need to sharpen up your thinking and show strength when dealing with powerful or awkward people. The other area where you could face some stiff opposition is from a family member who feels you have wronged them or haven't fulfilled a promise, and either way you will need to play the peacemaker.

The first half of May will entirely depend on how you determine the events of April. Things will either go well because you excelled yourself, or you may be wallowing in self-pity due to not putting yourself out enough to create the conditions you need for further progress. Now, the second half of the month is a different kettle of fish and is to be a very practical time when you're able to organise your life better, especially at work. Something you should pay more attention to is your health, as you tend to be lazy in that department. So to avoid any silly ailments which could take effect around the last quarter of May, make time for some exercising and set yourself a healthier diet, and this careful approach will be beneficial in the long run.

June should bring a welcome relief to the intensity of the hours you have put into your career over the past five months. Partnership or family matters are going to be featured strongly over the next four weeks. The Sun in your seventh house of marriage is set to make you compassionate and the caring side of your nature will be noticed by the people with whom you socialise. If single, it is likely you could find that special person through a friend who has your best interests at heart. Alternatively, should you be attached, then expect a montage of sexual, erotic and passionate pastimes, as you have a lot of loving to make up for.

An important date for you to look out for during July is the 12th when there is a Full Moon in Capricorn. This Lunar movement is responsible for the end of your current personal phase creating the need to make some serious decisions relating to your personal relationship. In all probability the prospect of starting a family is one such issue, or you might be considering marriage. Either way with Venus in your seventh house of partnerships, any decision you make with your lover will be a naturally happy one.

A tricky time around 5 August could see you being out-manoeuvred in a business dealing, so be forearmed and set your strategies out well at the very beginning of this month and you will succeed. The planet Mars stimulating your tenth house of ambition and social standing could play a part in your promotion prospects, so don't be too surprised if you get back from your summer holidays to the good news of a better position and a pay rise to boot.

Getting certain areas into perspective during September and October will prove troublesome, because it is another unsettled and challenging period. The biggest headache for you to overcome is getting others to see your point of view, something you are normally very proficient at. To get round this abnormality, you would be wise to let your business partner or an associate you trust do the talking for you, and this way the chances of you losing out will be minimal. Moving onto your personal life, try to keep the home fires burning if attached or you could find that your relationship will suffer. Remember most of your time this year has been taken up with your career.

Throughout November, Venus, Mars and Jupiter are conjunct in your eleventh house of friendship bringing your social life to the forefront. Often you seem to take more than you give from a friendship or relationship and November will be a good time to redress the balance. Certainly your energy is best taken up helping others in some way, so return a few favours and it will put you in good stead for when you next need some support yourself. As far as your career is concerned, you may feel as though there is a lot going on behind your back, but this behind-the-scenes activity is likely to have a positive effect on your long-term future, so don't let it worry you too much.

Right from the beginning of December you will be able to press on with important projects as well as finding time to socialise with friends or help your loved one with the run-up to Christmas. Between the 10th and the 22nd, you should find that with all the other zodiac signs (possibly with the exception of Virgo) concentrating their efforts on enjoying the seasonal partygoing, you can gain an advantage by setting your goals for 1996, so when the New Year starts you can leave them all standing.

Finally, your yearly outlook for 1995 may seem like all work and no play but do bear in mind the security benefits that this brings. It is your never-ending quest for success that your present partner, or any potential partner, loves you for.

AQUARIUS 1995

You potentially have a great year ahead, especially as revolutionary Uranus is entering Aquarius for the year. This super celestial line-up signifies a long exciting period and the need for you to be on your toes, so as not to miss out on the abundance of opportunities that will cross your path during 1996. Mercury is in the Air signs for most of the next twelve months so you should concentrate your efforts on being inventive or original to realise your goals and ambitions.

From 7 January onwards you should feel very strong mentally, something that has not happened for some months. The added bonus of communicative Mercury in your first house of personality will make you able to think on your feet quickly and, more importantly, you'll have the ability to make yourself understood both in the business sphere and within your current relationship.

When undertaking a creative project, 1 February

when the Sun is in your own sign of Aquarius is an ideal date to do so. All through the month you should be noticed by the people who matter because of your aptitude for independence and your steady supply of innovative ideas, although you must keep them to yourself around the middle of this period or a jealous rival may steal your thunder. Also, between the 9th and 14th, Mars in Leo could represent a tricky time for you and it could be hard to relax. Your personal or family life may be interrupted by your constant battling for the last word, so remember other people have opinions too.

If you are single, March will be a very beneficial month for your love life. With Venus rousing Aquarius, your free and easy magnetic appeal is sure to make you the centre of attention and you should have many admirers to choose from. The chances are you'll find what you are looking for in an arty location. Now, if you are attached, a long period of lust and a hot bed of inventive passion should be your main cause of mental stimulation, but if you're involved with an Earth sign, i.e. Taurus, Virgo or Capricorn, they will need to feel secure before fully letting rip.

April and May are going to be a taster of the Uranus in Aquarius planetary transition. Over the next eight years a revolution is about to happen in your world and you should prepare yourself for an exciting passage into the year 2000. You may have the sudden urge to break free from any current restrictions; independence and freedom will be important issues for you to consider. Use these two months to understand fully where you feel trapped or pressured before making any final decisions regarding either your love life, or your future career prospects. Be careful on 21 May for this is a day and a half. The Sun in Taurus being opposite Pluto in Scorpio are in turn being square to Mars in Leo and square to the Moon in Aquarius. This stressful Grand Cross may provoke a trigger point in relationships that are more related to work, but could also affect your personal union. The problem is that you are being stretched too far and pushed to the limit. Just like an elastic band, you could snap!

As soon as June arrives you should feel that normality has returned as the strains of the past months evaporate. Mercury is going to activate your fifth house of pleasure in a big way. By showing your intelligence, you will get on well with everyone you come into contact with. If you are involved in creative writing, then this period is one of the best for you to forge ahead with a book or making the most of any musical talents you have. If you use your abilities to the full, you could aspire to the level you ultimately desire and get the recognition you deserve.

Try to put your career second to the needs of your mate for July, though, because with the Sun and Venus in your seventh house of marriage, it is destined to be a tender time. Don't worry if you are still single as this month is also about meeting new friends and the beginning of love affairs. Impulsive sexual liaisons could lead to some bizarre fantasies, and you may even find yourself being outrageously adventurous in experiencing either group sex, or making love with your own gender, although this is even more likely if you are an Aquarian female.

Although you'd love to explore new countries all the year round if it were possible, August is the best month for you to take a holiday. Your physical energy along with your adventurous mind will be working in harmony, which should make for an exciting summer vacation. July provided a torrid patch of passion and August should see a continuation of those erotic escapades. If single, the outlook is equally sunny and if you are looking for a lover, even if it is only for two weeks, I promise you with sexy Mars in your ninth house of travel, wherever you go, you won't be short of admirers who will want to sample your intelligent mind and futuristic carnal ideas. The only headache you will have is who to choose – not a bad problem to have, eh Aquarius?

Around the first quarter of September you may have a run-in with a close friend and a silly quarrel could leave you on non-speaking terms. This is something that is likely to upset you a lot, because you put a lot of store and value on your friendships. In fact, you probably feel your best pal is as important to you as your lover. Nip this upset in the bud by resolving the argument quickly, even if you have to admit the blame when it wasn't your fault or you may lose this soul mate for good.

October contains one of your favourite words – socialising. All through this month the accent is on getting out and about and meeting new people. With the Sun and Venus in Libra, you are in demand especially if you are in new surroundings. This could lead to an awkward situation if you are attached because someone is likely to make a big play for you by massaging your delicate ego. If you fall for this weak ploy you certainly will live to regret it, for this secret is destined to become public knowledge when the Moon is next in Pisces. Play away from home at your peril, Aquarius.

Your eleventh house hosts the action in November due to Venus, Mars and Jupiter being there to expand your horizons. The emphasis for this month is on adventure, by way of playing sport, travelling to areas outside of your home town and lots of action of the sexual kind. This is also probably the best period of 1995 to trust in luck, so calculated investments should show quick dividends and maybe even a little flutter on the horses or dogs may provide you with some extra cash. If you have used the earlier creative months to write, paint or pen a musical score, then this is the best time to sell them to a publisher or art dealer.

Finally, what will December hold for you? Well with your first house of individuality and personality stimulated by the love planet Venus, it is going to be a great time when you can let your hair down and mix with the people you care about the most – your friends and your loved one. To be honest, December is going to be one big party for you as you adore the festivities and while say, Virgo, Capricorn and Leo are all still working away hard at it until the evening of the 24th, you will be on your hundredth party and looking for more, probably with a Geminian partner or friend. Do only what is necessary career-wise because 1996 holds a lot of changes for the better.

PISCES 1995

The next twelve months is a period when you need to recognise your responsibilities and limitations if you want success and contentment. This is more appropriate to you if your birthday is after 1 March and you would do well to adhere to this advice. Also, Pluto entering Sagittarius means that if you find escapism to be your usual way out of a difficult situation, you may be rudely awakened on more than one occasion. Remember, the ostrich never gains anything by sticking its head in the ground when facing adversity.

January and February will see Pluto occupying your tenth solar house of ambition and social standing creating a challenging time when issues affecting any balance of power need to be looked at carefully. This planetary phase is set to affect you not only for the next two months, but for a few years to come. Try to see this in a more positive light because the celestial influences could help you more than you think, especially when faced with some serious obstacles or troublesome authoritative types over the next eight weeks.

As Spring approaches, the Sun in your first house of personality is set to help you take steps to increase your security, especially around 1 March. The next four weeks will be a serious yet confident period and if you are in a position of responsibility, it is very important you let the people around you know what is required of them so you can set the scene for the rest of the year – this applies to your personal relationship equally, if you have one.

Although you have had to shoulder the burden of life's dilemmas for the last couple of years, Venus in Pisces through most of April should bring out a more caring, supportive side to a long-term partner which could also help inspire feelings of romance rather than resentment from you. If single, this is a good month to meet a new protective partner and more than likely it will be from helping out somewhere such as a church fête or a charity event that causes your paths to cross.

If you read too much into a situation during May, you could make some decisions that will prove costly. So be careful how you utilise your hard-earned cash and don't let someone fool you in thinking you can take advantage of a get-rich-quick scheme. It is a month when you should also have a close look at your health as the chances are that stress has played a big part in your life recently and you have had a niggling ailment for some time. So have a check-up, you may need a little medication, but whatever is troubling you is going to pass quickly.

You may be feeling a little below par during the early

part of June and if attached the temptation to criticise your loved one over trivial matters could lead to a much bigger confrontation, so try to resist any negative emotions you experience at the time. From the middle of the month onwards you could receive some uplifting news regarding a new job, or promotion, which will mean working closely with someone you have a lot of time for. If single, there may be a potential love match on the horizon, or at the very least a brief and beautiful affair.

Apart from a short tricky period around 12 July when Mars is in opposition with Saturn, the rest of your month is looking very good indeed. Going back to the 12th though, you must be careful not to force a showdown or over-exert yourself. By forcing someone's hand over an important issue you could easily lose out on an opportunity you have been waiting for. Patience will be your key word for these four weeks and by being so, you could gain more than you thought was ever possible.

Love, romance, sensitivity and general feelings of well-being should flow nicely during August and September, particularly as the Sun and Venus work their enchantment in your seventh solar house of marriage and partnerships. Sex is certain to be a big issue over the next eight weeks, especially if you are taking your annual holiday to a sun-kissed beach – your favourite habitat. You can expect to realise one or two of your erotic fantasies which you thought would stay hidden, but with the chemistry between you and your loved one being the best it's ever been, then you should have the security to be able to explore the deepest of sexual desires you both have been hiding from each other. Now, around 14 September when the Sun is in opposition with Saturn whilst in Pisces, you must recognise that there is still some way to go before you can expect the freedom to live exactly as you want. The trouble is you are constantly searching for the ideal world and unfortunately none of us live in such a place, human nature puts paid to that. However, by the end of this year you could be a lot closer to a better lifestyle both financially speaking and romantically.

October is to be one of your power months, I'm pleased to say. Mars in fearless Scorpio is to bestow some strong influences that will make you emotionally very potent, particularly when tackling some difficult problems. On the work front you now have the tenacity and energy to see awkward projects through to the end and if you are in business for yourself, a long-term contract you have been hoping to achieve could come to fruition before the month is over, or at least you will receive some positive news regarding this matter.

It is going to be a racy first week of November as Venus moves through sexy Scorpio. So strong is your quest for deviant erotic encounters, your partner may be forgiven for thinking he or she has found a new mate, but your loved one will be more than happy to indulge you in whatever takes your fancy. If you are single, you can expect much of the same as you are not going to be alone for most of this month. It may be a new lover or an old flame with whom you decide to share your impulsive intimate moments, but either way it will be fun and excitingly depraved. The rest of the month sees the world turning a bit too fast for your liking, yet there will be nothing much you can do about it. Venus, Mars and Jupiter in Sagittarius should prove helpful in making you appreciate a career challenge and giving you a purpose in working hard to conquer it. Around the 14th when Saturn is in Pisces, you may experience a temporary difficult period when conflict and clashes could affect that career plan. So be as flexible as possible, but don't let others take advantage of you, especially on the New Moon of the 22nd.

So, finally on to your December. Pluto in Sagittarius is to be responsible for many events and although this may be the beginning of a time when painful choices have to be made, it is a period when you can grow through facing up to any fears or dreads. This is a very long-term influence, which may not be immediately apparent to some Fishes, but you can use this transition in your favour. Be strong and your achievements will be plentiful, be weak and you could end up at the bottom of your murky pool watching other zodiac signs clean up. Christmas through to the New Year should be pretty much a happy period for you and whoever you spend it with. There may be one or two family altercations for you to endure, but they will amount to a few storms in tea cups, so to speak. If single, keep plenty of mistletoe handy, for you are destined to meet lots of possible suitors and you will subject them to the most gruelling of torrid tests. One will be a clear winner!

Answers to the
SEXTROLOGY QUIZZES

SEXTROLOGY QUIZ 1 (see page 177)

1. Sorry, trick question. The man was off his trolley, new to supermarket shopping and a Taurean.
2. B
3. A
4. A
5. B
6. B
7. C
8. D. Well, I wouldn't want to upset any readers before the sequel comes out.
9. A

SEXTROLOGY QUIZ 2 (see page 181)

1. A
2. B
3. B
4. C
5. C
6. A
7. A
8. A
9. A
10. A

SEXTROLOGY QUIZ 3 (see page 291)

1. C
2. B
3. A
4. B
5. C
6. A
7. A
8. C
9. B
10. C
11. A
12. C

SEXTROLOGY QUIZ 4 (see page 295)

1. B
2. C
3. C
4. B
5. B
6. B
7. C
8. A or B
9. B
10. A

BARBARA KAFKA
MICROWAVE GOURMET
THE DEFINITIVE MICROWAVE COOKBOOK

'An extraordinary, comprehensive book'
Jane Grigson, *Observer*

What do you use *your* microwave for?

To warm up coffee? Defrost bread from the freezer? Heat up ready-prepared supermarket meals? Bake a potato or two?

Yes, but what else can it do?

In this definitive guide to microwave cooking, Barbara Kafka shows, with a dazzling combination of culinary flair and scientific exactitude, how, by using a little care and imagination, you can make delicious meals out of fresh ingredients quickly and efficiently.

With over 600 recipes, a comprehensive dictionary of foods and techniques and advice on what the microwave can and cannot do, *Microwave Gourmet* covers everything from such basics as vegetable stock through classic dishes like Moules Marinières to rich dinner-party fare. Using precise easy-to-follow instructions, Barbara Kafka explains how to cook Paupiettes of Sole Stuffed with Salmon in three minutes, plum jam in thirteen minutes and artichokes in seven. As she herself says, 'It may not be a mystic experience, but it sure is quick and efficient.' Whether you are a beginner or an experienced microwave cook, *Microwave Gourmet* will prove to be as indispensable as your microwave itself.

'I feel fairly certain that it will make all other books on microwave cookery redundant' Paul Levy, *Observer*

'This intelligent person's guide to the microwave . . . is long overdue' *Sunday Times*

'The book I've turned to again and again has been Barbara Kafka's *Microwave Gourmet*' Sophie Grigson, *Evening Standard*

'This stupendously good book' *Cosmopolitan*

NON-FICTION/COOKERY   0 7472 3380 2

A selection of non-fiction from Headline

THE *INDEPENDENT* BOOK OF ANNIVERSARIES	George Beal	£8.99 ☐
MEAN BEANS	Cas Clarke	£5.99 ☐
ENCYCLOPEDIA OF FORENSIC SCIENCE	Brian Lane	£7.99 ☐
JUST THE ONE: The Wives and Times of Jeffrey Bernard	Graham Lord	£6.99 ☐
MALE SEXUAL AWARENESS	Barry McCarthy	£5.99 ☐
BURNS: A Biography of Robert Burns	James Mackay	£8.99 ☐
WORLD ENCYCLOPEDIA OF 20TH CENTURY MURDER	Jay Robert Nash	£8.99 ☐
PLAYFAIR FOOTBALL ANNUAL 1993-94	Jack Rollin (Ed)	£3.99 ☐
HEART AND SOLE	David Sole with Derek Douglas	£5.99 ☐

All Headline books are available at your local bookshop or newsagent, or can be ordered direct from the publisher. Just tick the titles you want and fill in the form below. Prices and availability subject to change without notice.

Headline Book Publishing PLC, Cash Sales Department, Bookpoint, 39 Milton Park, Abingdon, OXON, OX14 4TD, UK. If you have a credit card you may order by telephone – 0235 831700.

Please enclose a cheque or postal order made payable to Bookpoint Ltd to the value of the cover price and allow the following for postage and packing:
UK & BFPO: £1.00 for the first book, 50p for the second book and 30p for each additional book ordered up to a maximum charge of £3.00.
OVERSEAS & EIRE: £2.00 for the first book, £1.00 for the second book and 50p for each additional book.

Name ....

Address ....

....

....

If you would prefer to pay by credit card, please complete:
Please debit my Visa/Access/Diner's Card/American Express (delete as applicable) card no:

Signature .... Expiry Date ....